MAXIMUM DANGER

*Kennedy, the Missiles,
and the Crisis of
American Confidence*

ROBERT WEISBROT

Ivan R. Dee
CHICAGO

Library of Congress Cataloging-in-Publication Data:
Weisbrot, Robert.
    Maximum danger : Kennedy, the missiles, and the crisis of American confidence / Robert Weisbrot.
        p. cm.
    Includes bibliographical references and index.
    ISBN 1-56663-477-6 (alk. paper)
    1. Cuban Missile Crisis, 1962. 2. Kennedy, John F. (John Fitzgerald), 1917–1963. 3. United States—Politics and government—1961–1963. 4. United States—Foreign relations—1961–1963.   I. Title.

E841.W44 2001
973.922—dc21   2001037220

For Lucy, Rob, Daisy, and Julius

Acknowledgments

I AM INDEBTED to my editor, Ivan Dee, as much for his kindness as for his insight and precision. I am also grateful to two friends and mentors: William R. Cotter, for taking time to read several drafts and to provide, at every stage, a crucial blueprint for refining my ideas; and G. Calvin Mackenzie, for his lucid and penetrating criticisms of an early draft.

Kristin Elder, Eric Washer, Michael Wilmot, Mary Kathryn Brennan, and Emily Walker checked the text and notes for accuracy, a herculean labor that they performed with surpassing skill, tenacity, and good humor. Todd Curtis, Maribeth Saleem, Emily Mantel, Trang Nguyen, Alyssa Falwell, Kristofer Hamel, Suzanna Montezemolo, and Beth Scoville ably assisted my research in varied journals and magazines. Robert Fleiss shared his findings on earlier instances of Soviet-American brinkmanship.

Pat Burdick's expertise at Colby's Miller Library greatly speeded the flow of documents from many institutions. Margaret P. Menchen, Robert D. Heath, and other Miller staff members also provided crucial support. Thanks to Rurik Spence, Wendy Rancourt, and others at Information Technology Services, my computer and research files more than once made revivals worthy of Lazarus. The history department secretary, Sarah P. Ward, also gave valued assistance.

The staff at the John F. Kennedy Library in Boston, Massachusetts, expedited my work in countless ways and with unfailing courtesy; I owe a special debt to Stephen Plotkin for his guidance and generosity. I also wish to thank the staffs of the National Security Archive and the Library of Congress in Washington, D.C., and the National Archives in College Park, Maryland. I am especially grateful to the Christian A. Johnson Endeavor Foundation for funding my archival research.

Finally, I wish to express a personal word of appreciation to my parents, for relaying more valuable clippings, taped forums, and documentaries on the missile crisis than I would have imagined possible; to Linda Cotter, R. J. Stewart, and John Schulian, for their warm encouragement; and to Lucy and Rob Tapert, whose friendship has so deeply enriched my life. To Lucy and Rob, and to their children Daisy and Julius, this book is dedicated.

R. W.

Waterville, Maine
August 2001

Contents

Maximum Danger

CHAPTER ONE

Rethinking the Cuban Missile Crisis

ON AN AUTUMN DAY in 1962, Under Secretary of State George W. Ball observed "a particularly macabre background" for the decisions that brought Russia and America to the brink of war. It was the weather. "Though we might be about to blow up the world, nature had never seemed so luxuriant," Ball recalled. "The air was light and the sky crystal clear. As [Secretary of Defense] Bob McNamara and I walked through the White House Rose Garden that Sunday [October 21], I remarked: 'Do you remember the Georgia O'Keeffe painting of a rose blooming through an ox skull? That's exactly how I feel this morning.'"[1]

The enduring fascination with the Cuban missile crisis, the gravest collision in the history of the cold war, begins with this sense of sudden, unfathomable terror. On October 16, 1962, President John F. Kennedy had learned through CIA analysis of aerial surveillance that the Soviet Union was shipping nuclear missiles to Cuba, contrary to the Kremlin's repeated assurances and his own warnings. After nearly a week of secret deliberations, the president told a shocked nation of the weapons poised ninety miles from Florida and announced a naval "quarantine" of Cuba as a first step toward securing their removal. Americans braced for a Russian challenge as U.S. warships patrolled the Caribbean, the Strategic Air Command mobilized one step short of an all-out nuclear strike, and U.S. troops readied for a possible attack on the missile sites.

Whether the chances of war were really, in Kennedy's words, "between one out of three and even,"[2] the prospect of escalation by the nuclear superpowers cast a global pall. As schoolchildren practiced taking cover under their desks in case of a nuclear blast, parents strained for radio and TV updates on the approach of Soviet ships toward the blockade line around Cuba. McNamara left the president's office at dusk on Saturday night, October 27, thinking, "I might never live to see another Saturday night."[3] The sixty-eight-year-old Soviet premier, Nikita Khrushchev, spent "one of the most dangerous nights" sleeping on an office couch with his clothes on,"[4] and later said of the palpable aura of danger, "a smell of burning [was] in the air."[5] But on October 28 Khrushchev publicly agreed to withdraw all missiles in exchange for an American pledge not to invade Cuba.

The swift, bloodless achievement of American aims, relieving fears of imminent war between the nuclear superpowers, transformed Kennedy's image. Khrushchev's missile gambit had widely appeared as a bid to bully a young president of uncertain resolve. Instead the crisis vindicated Kennedy's mettle and became a symbol of national will to contain Communist aggression: in short, a compelling American parable of the cold war.

General Andrew. J. Goodpaster, chief of staff under President Eisenhower, recalled a "euphoria" in Washington over this display of "crisis management at its best."[6] Camelot's literary courtiers added elegant exclamations to the nation's exultant mood. Arthur M. Schlesinger, Jr., the Pulitzer Prize-winning historian, thought "it was almost as if [Kennedy] had begun to shape the nation in his own image," through a "combination of toughness and restraint, of will, nerve, and wisdom, so brilliantly controlled, so matchlessly calibrated, that dazzled the world."[7] The president's speech writer and special counsel, Theodore C. Sorensen, hailed an "effort that remains a standard for all time."[8]

Through the 1960s these portraits of the missile crisis as Kennedy's finest hour gleamed in the twilight of America's staunch anti-Communist consensus. But as cynicism toward national leaders deepened amid daily body counts in Vietnam and revelations about abuses of power by the president and the CIA, a new school of writers disdained nostalgia over Kennedy's "thirteen days." These revisionist scholars agreed with traditional historians of the missile crisis that Kennedy had acted boldly at the edge of Armageddon, but they asked why this should be remembered fondly, let alone with reverence, simply because we happened to survive.

A British observer of American mores, Henry Fairlie, found in Kennedy's militant oratory and fixation with global challenges a deeper failing of character. "If he did not actually enjoy leading his country to the edge of danger," Fairlie wrote, "one could not tell so from his words or from his actions."[9] Thanks to the president's continuing references to imminent Communist threats and his aggressive policies toward Cuba, the Congo, Laos, Vietnam, Berlin, and elsewhere, "From midday on 20 January 1961 until midday on 22 November 1963, the people of the United States lived in an atmosphere of perpetual crisis and recurring crises...."[10]

Some writers sought clues to Kennedy's political conduct in

5

newly unearthed evidence of scandals in Camelot, ranging from Kennedy's compulsive womanizing to his obsessive involvement in CIA plots against Castro (possibly including its recruitment of Mafia hit men). They recast the young prince of American memory as simply a glib pretender driven by amoral ambition, unbounded family yearnings for glory and power, and desperation to prove his manhood. History, in these accounts, was above all the story of greatly flawed men: "the Kennedys, not the Russians, were ready to go to nuclear war over Cuba," and the "compulsions" to risk war "were more within the leaders than upon their nations."[11]

Despite a growing recognition that Kennedy tried to avoid war once the crisis was under way, historians still widely depict him as dangerously reckless. In his riveting narrative *The Crisis Years: Kennedy and Khrushchev, 1960–1963*, Michael R. Beschloss argues that the president was flawed by a craving to prove himself through confrontation. "At some level of Kennedy's thinking," Beschloss observes, "there was always the conviction, as he wrote in *Profiles in Courage*, that 'great crises make great men.'"[12] Lacking the experience and poise of Dwight D. Eisenhower, his predecessor in the White House, Kennedy "aroused the Western world to an hour of imminent danger that did not exist."[13] Beschloss concedes of the missiles that "anyone who was President" arguably "would have felt compelled to demand their removal," but he faults Kennedy for a rash "blanket warning" to the Russians in the late summer of 1962 that "locked him into a specific course of action. . . ." His public belligerence "had the effect of foreclosing any presidential action if missiles were found in Cuba short of risking nuclear war."[14]

The belief that President Kennedy's actions during the missile crisis chiefly reflected his singular character, judgment, and leadership may be the last great myth surrounding this clash of superpowers. For more than three decades writers have vari-

ously highlighted Kennedy's efforts to rid Cuba of Soviet nuclear weapons as a triumph of heroic statesmanship, a near
tragic indulgence in *machismo*, or, increasingly, a mixture of the
two. (Popular culture has rendered a more consistent verdict:
the 1974 TV drama *The Missiles of October* and the recent big-
budget Hollywood thriller *Thirteen Days* portray President
Kennedy and his brother Robert as the sort of larger-than-life
patriots sorely missed in politics today.) On closer inspection,
however, one finds that Kennedy explored no new policy fron-
tiers but rather etched a mainstream profile in caution, bounded
securely by diplomatic precedent, partisan pressure, and the values of American political culture during the cold war.

Accounts of Kennedy's unique grace—or disgrace—under
Soviet pressure have centered on whether the president personally was right or reckless in committing to three bold policies:
treating the placement of Soviet missiles in Cuba as a crisis; relying on military action (a blockade of Cuba), not simply diplomacy, to remove the missiles; and resisting a formal agreement
to withdraw American missiles from Turkey, as the Soviets had
demanded in exchange for dismantling comparable weapons in
Cuba. Yet in each of these areas President Kennedy's policies
were largely inherited from the previous administration and
hardened by a formidable public consensus that crossed party
lines as well as regional and sectional borders.

Kennedy's insistence that the Soviet placement of missiles in
Cuba was intolerable coincided with policies and public opinion
that had crystallized long before his emergence in 1960 as the
Democratic presidential candidate. American cold war attitudes
were becoming more alarmist and belligerent, based on perceptions of proliferating global crises caused by Communist threats
and subversion, growing Soviet nuclear and missile capabilities,
and Cuba's increasing reliance on Soviet trade and aid, under its
left-leaning president Fidel Castro. The appearance in Cuba of

7

Russian military equipment and "technical personnel" further provoked fears that America was slackening in its anti-Communist vigilance and permitting a blatant violation of the Monroe Doctrine, which since 1823 had warned foreign powers against encroaching in the Western hemisphere. Before Eisenhower left office in January 1961, his administration had sanctioned covert efforts to topple Castro, and in scattered private remarks he had treated as self-evident that any Soviet attempt to build an offensive military base in Cuba would require a U.S. military response.

Kennedy's Cuban policy built on his predecessor's, though with scant initial success. In April 1961 the president's hesitant approval of a disastrous CIA-sponsored invasion of Cuba by exiles seeking to oust Castro was a shock to his image and his ego, as well as his hopes of ending a Russian foothold in Latin America. Yet this defeat did not significantly alter U.S. policy toward Cuba, which remained to undermine Castro by all means short of occupation by American forces, and to deter the Soviets from converting the island into an offensive military base.

When President Kennedy learned that the Russians had covertly deployed missiles in Cuba capable of destroying American cities as far as Texas, he had, in theory, a wide choice of ways to secure their removal: private diplomacy, appeals to the United Nations, a blockade of Cuba, an air strike on the missile sites, an invasion of the island. But with rare exceptions, no one in the administration—and few Americans generally—believed diplomacy alone to be an adequate response to a nuclear intrusion ninety miles from the U.S. mainland. Of the possible military responses, Kennedy believed a blockade to be the mildest, offering the best chances for a peaceful settlement. For these same reasons, calls for a blockade of Soviet arms to Cuba (but not an air strike or an invasion) had earlier gained strong support among Democrats and Republicans in Congress, and among newspapers and magazines throughout the country and across a broad political spectrum. Once again, President Kennedy's course built on widely shared perceptions of vital national interests, tempered by a concern to curb the dangers of unchecked escalation.

Early in the crisis Adlai Stevenson, Kennedy's ambassador to the United Nations and twice the Democratic party's candidate for president, privately urged withdrawal of American Jupiter missiles from Turkey in exchange for the Soviets' removing their missiles from Cuba. Stevenson's advice was emphatically rejected, and when the Russians later pressed for such a trade, Kennedy publicly refused. Yet we know now that Kennedy and his aides repeatedly considered this proposal in their secret deliberations, and in fact it became a crucial though hidden addendum to a larger, public settlement. Kennedy's policy shifts on this issue appear, at first glance, to suggest the exceedingly personal and contingent nature of diplomacy during the crisis. On fuller consideration, though, these maneuvers underscore the extent to which the president's policies reflected his caution in both foreign policy and domestic politics.

The missiles in Turkey were a logical bargaining chip in the crisis, for they were by all accounts obsolete and militarily useless, whereas their proximity to the Soviet Union was a diplomatic embarrassment, tending to discredit professions of outrage over Russian missiles near Florida. Yet before Kennedy could include them in any deal, he had first to take a firm military stand, to signal American resolve and avoid appearing to reward the covert Soviet nuclear deployment. The president also feared alienating Turkey and straining the NATO alliance by reversing commitments dating to the Eisenhower administration; and feared as well incurring Republican charges of weakness toward the Communists. By pledging to withdraw the Jupiter missiles yet concealing this from all but a handful of Soviet and American officials, Kennedy reconciled several compelling but seemingly incompatible aims. His compromise cost nothing in military security, defused the risks of escalation, and achieved what Americans most wanted—removal of missiles from Cuba, all the while preserving his image at home and abroad as an uncompromising anti-Communist leader.

Kennedy's cautious attempts to accommodate both domestic pressures and Soviet interests may best be appreciated in relation to each other. Too often scholars have tended to equate Kennedy's top-secret deliberations and formal authority as commander-in-chief with vast practical latitude in responding to the missiles in Cuba. In fact the political context, though at times depicted mainly as a dramatic backdrop to Kennedy's decisions, acted more like a vise tightly wound around the entire decision-making process. In this light the president's policies, however fraught with risk, appear temperate and even unseasonably restrained compared with the alarums and calls for bold action by Democratic and Republican officials, the media, community leaders, and the general public. Within a sharply limited realm for maneuver, Kennedy sought to curb the risks of escalation while forging a consensus from an electorate and a political establishment consistently more militant than he.

That Kennedy assiduously gauged public sentiment should scarcely occasion censure, for no leader can effectively march to the beat of his own drummer unless others join the procession. As Franklin Roosevelt confided in October 1937, after isolationists in Congress and the press had denounced his call for a "quarantine" of aggressor states, "It's a terrible thing to look over your shoulder when you are trying to lead—and to find no one there."[15]

With his keen sense of history, President Kennedy discerned that democratic leaders are subject to constraints that even scholars may find elusive. In 1962 he had started to fill out a poll evaluating American presidents, then decided the project was fruitless. According to Arthur Schlesinger, Jr., son of the distinguished historian who had sent the poll, the president objected that "some of his greatest predecessors . . . were given credit for doing things when they could do nothing else; only the most detailed study could disclose what difference a President had made by his own individual effort." As for ranking leaders, he exclaimed, "How the hell can you tell? Only the President himself can know what his real pressures and his real alternatives are. If you don't know that, how can you judge performance?"[16]

Such skepticism need not preclude a study of Kennedy's own leadership, but it should discourage interpretations detached from the dominant political values and concerns of his era. Persistent attempts to divine the president's character from his policies and to attribute his actions to unique personal traits too often float free of historical context. If Kennedy was obsessed with personal honor, Red shadows over Cuba, a nonexistent "missile gap," Khrushchev's arrogance, and reliance on military responses, he did no more than reflect the harsh and largely unyielding terrain of American politics during the early 1960s. The public mood was alarmist, even apocalyptic, for a nation officially at peace, and no public figure could expect to contravene that mood and still retain credibility.

The surest way to see Kennedy's role more clearly may therefore be, paradoxically, to pull back from the relentless close-ups that have formed our standard images of him. In accounts of the missile crisis, foreign policy tends to appear an exceedingly personal enterprise, in which, for good or ill, "one human being alone exercised the responsibility to decide a matter that could have determined the fate of 185 million others."[17] Yet the impact on Kennedy of those 185 million citizens and their political system warrants a closer, more respectful look.

CHAPTER TWO

Cold War Alarms
and the 1960 Campaign

1. Fear and Loathing of Khrushchev on the Campaign Trail

EARLY IN 1960 Americans were enjoying the last months of a brief thaw in the cold war. Nikita Khrushchev's visit to the United States the previous September had seemed a heartening portent, and the four-power summit scheduled for mid-May in Paris offered hope of a nuclear test ban and an easing of tensions over Berlin. A relative lull in foreign crises burnished President Eisenhower's aura of firm, experienced leadership, and the eventual Republican presidential nominee, Vice President Richard Nixon, basked in the glow. John F. Kennedy and his rivals for the Democratic nomination downplayed foreign affairs in favor of such bread-and-butter domestic issues as the "Eisenhower" recession, rising unemployment, and proposals for aid to education and raising the minimum wage. Then, beginning May 1, a series of international incidents revived the cold war and transformed the landscape of American electoral politics.

May 1 was a day of proletarian celebration in the Soviet Union. In 1960 it also became a cold war milestone as a Russian surface-to-air missile downed an American U-2 spy plane filming military installations from an altitude of eighty thousand feet. On May 6 Khrushchev discredited the U.S. denials of espionage by triumphantly producing the captured pilot, Francis Gary Powers. On May 9 Eisenhower accepted responsibility for authorizing the mission and implied that such flights would continue. On the eve of the Paris summit, Khrushchev angrily demanded an apology for the violation of Soviet air space, then scuttled the talks when Eisenhower would not comply.

As Democrats convened in early July and Republicans in early August to select their presidential nominees, Soviet-American relations continued to deteriorate. On July 11 the Russians announced the downing of an RB-47, another U.S. spy plane, and held the two pilots prisoner, though the plane had been thirty miles beyond Soviet air space. The following day Khrushchev dismissed the Monroe Doctrine as obsolete, which brought a stern rebuttal from the State Department.

Africa too felt the tremors of Soviet assertion in the "third world" when Khrushchev disparaged a UN peacekeeping force in the newly independent but anarchy-plagued Congo as a front for Western colonialists. During the summer of 1960 the Congo's deposed but defiant prime minister, Patrice Lumumba, invited Russian troops to expel the Congo's remaining Belgian soldiers. In September Khrushchev sent fifteen planes to Lumumba, prompting Eisenhower to take "a most serious view of this action,"[1] and urge instead that the Soviets support the UN.

A *Newsweek* survey in July revealed that the international situation "towers above all others as the No. 1 issue of the coming Presidential campaign."[2] "Probably not since Hitler has the average American been more concerned about the course of world affairs," Robert Spivack wrote in the *Nation* as the election approached.[3] Whoever won the presidency, *Time* observed, the next administration must "build defense and foreign policies designed not to settle the cold war but to win it."[4]

The resurgence of the cold war appeared to favor Nixon politically. He had investigated suspected Communist agents as a congressman in the 1940s and later, as Eisenhower's vice president, had pressed a hard line toward the Soviet Union and Communist China. James Reston of the *New York Times* reported from Washington in September 1960 that "every crisis overseas is generally believed here to help Mr. Nixon."[5] Writing in the *Nation*, William Carleton also found the American people in a "get tough" mood and receptive to Nixon for his proven ability to "talk back" to the Communists.[6]

While Nixon emphasized his experience as a member of Eisenhower's administration, Kennedy evoked perceptions of America's slipping prestige and vigor in world affairs. He called for sacrifice to meet worsening dangers, and identified the great challenge facing Americans: "whether freedom will conquer or whether the Communists are going to be successful." The candidate's often shrill warnings later prompted some writers to ask what inner demons, insecurities, and grandiose ambitions drove him. Yet Kennedy's militant and at times militaristic campaign utterances scarcely revealed his character or a distinctive ideology but rather formed the irreducible legitimating credentials for national office.

The journalist Theodore H. White found the entire Democratic National Convention awash in the crisis of containment: "this world of challenge and chaos and Communism, was the central theme of all oratory; and the speakers—in caucus, on TV, in convention, later—seized on the theme, repeated it, hammered it, flattened it, until the entire Convention seemed a continuous drone of great worries. . . ."[7] Frank Church of Idaho, still far from the post-Vietnam disillusionment that fueled his later Senate investigations of CIA abuses, focused his keynote address on the danger from "world Communism" and the "Red empire."[8]

If the Democrats had gotten "religion" about the Communist menace, Republicans two weeks later turned their convention into a gathering of fundamentalists. Nixon's running mate, Henry Cabot Lodge, declared, "The basic contest is the life and death struggle between the Communists on the one hand and those who insist on being free on the other. This is what gives this election of 1960 its compelling, overwhelming importance to us and to the world."[9] His words could have been taken from the editorial pages of almost any newspaper (or almost any speech from the Democratic convention), and they aligned perfectly with Nixon's fifty-minute acceptance speech on the world crisis. The United States, Nixon said, could not "tolerate being pushed around by anybody, any place." He promised a "strategy of victory for the free world" against the Communists.[10]

In addition to touting Nixon's experience in foreign affairs, Republicans exploited a familiar partisan theme: the alleged softness of Democratic candidates toward Communist influence. The prominence of liberal foreign policy advisers on Kennedy's campaign team, including Chester Bowles and Arthur Schlesinger, Jr., added grist to charges that the candidate relied more on fuzzy notions of social reform than on a readiness to face down Communist threats with superior force. Republicans also trotted out against Kennedy the most deadly bywords for foreign policy shame during the early cold war: "Munich" and "appeasement."

The "lessons of Munich" served as the historical guidepost by which Americans navigated policy during the cold war. Recalling the vain British and French bid for "peace in our time" by acceding to Adolf Hitler's claims on Czechoslovakia in 1938, the "lessons" became clear after Hitler embarked on new conquests that led within a year to the outbreak of World War II. The disastrous consequences loosed by this strategy of appeasement discredited the notion that democracies could sate an aggressive dictatorship through goodwill and accommodation. With the defeat of Hitler in 1945, parallels between Nazi Germany and the Soviet Union—one enemy just defeated, the other newly emerging—circulated among American policymakers. So did warnings against compromise with Communist "totalitarians" because, as history had shown, such attempts were both dishonorable and doomed.

Charges of appeasement became a commonplace of American political discourse and could taint even hardened cold warriors. George C. Marshall and Dean Acheson, former secretaries of state under President Truman, were savaged by Republicans as "appeasers": Marshall for "losing" China to Communist revolutionaries in 1949, Acheson for failing to deter a Communist attack on South Korea the following year. Years after leaving office, Acheson, a key architect of America's strategy to contain Soviet influence, was still vilified by Republican partisans like Nixon, who accused him of standing for "retreat and appeasement."[11]

Not even the hero of Normandy, Dwight D. Eisenhower, was immune. Governor Nelson Rockefeller of New York, an early aspirant for his party's presidential nomination in 1960, privately called Eisenhower's defense program "almost Chamberlain-like," alluding to the British prime minister who had bargained with Hitler.[12] On January 16, 1961, John W. Mc-

Cormack, the Democratic leader in the House of Representatives, accused the departing president of "very weak leadership on the world level," adding, "And Hitler showed that the road to appeasement is the road to war."[13]

Kennedy too tried to offset Nixon's claims to superior experience in foreign policy by deriding him as "experienced in policies of retreat, defeat and weakness."[14] But, as in earlier campaigns, Republicans played the "appeasement" card with greater zeal and impact. Unproven in foreign affairs, Kennedy made an inviting target for Republicans looking to bury him under their lessons of history beside Marshall and Acheson. Congressman Walter Judd of Minnesota set the tone in his keynote address at the Republican National Convention, reviling Democrats as appeasers and alluding to the Communist Chinese seizure of power while Truman was president: "It wasn't under the Republicans that 600 million people disappeared behind the Iron Curtain."[15]

Nixon was a past master at tarring Democrats as appeasers, and he found his opening when Kennedy criticized Eisenhower's seeming commitment to defend the tiny offshore islands of Quemoy and Matsu against the Red Chinese. These islands were ruled by Chiang Kai-shek's Nationalist Chinese government in Formosa but lay nearer to the People's Republic of China, which claimed and periodically shelled them. Kennedy argued that to risk war with China over two insignificant and "strategically indefensible" islands showed a dangerous lack of proportion. Better, he said, to persuade Chiang to withdraw his forces voluntarily. Such efforts to limit America's anti-Communist intervention were like red meat to Nixon, who sprang at Kennedy on October 7, toward the end of their second presidential debate.

Kennedy's statement, Nixon gloated, was comparable to

Acheson's alleged abandonment of Korea in 1950. Nixon insisted that the United States should never yield an inch of the "free" world to Communists by force or threat. Kennedy answered with a statement on October 10 that admonished Nixon for looking "to the defense of every rock and island around the world," a policy that could "involve American boys in an unnecessary and futile war."[16] This reasoned judgment did Kennedy little good, however, at a time when "appeasement" was virtually the third rail of national politics. In their third debate, on October 13, Nixon asked whether Kennedy would also give up West Berlin, another "indefensible" outpost. Unfurling the lessons of Munich to their full height, Nixon charged Kennedy with "a policy of retreat and surrender" and said, "We tried this with Hitler, and it didn't work."[17]

Soon the media joined in the hunt for Kennedy's Red October lapse. Ernest K. Lindley of *Newsweek* wrote that "Kennedy's policy on Quemoy and Matsu is not only weak, and thus likely to damage our prestige, but dangerous in that it almost invites another Red Chinese assault. . . . Principle is at stake."[18] Another *Newsweek* columnist, Henry Hazlitt, found evidence of "a tendency toward retreat and appeasement":

> [Kennedy's] preference for [liberal] advisers like [Adlai] Stevenson and [Chester] Bowles, his suggestion that the President should have halted the U-2 flights earlier and expressed regrets to Khrushchev, his opposition to United States resumption of underground nuclear tests, his suggestion that we should publicly declare in advance that we have no intention of defending Quemoy or Matsu—all point in the same direction."[19]

According to the historian Robert A. Divine, "The episode . . . taught Kennedy how risky it was to try to deal candidly with substantive international issues in a presidential campaign."[20] The senator backed away from his original position and emphasized instead his commitment to defend Formosa and the Pescadores, another nearby island group. Privately he admitted to aides his mistake in pitting a "sophisticated" foreign policy argument against Nixon's emotional stand.[21]

If Kennedy often campaigned as though engaged in a personal duel with Soviet Premier Khrushchev, his behavior again simply acknowledged changing political realities. Never before had a foreign leader so brazenly injected himself into a U.S. presidential campaign by the force of his personality. Although Joseph Stalin had ordered millions shot or jailed as "enemies of the people" and had increasingly clashed with the West, his public demeanor had been impeccable, his speeches few, dignified, and unremarkable. In rare meetings with U.S. diplomats during World War II, Stalin's courtliness and seeming candor had made otherwise hardened leaders speak of "Uncle Joe" in relieved, even effusive tones. By contrast the stocky, bald, deep-voiced, aggressively voluble Khrushchev, chairman of the Soviet Council of Ministers and first secretary of the Communist party, was unpredictable in his every gesture: one minute calm and jovial, the next angrily gesticulating. He presented an image that Western leaders found disconcerting, and symbolic of Russia's growing dynamism and menace.[22]

Cunning and ruthless, Khrushchev was still far from being the implacable ogre of Western imagination. At Moscow's Twentieth Party Congress in 1956 he denounced Stalin's terror and "crimes" against the Russian people in a widely leaked "secret" speech. He also renounced the doctrine that war between Communist and capitalist states was "fatalistically inevitable,"[23] stressed instead "peaceful coexistence," and shifted resources from military to consumer growth. Yet in trumpeting Soviet parity with the West in technology, military power, economic growth, and political stature, the Soviet chairman aggravated the very cold war fears he wished to calm.

Khrushchev's earthy, impulsive nature at times overwhelmed his regard for diplomatic protocol in ways that ranged from farcical to frightening. During his visit to the United States in 1959, he complained of his exclusion from Disneyland (for security reasons). Earlier, beginning in the late 1950s, he had boomed repeated threats that Soviet rockets could destroy France, England, even the United States if the "imperialists" dared aggression.

The most notorious of Khrushchev's challenges to the West, "We will bury you," was much misunderstood. Coaxed by many rounds of vodka at a Polish embassy reception in Moscow in November 1956, his words were an invitation to peaceful competition, not an intimation of war.[24] Khrushchev was alluding to the march of history, which, as a good Bolshevik, he trusted would vindicate communism and leave capitalism a lifeless relic. Still, in a time of high tension between rival military alliances, his remark did little to promote East-West ties.[25]

"Standing up to Khrushchev" became a valued political currency during the 1960 campaign. Nixon alluded with telling effect to his impromptu "kitchen debate" with Khrushchev at an American exhibit in Moscow in July 1959, when he waved a finger in the chairman's face.[26] Nixon's running mate Henry Cabot Lodge had also impressed Americans "as the man who stood up to Premier Khrushchev"[27] during his tour of America in 1959, and, as ambassador to the UN, by "talking tough" to the Russians in disputes over the U-2, the RB-47, and the Congo. Kennedy could scarcely have avoided competing in this political and psychological arena while Nixon told voters that JFK was "the kind of man 'Mr. Khrushchev would make mincemeat of.' "[28]

Kennedy early learned the cost of courtesy to Khrushchev

while seeking his party's presidential nomination. In May he remarked in Oregon that a timely apology by President Eisenhower for the U-2 spy mission might have saved the summit
conference. Criticisms soon rained down on the young candidate, heaviest from the Republican right (Hugh Scott of Pennsylvania attacked Kennedy's "appeasement" on the Senate
floor[29]) but also from disheartened supporters. Arriving for a
campaign stop in Denver,

> Kennedy was met at the airport by a teen-aged girl with a
> Kennedy-for-President placard and a perplexed expres-
> sion. . . . "Why," she asked, "did you say that President
> Eisenhower should apologize to Khrushchev?" Startled,
> Kennedy muttered that he had not meant that the U.S.
> should "apologize," only that it should have expressed
> "diplomatic regrets."

While Kennedy continued to explain away his civility, the
South's favorite son, Lyndon Johnson, scouting for delegates
through the West, "won the loudest applause by booming out:
'Would you apologize to Khrushchev?' Invariably, the audiences
boomed back: 'NO!' "[30]

Like the rest of the country, Kennedy had little choice during the height of the fall campaign but to focus on Khrushchev,
who arrived in the United States on September 19, 1960, for an
uninvited and increasingly unwelcome twenty-five-day appearance. Having addressed the United Nations General Assembly,
the Soviet chairman stayed to wreak havoc. After heckling
British Prime Minister Macmillan, he expressed displeasure
with the Western leanings of a Filipino delegate by removing
his shoe and pounding a table. (Soviet officials at first dismissed
word of this sabotage as "Western propaganda."[31]) Khrushchev
assured UN members that his cause was peace, but, as so often,
he proved better at shocking his listeners than soothing them.

2. "The Delicate Balance of Terror"

ONE NEED NOT rummage through the recesses of Kennedy's psychology to fathom his extreme sensitivity to changes in Soviet missile strength. Americans had only fitfully emerged from a panic beginning in October 1957, when the Russians sent the satellite Sputnik into orbit, shattering American confidence in its technological superiority and strategic defenses. "The national ego had not been so affronted since Pearl Harbor," Ben Pearse of the *New York Times* summed up the national trauma.[32]

The national ego took a further pounding from a report, *Deterrence and Survival in the Nuclear Age*, submitted in November 1957 by a presidential advisory committee. Chaired by the San Francisco lawyer H. Rowen Gaither, the committee had set out to investigate civil defense measures but had hurriedly shifted focus after Sputnik to warn, "The evidence clearly indicates an increasing threat which may become critical in 1959 or early 1960."[33] By then

> the USSR may be able to launch an attack—with ICBMs [intercontinental ballistic missiles] carrying megaton warheads, against which SAC [the Strategic Air Command] will be almost completely vulnerable against present programs.... The next two years seem to us critical. If we fail to act at once, the risk, in our opinion, will be unacceptable.[34]

Media leaks from this jeremiad over slipping U.S. security soon created ripples of panic. On December 20, 1957, the *Washington Post* reported under the front-page headline "Enormous Arms Outlay Is Held Vital to Survival,"

> The still top-secret Gaither Report portrays a United States in the gravest danger in its history.... It finds Amer-

ica's long-term prospect one of cataclysmic peril in the face
of rocketing Soviet military might and of a powerful, growing Soviet economy and technology which will bring new
political, propaganda, and psychological assaults on freedom all around the globe.[35]

Such public laments echoed years of high-level wailings
hitherto confined largely to classified or arcane rumblings in the
corridors of government, the Pentagon, and national security
"think tanks." In April 1950 the State Department's Policy
Planning Council had composed the decade's first and foremost
prophecy of doom.[36] Labeled NSC-68, the voluminous memo
warned of the "Kremlin's design for world domination,"[37] urged
a vast and immediate expansion of nuclear and conventional
forces, and proclaimed, "The issues that face us are momentous,
involving the fulfillment or destruction not only of this Republic but of civilization itself."[38] NSC-68 pronounced 1954 the
"critical date"[39] by which the Soviets would be able to launch a
surprise attack "of such weight that the United States must have
substantially increased . . . air, ground, and sea strength, atomic
capabilities, and air and civilian defenses to deter" or survive a
war.[40]

Shrill and hyperbolic, NSC-68 nonetheless became official
policy in September 1950, soon after the outbreak of the Korean War, a time when few appraisals of Communist productiv-
ity and intentions erred on the side of serenity.[41] As in shooting
wars, psychological mobilization during the cold war admitted
little room for nuance or ambiguity.[42] Instead NSC-68 set a
standard for urgency that later policy papers (as well as candidates for national office) rivaled as Soviet nuclear might increased.

In February 1955 a scientific advisory panel chaired by the
president of MIT, James Killian, submitted to President Eisen-

hower a two-volume report, *Meeting the Threat of Surprise Attack*, that looked to an unrelenting arms race even beyond the point "where each could destroy the other." "We need not assume that this stage is unchangeable or that one country or the other cannot move again into a position of relative advantage," the Killian panel declared. "The search for 'technological breakthroughs' must continue."[43] The Gaither report two years later, though tethered to immediate concerns over Sputnik, built on this obligatory refrain in American political discourse that cold war dangers were approaching a critical level.

American rocket failures after Sputnik deepened public frustration and fears. In November 1957 the navy fired its answer to Sputnik, a three-stage rocket called Test Vehicle 3—but the missile "[rose] 4 feet, then settle[d] awkwardly on its steel launching platform, tumble[d] to the beach, and explode[d] in a spectacular fireball. 'Oh, it's awful,' wail[ed] a veteran woman bird watcher looking on. 'It's failed. It's failed terribly.' "[44] As worldwide ridicule punctured the aura of "Yankee ingenuity," the Democratic Senate majority leader, Lyndon Johnson, mourned the rocket and American rocket science, asking, "How long, how long, O God, how long will it take us to catch up with Russia's two satellites?"[45]

Khrushchev vigorously stirred these anxieties. "If a war should break out," he told visiting British members of Parliament soon after the Sputnik launch, ". . . socialism will live on while capitalism will not remain," though he piously assured them that Communists never thought of achieving goals by such means.[46] *Time* magazine noted the Kremlin's "new offensive technique: 'missile diplomacy,' " in which "Every day of every week Moscow rolls out pronouncements" of successful experiments with intercontinental ballistic missiles. In this new age of the missile, Khrushchev liked to say, Europe might become "a veritable cemetery," and the United States had become just as vulnerable.[47]

Soon after the Sputnik flight, Washington set 1960 as the target date for catching up in missiles, based on intelligence reports that Russia would by then have intercontinental ballistic missiles in operation.[48] While *Time* named Khrushchev its "man of the year" for 1957,[49] the Democratic National Committee, in a statement signed by former President Truman, accused the Republican administration of "complacency" and "failure."[50] According to a survey by *Newsweek* published just after the Sputnik launch, most Americans favored a crash program to put the United States ahead in the missile race and were prepared to forgo a tax cut to achieve this.[51]

Capitol Hill resounded with so many calls for greater military spending that the new session was informally dubbed "the Sputnik Congress."[52] Senator Johnson meanwhile told his Democratic caucus early in 1958 that the issue of national security would "dominate the Congresses of free men for lifetimes to come."[53] Later that year the prestigious Rockefeller Panel distilled more than a year's "expert" testimony into an urgent call to raise military spending by $3 billion annually at least until 1965, or "the world balance of power will shift in favor of the Soviet bloc." This would be catastrophic because "Communism, by its nature, is ready to strike the first blow . . . while the U.S., by its nature, must be defensive. . . ."[54]

President Eisenhower's secretary of defense, Neil H. McElroy, assured the Senate Preparedness Subcommittee in 1959 that America's strategic bombers and development of a submarine-launched "Polaris" missile guaranteed an adequate deterrent. Yet he drew greater attention by conceding that the Soviets would likely have a three-to-one lead in intercontinental missiles during the next several years.[55] Democrats like Senator Stuart Symington of Missouri, an early contender for the 1960 Democratic presidential nomination, saw both an imminent threat and an invitation to cast the Republican party as weak on national security.

For the national security experts clustered in the RAND Corporation, a nominally private think tank in Santa Monica formed by the air force, the perils of the late 1950s spurred a golden age of theoretical ferment. The most influential thinker within RAND and among informed laymen in academe and politics was Albert Wohlstetter, whose analytical clarity and reasoned tone helped make fear of vulnerability to a Russian nuclear attack intellectually respectable. In January 1959 his article in *Foreign Affairs*, "The Delicate Balance of Terror," explained that even a large U.S. nuclear force might not deter war if the Russians felt confident of destroying enough bombers and missiles, especially those stationed overseas, in a surprise strike. "We must expect a vast increase in the weight of attack which the Soviets can deliver with little warning," Wohlstetter wrote, and therefore "at critical junctures in the 1960s, we may not have the power to deter attack."[56] The United States could do much to secure its nuclear forces, but only if the country awakened to the peril:

> The notion that a carefully planned surprise attack can be checkmated almost effortlessly, that, in short, we may resume our deep pre-sputnik sleep, is wrong and its nearly universal acceptance is terribly dangerous. . . . Deterring general war in both the early and late 1960s will be hard at best. . . .[57]

Also in 1959 Bernard Brodie, the earliest pioneer in nuclear weapons theory, emphasized in his book *Strategy in the Missile Age* the shrinking limits of safety in the cold war:

The fact is that deterrence can fail. The great advantage of striking first, at least under existing conditions, must be viewed as an extremely strong and persistent incentive to each side to attack the other. As long as this incentive exists, the danger of total war arising out of a crisis situation—or even from a premeditated attack by the Soviet Union—cannot be considered trivial or remote.[58]

In the presidential election year 1960, the RAND Corporation's distinctive blend of reason and terror attained still broader influence and notoriety. The catalyst was a balding, rotund mathematical physicist named Herman Kahn, who had an ear for lively phrases ("Doomsday Machine," "thinking about the unthinkable") and a bent for provocative, at times humorous, references to scenarios of nuclear deterrence and destruction. In a 750-page tract *On Thermonuclear War*,[59] published by the Princeton University Press, Kahn portrayed nuclear war as a fact of life that Americans must prepare for, through construction of fallout shelters and periodic mass evacuations; resort to, if the Russians dared invade Western Europe; and control, by employing such "restrained" tactics as initially targeting Russian missiles rather than cities, or destroying "only" a single Russian city. Waged judiciously, Kahn suggested, a nuclear war might entail no more than a few million casualties on either side. Denounced as ghoulishly immoral (and later parodied in the dark cinematic satire *Dr. Strangelove*), Kahn nonetheless lectured to rows of generals, transfixed lay audiences, and became the cold war's most widely read thinker on nuclear strategy.

However Americans felt about the self-consciously outrageous Kahn, few disputed his core conviction, one shared by virtually all of RAND, the Pentagon, and the government: the United States was unavoidably passing through a period of supreme peril. The root problem, in this view, was not wild-eyed generals or even accidental missile launches. Rather, the accelerating technology of destruction had outpaced the ability of diplomats to resolve conflicts between the Western democracies and the Communist bloc. Compounding these tensions was the prospect of vulnerability to a disarming "first strike," a fear that might tempt rather than inhibit an attack by either side. American (and Soviet) leaders were therefore doomed to grope through a thicket of untested strategic options in hopes of stumbling on the right, or most fortunate, balance between vigilance and restraint.

As newsmagazines in 1960 gripped readers with such headlines as "If the Enemy Should Attack,"[60] Khrushchev stoked these fears by boasting of ever more numerous and powerful weapons.[61] "We are several years ahead of all other countries in the development and assembly-line production of intercontinental ballistic missiles," he told applauding delegates at the Supreme Soviet in January. "The United States of America is [no longer] the world's strongest military power." And the shift from West to East was building momentum. "Though the weapons we have now are formidable," he said, "the weapon we have in the hatching stage is . . . even more formidable." It was, he gloated, "fantastic."[62] At the UN in September he proclaimed that Soviet factories were turning out nuclear missiles "like sausages."

For all Khrushchev's claims and the Pentagon's laments, the so-called missile gap, like earlier cries of a "bomber gap" in the mid-1950s, was illusory. By 1960 the United States held a substantial edge in both nuclear warheads and delivery systems, but President Eisenhower refused to reveal the CIA's evidence confirming this. He thought it would provoke an acceleration of the Soviet missile program and an uproar over intrusions into Soviet air space (a fear borne out by the downing of Francis Gary Powers). Then too, even had Eisenhower disclosed details of

U.S. nuclear superiority, no one could say with certainty what the Russians would soon deploy. The cost of Eisenhower's restraint was nonetheless high, for his vague assurances failed to calm the public. Instead they guaranteed that whoever won the Democratic presidential nomination in 1960 would make the "missile gap" central to his calls for change.

Kennedy had barely emerged from the Democratic National Convention in July 1960 when Nixon tacitly conceded that U.S. military readiness would be an irresistible campaign issue. At a partisan summit meeting with an early aspirant for the Republican nomination, New York Governor Nelson Rockefeller, Nixon agreed on the need to upgrade the nation's "military posture" by calling "for more and better bombers, an airborne SAC alert, more missiles, dispersed bases, greater limited-war capability and 'an intensified program for civil defense.' "[63]

Kennedy was perhaps the most widely touted politician among national security specialists. His interest in military vigilance had been evident as early as 1940 with the publication of *Why England Slept*, a reworking of his senior thesis at Harvard on the disastrous failure to rearm against Hitler's Germany. As a member of the House of Representatives since 1947 and the Senate since 1953, he had consistently supported strong nuclear and conventional forces.

Far from inventing the "missile gap" issue during the 1960 campaign, Kennedy was a modest latecomer to this cause. He had largely ignored the subject for a full year after the Soviets launched their first Sputnik satellite, preferring to build support over domestic issues. Even after finally giving a major Senate address on national defense in August 1958, Kennedy once more relinquished the issue to Democratic colleagues—and presidential aspirants—in the Senate, such as Stuart Symington of Missouri and Lyndon Johnson of Texas, preferring to concentrate on labor legislation to bolster his union support. The demands of national campaigning finally pulled him into the maelstrom of partisan sniping over missile strength, but he merely "embraced the issue made popular and appealing by others."[64]

Yet Kennedy appeared—for a politician—surpassingly informed, articulate, and intellectually self-assured in discussing the "missile gap." These were precisely the traits most likely to make the analysts at RAND raise their slide rules in salute. His speeches employed the term "missile gap" as a shorthand reference to larger questions of military readiness than simply relative numbers of missiles. The United States, Kennedy argued, must safeguard its bombers and missiles against a Soviet attack. The country must also upgrade its conventional forces rather than rely on "massive retaliation" against Russia to deter or punish even marginal acts of Communist aggression or subversion. This preference for "flexible response" endeared Kennedy to national security analysts who believed that the growing Soviet nuclear arsenal made it desirable to confine rather than brandish the "ultimate weapon."

Kennedy's speeches at times sounded uncannily like the cutting-edge discourses of RAND experts—and with good reason. From late 1959, Wohlstetter and other RAND notables had discreetly contributed ideas and passages to Kennedy's Academic Advisory Group, which already boasted such luminaries in strategic thought as Harvard's Henry Kissinger. The Massachusetts senator cast his concerns to upgrade the nation's military as a rebuke to the Eisenhower-Nixon administration and as part of his challenge to "get America moving again." But among the strategic community from Santa Monica to Cambridge to Washington, D.C., who had honed these same points for years, the candidate's challenge was simply a bracing dose of common sense.[65]

3. "Standing Up to Castro"

KENNEDY'S CAMPAIGN DISCOURSES on "standing up to Castro" similarly revealed neither personal adventurism nor animus but rather formed a belated salute to political necessity. Early on many Americans had sympathized with the exuberant, idealistic Castro after his triumph over the corrupt dictator Fulgencio Batista in January 1959. Kennedy himself had implicitly criticized U.S. support for Batista in a speech late in 1958, deploring "military assistance" that "tightens the grip of dictatorial governments, [and] makes friends with those in power today at the expense of those who may be in power tomorrow. . . ."[66] The senator's 1960 campaign book, *The Strategy of Peace*, dared to recognize Castro as "part of the legacy of [Simón] Bolívar," the nineteenth-century hero of Latin American freedom struggles. Kennedy added that Castro might "have taken a more rational course after his victory had the United States Government not backed the dictator [Batista] so long and so uncritically" or had Eisenhower received Castro more warmly on his visit to Washington in April 1959.[67]

By 1960, however, Castro had spent his reserves of American goodwill with tirades against U.S. imperialism and the executions of several thousand "enemies of the people." His agitated manner and unruly beard (recalling his days as a guerrilla fighter in the Sierra Maestra mountains) also played into American stereotypes of boisterous, not quite civilized Latins. But it was his hard left turns—appointing Marxists like his brother Raul to key government posts, seizing U.S. businesses with scant compensation, and inviting Moscow to offset Cuba's dependence on its giant neighbor to the north—that magnified his menace to Americans intent on stopping the Red Tide from poisoning the Western Hemisphere.

Both Castro and Khrushchev kept American agitation over Cuba at a boil during the 1960 campaign. In June the Soviet leader agreed to visit Cuba and pledged support for Castro's "struggle against American imperialist colonialists." In July Castro nationalized two U.S.-owned oil refineries that refused to process crude oil imported from the Soviet Union. In a spiral of retaliation, President Eisenhower reduced the Cuban sugar quota by 700,000 tons, and Castro soon after expropriated more U.S. properties. The Soviet Union promptly announced that it would buy Cuba's sugar surplus. On July 9 Khrushchev further raised the stakes by declaring, "If need be, Soviet artillerymen can support the Cuban people with their rocket fire, should the aggressive forces in the Pentagon dare to start intervention against Cuba."[68]

On July 12 three hundred international journalists gathered at the Kremlin heard Khrushchev mock the Monroe Doctrine, which American presidents had repeatedly invoked since 1823 to warn overseas powers against interfering in Latin American nations. The Soviet leader pronounced the policy "dead," saying it "should best be buried . . . so that it should not poison the air by its decay." In reply, the State Department affirmed that the Monroe Doctrine was alive and well defended by American forces. It then gave the doctrine a cold war flourish by declaring, "The U.S. will not permit the establishment of a regime dominated by international Communism in the Western Hemisphere."[69]

Khrushchev and Castro dramatized their solidarity in September while in New York City to speak at the United Nations. The two leaders embraced outside the Hotel Theresa in Harlem, the only place to extend Castro lodging. They embraced again the next morning at the United Nations before each addressed the General Assembly.[70] The symbolism was clear: Cuba had become the first Latin American country to lean toward Moscow in the cold war.

Daring Khrushchev to cross U.S. interests in Latin America was, for any politician in 1960, a mark of sober statesmanship. Few voters or opinion leaders considered the Monroe Doctrine anachronistic, let alone imperialistic. On the eve of Kennedy's presidential nomination in July, the *New York Times* measured the doctrine as still "a valid, enduring, basic expression of intent to safeguard" the hemisphere "against any attempt by a European (we would now add Asiatic) power to get control of any nation of the North or South American continents. . . . It is a national expression of policy sustained by generations of Americans as of vital necessity to our own security as well as to the security of the hemisphere."[71]

The view that Khrushchev threatened vital American interests in Cuba found vocal friends in Congress, beside whom both Kennedy and Nixon appeared more like somnolent sentries. Kenneth Keating, a Republican senator from New York who later vexed President Kennedy with warnings of missiles in Cuba, pressed this subject as early as the spring of 1960, calling the Soviet presence in Cuba "the boldest challenge to freedom we have known in 60 years." Kennedy's friend and Democratic Senate colleague from Florida, George Smathers, insisted there could no longer be any doubt that Cuba under Castro was in effect a Soviet satellite.[72]

As early as 1960 some Americans spoke of forcibly resisting a possible Soviet military buildup in Cuba. The *Atlanta Constitution* stated in July, "If Cuba really does sign a mutual defense pact with the Soviets giving the latter military bases, our world position will deteriorate alarmingly. . . . The time for patience will come to an end quickly should we wake up to find the Soviet Union with rockets and submarine bases in the Caribbean.

The Monroe Doctrine, the newest aspect of U.S. policy to be challenged by the Russians, must be upheld. And it will be upheld even if it means war."[73] Senator Herman Talmadge of Georgia summed up the stakes, "We can't afford to have a Russian missile base 90 miles from Florida."[74]

Although Kennedy is remembered for stirring up public concerns over Cuba, he actually lagged in addressing them. The columnist William S. White observed that the young Democratic candidate had begun his campaign with "mainly intellectual criticisms of Republican handling of foreign policy," but these "did not seem to be cutting too deeply into public consciousness" or offsetting Nixon's derision of him as too soft and inexperienced to stand up to Khrushchev.[75] Then Kennedy found that assailing the incumbents for permitting a pro-Soviet regime in Cuba—echoes of Republican tirades that the Democrats had "lost" China to the Communists—gave his candidacy new vigor and respectability.

In his rhetorical charges back up San Juan Hill, Kennedy followed a path already tested by his running mate, Lyndon Johnson. During the late summer of 1960, Johnson charged the Republicans with losing Cuba to the "Red Bloc"; the overwhelming responses at each of Johnson's stump speeches led Kennedy to pick up on the issue.[76] Nixon had by then staked his own claim to champion Latin America against Soviet communism, declaring in his acceptance speech on July 28, "When Mr. Khrushchev says the Monroe Doctrine is dead in the Americas, we say the doctrine of freedom applies everywhere in the world."[77]

Even had Kennedy wished to quiet the Cuban issue as too inflammatory for measured debate in the midst of an election campaign, public opinion would not have brooked any apparent complacency over Castro's ties with Khrushchev. The candidate confided to his friend Senator Smathers that "voters asked him more often about Cuba and Castro than any other foreign issue."[78]

Newsweek fairly reflected public sentiment by observing in early July 1960 that "the bearded and bearding Premier of tiny Cuba ... posed a more immediate threat to world peace than West Berlin, Formosa, Korea, and the Middle East fused together."[79] Not to be outdone by its rival, *Time* a week later referred to Cuba as "Khrushchev's Protectorate" and reported that Castro's brother and trusted aide, Raul, had confided to intimates before leaving Havana for Communist Czechoslovakia, "My dream is to drop three atomic bombs on New York."[80]

Privately Kennedy admitted unease at criticizing Eisenhower's Cuban policy when he himself had no plans to do anything differently. Then the realities of campaigning set in, and he added, "What the hell, they [the Republicans] never told us how they would have saved China."[81] On October 20, though, Kennedy made a rare concrete departure from Eisenhower's policies. Dismissing the administration's announcement a day earlier of a ban on most exports to Cuba as "a dramatic but almost empty gesture," Kennedy proposed "to strengthen the non-Batista democratic anti-Castro forces in exile, and in Cuba itself, who offer eventual hope of overthrowing Castro. Thus far these fighters for freedom have had virtually no support from our Government."[82]

Nixon, who believed Kennedy had been briefed on the CIA's plans for Cuban exiles to invade the island,[83] was outraged by his opponent's charge. But to protect the CIA scheme he had secretly advocated, Nixon feigned indignation at the idea of intervention in Cuba, scoring Kennedy's "dangerously irresponsible recommendations."[84] Kennedy's Cuban gambit also drew friendly fire from the liberal press, in part for raising matters best left covert. Yet his call to aid Cuban "fighters for freedom" stemmed largely from inadvertence. A recent Harvard Law

School graduate, Richard N. Goodwin, had drafted the statement without knowing of the CIA's parallel plans. Nor, Goodwin recalled, had he cleared his words beforehand with the candidate, who was asleep. (Kennedy genially quipped to Goodwin and Theodore Sorensen, "OK, if I win this election, I will have won it myself, but, if I lose, you fellows will have lost it."[85])

Buffeted by Nixon and the media, Kennedy retreated four days later with a clarifying statement, "I have never advocated, and I do not advocate, intervention in Cuba in violation of our treaty obligations." The candidate merely wished to "let the forces of freedom in Cuba" know that "the United States sympathized with them."[86] Just as the tempest over Quemoy and Matsu had exposed Kennedy's vulnerability to charges of appeasement, his brief lurch toward a distinctive approach to Castro revealed that any policy initiative on Cuba risked dividing the electorate. Here too, as in his statements on communism, Khrushchev, and the missile gap, Kennedy struggled to hold the political center, not to alter it.

According to Robert A. Divine, Kennedy gained his razor-thin plurality in the election despite failing to offset fully the doubts about his experience, firmness, and judgment in foreign affairs. In substance, though, Kennedy's "New Frontier" observed the familiar boundaries of America's bipartisan cold war consensus:

> For all the rhetoric of a new generation of leadership, Kennedy offered no new departures in American foreign policy. Instead, he simply expounded the doctrines of [former Secretaries of State] Dean Acheson and John Foster Dulles in his constant description of a world divided between freedom and slavery and in his relentless hammering at the need to get the nation moving again in world affairs. . . . Like Roosevelt, Truman, and Eisenhower, he would [as

President] have to learn to turn his back on the myth of a world torn between good and evil which had been foisted on the American people in every election since 1940."[87]

4. Transition in a Time of Crisis

HAVING RIDDEN a rising wave of anxieties and aspirations to the White House, the president-elect found it no simple matter to rein them in. Nor was there a respite from the global crises that had given Kennedy's calls for national sacrifice such conviction. Days before leaving office, President Eisenhower remarked that only strength of arms and will could check Communist belligerence. Looking back on his eight-year legacy, he called his main contribution a "firmness and readiness to take the risk" [of war] that prevented a destructive clash with the Communist bloc."[88]

General C. P. Cabell, the CIA's deputy director, concurred on the urgent dangers that faced the incoming administration. "What do the Communist leaders really want?" he challenged an audience in early January 1961. "The answer is, simply, the world. . . . Theirs is the language of total war. . . . We have been warned before, by Hitler, of plans for world domination. We cannot ignore the present, clear Communist warning. . . ."[89]

In January 1961 *Newsweek* expressed the national media's sympathy for the man about to inherit a world in flames:

John Fitzgerald Kennedy will have good reason to shudder when he takes his first look at the "in" basket on the White House executive desk. . . . From his first day in office, he will confront an all but overpowering array of problems and dangers arising in every corner of a world in up-heaval. . . . In each and every crisis, the world will look to the White House.[90]

Columnists widely agreed that Kennedy would have to repel Communist aggression more boldly than his predecessor. Weeks before the inauguration, Rowland Evans, Jr., wrote in his syndicated column that the new president's "paramount challenge . . . is to end the creeping doubt abroad about the will and vigor of the United States to win the cold war. . . ."[91] And Clarence Manion warned in the *Houston Chronicle* of a "Communist war against us . . . directed by a unified, Kremlin-controlled command which flashes simultaneous orders to its slavishly obedient forces in Laos, Berlin, Algeria, the Congo, Cuba and elsewhere."[92]

In the weeks leading to Kennedy's inauguration the media stirred a cauldron of concern over Latin America, portraying Castro as Khrushchev's man in Havana.[93] Associated Press news analyst Daniel James forecast "heightened uncertainty and tension" and "serious trouble" for fourteen of the twenty Latin American republics, stemming from "deteriorating economic aid and social conditions" but also from subversion by Castro and "intensified Soviet Russian–Red Chinese activities." James warned that "the emboldened czars of world communism have . . . designated the entire Latin American continent as their No. 1 target." Castro topped the list of dangers with his "aggressive campaign" to " 'sell' his revolution. . . . If not stopped soon, we can expect chain-reacting explosions in the Caribbean which no one will be able to control."[94]

Castro's image in the American press during Eisenhower's waning days in office was that of great potential betrayed—much like the American view of Cuba's revolution. Castro "could have become the greatest hero [of] Latin American

38

democracy," the *Birmingham News* lamented. ". . . But he threw it all away in Communist insanity."[95] "Indiscriminate arrests, torture and executions" were bad enough, the *Houston Chronicle* observed, but Cuba now endured "the cult of the filthy, as personified by the bearded messianic one."[96]

"To what lengths will Castro go?" asked the *New Orleans Times-Picayune*, which could not answer because this unpredictable provocateur might dare anything, "whether or not it comes within the bounds of rational action."[97] What mattered, in any case, was the Cuban leader's subservience to the Kremlin: when that "swine" Khrushchev "put on a world championship exhibition of boorishness" at the UN, he came "with Castro in tow."[98] In its report on Kennedy's urgent tasks, *Newsweek* tacitly suggested that the president-elect had a right and a duty to oust Castro, though it remained discreet about the means.[99]

CHAPTER THREE

The New Frontier
Under Siege

TO A LATER GENERATION of scholars, Kennedy's Inaugural Address, pledging to defend freedom "in its hour of maximum danger," needlessly alarmed the American people with shrill cold war refrains. But in a time when Americans were already profoundly alarmed, Kennedy's speech impressed listeners for its restraint and openness to agreement with the Russians across a daunting ideological expanse. His overtures, said the *New Orleans Times-Picayune*, "completely shorn of all belligerence and threats," cut a striking contrast with Khrushchev's "manifesto" two weeks earlier "for continuance of bitter struggle for Red supremacy and triumph, worldwide."[1]

Kennedy's Inaugural exhortation, "Let us never negotiate out of fear; but let us never fear to negotiate," may seem unremarkable in this post–cold war, post-Soviet era. But less than two weeks before his inauguration, the pollster Samuel Lubell found that while the election had stirred hope among some voters that "a new man may get somewhere" with the Russian, the prevalent feeling was that "no one can negotiate with Khrushchev."[2] The new president sensed the mood of pessimism and intransigence toward the Soviets and tried in his first official speech to recognize public concerns yet soften them. Soviet Foreign Minister Andrei Gromyko, evincing no unease over the speech, thought Kennedy "in great form."[3]

Kennedy came to office with a remarkably open view of the Russians. In 1939 a future ambassador to the Kremlin, Charles Bohlen, had hosted the young Harvard grad at his Moscow home and been "struck by Kennedy's charm and quick mind, but especially his open-mindedness about the Soviet Union, a rare quality in those pre-war days."[4] Twenty years later, as a front-runner for the Democratic presidential nomination, Kennedy told the historian James MacGregor Burns that while the Soviets were intent on expanding their power, the cold war was aggravated by mutual misunderstanding: "You have two people . . . who are both of goodwill, but neither of whom can communicate" with the other.[5] Such moderation impressed Soviet intelligence agents, who cabled Moscow expectantly from their embassy in Washington upon Kennedy's nomination in 1960:

Considering that . . . there is a conflict of "basic national interests" between the United States and the USSR and that because of this one cannot expect [any] fundamental change in their relations, Kennedy nevertheless grants the possibility of a mutually acceptable settlement . . . on the basis of a joint effort to avoid nuclear war. . . . Kennedy, in principle, is in favor of talks with the Soviet Union, rejecting as "too fatalistic" the opinion that "you can't trust" the Soviet Union, that it "doesn't observe treaties," and so on.[6]

On February 11, 1961, just weeks after entering the White House, Kennedy tapped four veteran diplomats for their insights into Soviet-American relations: Llewelyn Thompson, his ambassador to Moscow (named in 1958 by Eisenhower), and three of Thompson's venerable predecessors: Averell Harriman, George Kennan, and Bohlen. Afterward Bohlen wrote to Thompson, "I never heard of a President who wanted to know so much." Kennedy appeared "extraordinarily free from preconceived prejudices, inherited or otherwise . . . almost as though he had thrown aside the normal prejudices that beset human mentality." In contrast to his somber State of the Union message in January 1961, Kennedy, according to Bohlen, "saw Russia as a great and powerful country and we were a great and powerful country, and it seemed to him there must be some basis upon which the two countries could live without blowing each other up." Bohlen's sole concern was that Kennedy might discount unduly the Soviet Communist challenge to Western interests.[7]

Yet while the new president looked to scale back the hallmarks of East-West tension—armed confrontation, invective, and fear—he soon found the momentum of cold war politics more potent than he had imagined. Deep-rooted tensions over Berlin; spiraling technology in nuclear weapons; competition for the allegiance of developing nations; expanding Soviet ambitions for influence beyond Eastern Europe to all points of the globe; a bid for leadership of the socialist world by the intensely anti-Western Chinese Communists; and NATO's fractious, nervous responses to U.S. initiatives, all proved resistant or impervious to changes in the White House. So, largely, did cold war attitudes on Main Streets across the country and on Capitol Hill. The precedents set by earlier administrations also sharply impinged on presidential decision-making. Nowhere was this so glaring as in President Kennedy's emerging policy toward Cuba.

1. The Bay of Pigs and After

THE ELECTION RESULTS had left the partisan politics of the Monroe Doctrine intact save that Republicans could now indulge in the same demands for executive action against Castro that Democrats had made of Eisenhower. Therefore the new president had, at the least, to match his predecessor's efforts to dislodge Castro. By January 1961 those efforts ranged from diplomatic isolation and economic embargo to covert war.

Kennedy quietly acquiesced in one of Eisenhower's final acts as president: on January 3, 1961, he severed relations with Cuba after Castro charged the American embassy in Havana with espionage and ordered a reduction of its staff. "There is a limit to what the United States in self-respect can endure," Eisenhower explained in a statement handed to reporters. "That limit has now been reached."[8] Although the historian Thomas G. Paterson argues that Kennedy, by failing to repudiate this act, fumbled away his options for rebuilding ties with Castro,[9] in fact his options were already meager.

Americans were elated by Eisenhower's stand, and most newspapers judged the president had no alternative.[10] A typical editorial pronounced the break "inevitable" and even an "anti-climax" in view of Castro's heaping "insult upon injury upon this country, seizing our investments of more than a billion dollars, mistreating our nationals, attacking our motives and lying about our deeds."[11] Kennedy resisted pressures to endorse Eisenhower's move, but he could scarcely have renounced it without undercutting his own credibility before ever taking office.

Kennedy's critics have feasted on Defense Secretary Robert McNamara's candid recollection that the administration was "hysterical about Castro at the time of the Bay of Pigs [in April 1961] and thereafter."[12] The unraveling of the CIA-sponsored landing at the Bay of Pigs on April 17, 1961, dubbed by Theodore Draper "a perfect failure,"[13] indeed shocked Kennedy and left him defensive about his most exposed foreign policy weakness. Nor did it help that Castro had mocked Kennedy during the 1960 campaign as an "ignorant, illiterate, beardless kid."[14] But the hysteria reverberating through the White House originated from many quarters.

Breaking diplomatic relations with Cuba whetted public hopes for openly toppling Castro. The *Birmingham News* declared that Castro's "outrageous conduct . . . warranted a break long ago." The paper discounted Cuban charges of an imminent U.S. invasion, saying, "it is too much to hope for," but added, "in the name of all American liberty": "oh, the temptation!"[15] Breaking relations, a Texan chided, was no more a cure for communism than taking a boy out of school would keep him from becoming a delinquent. Instead the United States should "dispatch an ultimatum of complete military surrender of all Castro forces and set about making Cuba our 51st state. Viva America!"[16]

Demands to shear Castro of his power greeted Kennedy as he assumed office. An editorial in the right-wing *Dallas Morning News*, on January 21, 1961, referred to Cuba's "crazed chieftain" and "bearded madman."[17] William B. Ruggles, reviewing a new study of Castro, *Red Star Over Cuba* by Nathaniel Weyl, thought the Cuban leader's mental state uncertain but his politics an open book, one that America should soon close: "Fidel Castro, sane or otherwise, daily demonstrates that he is only a front for penetrative Communism. . . ."[18]

Thomas G. Paterson, who faults Kennedy's "fixation" with Cuba, nonetheless observes that from the outset of his presidency he faced unrelenting and pervasive pressure to act against Castro: "Hardly a press conference went by without an insistent question about Cuba." The demands came from "Republicans and Democrats alike," the vocal Cuban exile community in Florida, businessmen protesting the nationalization of a billion dollars' worth of American-owned property, George Meany of the AFL-CIO deploring severe restraints on the Cuban labor federation, and the Joint Chiefs, who urged an invasion of the island. "Everyone seemed eager to know when Kennedy would knock Castro off his perch, and many expected the President to act before the next election."[19]

For all the later talk of Kennedy's "vendetta" against Castro, his actions as president observed the contours of earlier policies. The history of U.S. relations with Latin American nations before the missile crisis had been pockmarked by 90 instances of open military intervention in the 164 years between 1798 and 1962.[20] Cuba was a much trod-upon cornerstone of this aggressive approach to hemispheric security. The United States had sent marines to Cuba in 1898, 1906, 1912, and 1917, while during the 1940s and 1950s it had propped up as president an army strongman, Fulgencio Batista, corrupt, ruthless, but relentlessly subservient to America's sprawling economic interests on the island.

Kennedy's approval of a CIA operation to train a contingent of armed Cuban exiles to reclaim their island originated in policies by the Eisenhower administration. In March 1959, even before Castro seized U.S. property and opened diplomatic relations with the Soviet Union, the National Security Council considered ways to bring "another government to power in Cuba."[21] On March 17, 1960, shortly after Cuba signed a trade agreement with the Soviet Union, Eisenhower authorized "A Program of Covert Action Against the Castro Regime" which included sponsorship of a paramilitary force outside of Cuba for future military action.[22]

The CIA's assassination plots against Castro during the Kennedy years similarly extended operations first authorized in 1960 by a high Eisenhower administration official.[23] Like Kennedy, Eisenhower more clearly enjoyed plausible deniability in these schemes than innocence.[24] But the exigencies of waging the cold war and a hatred of communism discouraged cavils over acceptable behavior, for as Eisenhower noted of the CIA, "Our traditional ideas of international sportsmanship are scarcely applicable in the morass in which the world now flounders."[25]

Whether Eisenhower would have approved the CIA's blueprint for a rebel landing in Cuba is uncertain.[26] He had always insisted that this was simply an option, not an obligation. Still, in November 1960 Eisenhower had stood ready to order the first open U.S. military intervention in Latin America in more than a quarter-century when a brewing rebellion in Guatemala threatened the security of Cuban rebels training there under CIA tutelage.[27] And according to notes of a White House conference with President-elect Kennedy on January 19, 1961, a day before leaving office, Eisenhower "said with reference to guerrilla forces which are opposed to Castro that it was the policy of this government to help such forces to the utmost. . . . It was his recommendation that this effort be continued and accelerated."[28]

Kennedy shared Eisenhower's hope that a paramilitary operation would bring Castro down, differing mainly in his handling, or mishandling, of the CIA's venture. Startled to learn in

March 1961 that the agency's aims had burgeoned from a modest infiltration of guerrillas to a full-fledged invasion, the president scaled back plans for air support and other actions that might expose U.S. complicity. Kennedy's halfhearted commitment to the invasion ended in full-fledged disaster. Some 1,400 armed Cuban exiles landed at the Bay of Pigs on April 17, 1961, and were quickly pinned down by Castro's forces. Despite urgent pleas by CIA and military leaders, Kennedy refused to order U.S. air or naval strikes, or to commit U.S. ground troops, for fear of touching off a wider conflict with the Russians.[29] By April 19 the battle was over: the invaders had lost 114 dead and 1,189 captured; barely 100 escaped by sea.

Eisenhower was appalled to learn of his successor's restraint. Invited to Camp David in the wake of this debacle, the former president berated Kennedy for failing to follow through: " 'Why on earth' hadn't he provided the exiles with air cover? Kennedy said he had feared the Soviets 'would be very apt to cause trouble in Berlin.' " This, Michael Beschloss writes, drew from Eisenhower "one of the chilling stares that the public never saw" as he lectured his young successor: "That is exactly the *opposite* of what would really happen. The Soviets follow their own plans, and if they see us show any weakness, then is when they press us the hardest. . . . The failure of the Bay of Pigs will embolden the Soviets to do something that they would not otherwise do."[30]

According to Eisenhower's notes of the meeting, "The next thing that [Kennedy] wanted to talk about were the direction and prospects for future action. I was unable to give him any detailed suggestions, but did say that I would support anything that had as its objective the prevention of Communist entry and solidification of bases in the Western hemisphere."[31]

Former Vice President Richard Nixon, called to the White House, advised Kennedy to "find a proper legal cover" and go in militarily to topple Castro. Kennedy demurred, saying, "Both Walter Lippmann [the columnist] and Chip Bohlen have reported that Khrushchev is in a very cocky mood. . . . This means that there is a good chance that if we move on Cuba, Khrushchev will move on Berlin." But Nixon, like Eisenhower, pounded on the need for strength: "Khrushchev will prod and probe in several places at once. When we show weakness, he'll create crisis to take advantage of us. We should act in Cuba. . . ."[32]

Although Eisenhower and Nixon took the nonpartisan high road by forgoing public criticism of the president, the Cuban fiasco set a pack of Republicans baying at Kennedy's refusal to use troops, even in extremis, to uphold the national security. Nelson Rockefeller and Barry Goldwater, two likely contenders for the Republican presidential nomination in 1964, fed eagerly on Kennedy's caution. Rockefeller charged that Kennedy had failed "to make good on the Monroe Doctrine" by adequately supporting the Bay of Pigs invasion;[33] Goldwater said the episode should fill each American with "apprehension and shame."[34]

Kennedy often bitterly reproached himself for the misjudgments underlying the failed invasion. Yet he never regretted his refusal to allow open U.S. military intervention. Hosting a friend that summer at Hyannis Port, Kennedy explained, "We're not going to plunge into an irresponsible action just because a fanatical fringe . . . puts so-called national pride above national reason. Do you think I'm going to carry on my conscience the responsibility for the wanton maiming and killing of children like our children we saw here this evening?"[35]

From a decidedly different vantage point, CIA Director Allen Dulles years later told Tom Wicker of the *New York Times* that Kennedy had shown only a reluctant interest in the Bay of Pigs operation:

In order to get him to go along, Dulles had to suggest repeatedly, without ever saying so explicitly, that, if Kennedy canceled the project, he would appear less zealous than Eisenhower against communism in the hemisphere. "This was a mistake," Dulles said. "I should have realized that, if he had no enthusiasm about the idea in the first place, he would drop it at the first opportunity rather than do the things necessary to make it succeed."[36]

Few Americans, however critical of Kennedy's judgment and resolve, questioned the ethics of sponsoring an invasion of Cuba by anti-Communist forces. In contrast to the moral criticisms scholars have since expressed, Kennedy's countrymen typically expected more ruthless actions with concrete results, not passive musings on Castro's rights as a legitimate head of state. *Newsweek*, gleaning a silver lining in the debacle, saw a "long-term gain for the U.S." in its conduct of paramilitary operations and international political action. This learning experience in sponsoring guerilla warfare was crucial because, unlike the Communists, who were "past masters . . . at capturing a country without firing a shot," neither the American CIA nor the armed services "are now capable of directing operations involving nationals of other countries."[37]

After the defeat a Gallup survey showed that a majority of respondents who expressed an opinion favored continued aid to anti-Castro forces with money and war materials.[38] "Self-determination" was not an issue, for only 14 percent of respondents believed Castro would win "a free and honest election" while 71 percent said he would not.[39] In a Gallup poll in late September 1962, only 22 percent of respondents thought the U.S. government should adopt a policy of "keep out, hands off" Cuban affairs.[40] *Time* pronounced the doctrine of nonintervention "especially unsuited to the world of the 1960s," when the West faced "the implacable challenge of Communism."[41] Kennedy's contemporary critics, in short, thought him feckless, not reckless.

The prevalent view of Castro as a tyrant who richly merited a violent end was faithfully dramatized on national television months after the failed Bay of Pigs invasion. In October 1961 the acclaimed anthology *The Twilight Zone* featured a withering morality tale of a revolutionary named "Clemente," replete with Castro's trademark jungle fatigues, sprawling black beard, and ever-present cigar. Clemente's story begins in seeming triumph, with his seizure of the presidential palace. But his rapid descent into madness, megalomania, and murder—sins that Americans routinely attributed to Castro—leads the dictator to betray his former comrades, his revolution, and his people until, seeing "enemies" everywhere, he takes his own life. Aired by the premier TV network, CBS, the episode fairly distilled opinion of Castro as an illegitimate, possibly insane ruler. Nor was the show's creator, Rod Serling, content in his final voice-over to keep this tale at a safe remove from real-world struggles:

> Ramos Clemente, a would-be god in dungarees, strangled by an illusion, that will-o'-the-wisp mirage that dangles from the sky in front of the eyes of all ambitious men, all tyrants—*and any resemblance to tyrants living or dead is hardly coincidental,* whether it be here or in the Twilight Zone.[42]

Years later the show's producer, Buck Houghton, ruefully recalled the excesses of the "Castro" episode, saying, "I think we had a fairly simplistic view of Castro at that time."[43] In this *The Twilight Zone,* however shadowy and allegorical, was a realm Americans found familiar and convincing.

2. Vienna and Berlin: Kennedy's Education in Crisis Politics

FOLLOWING the Bay of Pigs, President Kennedy talked about staying focused on "the substance of power" rather than "the shadow." For Kennedy this meant limiting conflicts between the superpowers while defending vital national interests, as in West Berlin. In June 1961 a two-day summit meeting with Khrushchev offered a chance to clarify American aims, reassure the Russians, and lower the temperature of crisis points from Berlin to Laos. But hopes for a meeting of minds vanished in the chasm between the two governments' agenda. Aggravating the deadlock, Khrushchev's combative manner shocked Kennedy and mocked his faith that discreet, businesslike accommodation could neatly manage the volatile clash of superpowers.

At Vienna Kennedy treated the Soviet chairman as an honorable and equal partner for peace, crediting his good motives and equating their dilemmas and challenges. Instead of trumpeting the vast U.S. lead in nuclear weapons, he volunteered that "the present balance of power between Sino-Soviet forces and the forces of the United States and Western Europe [was] more or less in balance," a gallant fiction that Khrushchev, in a rare show of harmony, immediately seconded.[44]

Kennedy's proposed solution to the dangers of the cold war was a mutual effort to anticipate and avert confrontations. Competition between their nations might be unavoidable, Kennedy said, but "The struggle in other areas should be conducted in a way which would not involve the two countries directly and would not affect their national interest or prestige. As Mr. Khrushchev knows from history . . . it is very easy to involve countries in certain actions. We might get involved in a struggle which would affect the peace of the world and the interests of our peoples."[45]

When Khrushchev rejoined that the West liked to warn of "miscalculation" simply to blame the USSR,[46] Kennedy looked for neutral, even self-denigrating ways to win over the Soviet chairman: "As Mr. Khrushchev knows, history shows that it is extremely difficult to make a judgment as to what other countries would do next." Alluding to the century's two world wars, Kennedy said, "Western Europe has suffered a great deal because of its failure to foresee with precision what other countries would do." And during the Korean War, "the United States had failed to foresee what the Chinese would do. However, misjudgment can be avoided and the purpose of this meeting is to introduce precision in judgments of the two sides and to obtain a clearer understanding of where we are going."[47]

Kennedy confessed his own "misjudgment with regard to the Cuban situation" as an example of the difficulty of gauging events. He then emphasized as their paramount task in Vienna, "to introduce greater precision" in predicting each other's actions "so that our two countries could survive this period of competition without endangering their national security."[48]

Seeking at least symbolic accords that could lessen tensions, Kennedy pressed for close UN supervision of a cease-fire in Laos, where Russia and America supplied rival factions yet lacked a compelling strategic interest. He hoped too for progress toward a nuclear test ban that would discourage proliferation and curb radioactive fallout. For Khrushchev, however, a cease-fire in Laos held scant urgency compared with gaining Western concessions on Berlin. And the chairman shunned a test ban decoupled from wider issues of disarmament, fearing a ban alone would freeze America's lead in nuclear arms while inspections could expose that lead and help the U.S. target Soviet installations.

Already mired in policy differences, the summit under-scored how clashing styles of leadership could misshape foreign relations. The U.S. ambassador to Moscow, Llewelyn Thompson, who knew Khrushchev better than any other American, had cautioned Kennedy against being drawn into debates over ideology. The chairman was too steeped in Marxist dialectic and, like all true believers, would concede nothing. This advice fit the president's own focus on practical steps to avoid stumbling into conflicts. But he had not reckoned with the force—and fury—of Khrushchev's personal diplomacy.

Buoyed by socialist currents among developing nations and by Soviet triumphs in missile development, space launches, and economic growth, Khrushchev saw his country—his "system"—advancing inexorably. Kennedy's recent humiliation by Castro's Cuba appeared further proof that "reactionary" capitalism was doomed. And the Soviet chairman had come to Vienna to press the point.

"The Soviet Union is for change," Khrushchev lectured Kennedy. Communism was challenging capitalism just as the French Revolution once challenged feudalism, he said, and he likened America to the "Holy Alliance" that had tried to crush that revolution—in vain.[49] Deploring American hostility to popular revolutions, the chairman tendered Kennedy some unsolicited advice in developing a more effective Cuban policy based on a sound grasp of history:

A mere handful of people, headed by Fidel Castro, over-threw the Batista regime because of its oppressive nature. During Castro's fight against Batista, US capitalist circles, as they are called in the USSR, supported Batista and this is why the anger of the Cuban people turned against the United States. The President's decision to launch a landing in Cuba only strengthened the revolutionary forces and

53

Castro's own position, because the people of Cuba were afraid that they would get another Batista and lose the achievements of the revolution.

To better convey the lesson, Khrushchev thoughtfully highlighted Kennedy's ongoing failure: "Castro is not a Communist but US policy can make him one."[50]

It was an astonishing performance by Khrushchev, delivered with breathtaking conviction: the dictator of the world's largest empire, scarcely five years after revealing the mass purges, executions, deportations, and imprisonment under Stalin, had seized for Soviet communism the moral high ground of popular rule and individual rights. Equally astonishing was Kennedy's forbearance. Instead of replying in kind, he retreated before Khrushchev's ideological hailstorm, hoping to lead the chairman back to areas of possible agreement.

When Khrushchev insisted that tyrants like "the Shah will certainly be overthrown,"[51] the president acknowledged that "if certain governments should fail to produce better living for their people," they "would be doomed. But in all these developments, the President reiterated, we should avoid direct contact between our two countries so as not to prejudice the interests of their national security."[52]

Khrushchev's insult that U.S. commitments to Laos and other remote areas sprang "from megalomania, from delusions of grandeur," also failed to provoke Kennedy to indignant denials or countercharges. "The President said that, frankly speaking, he had assumed office on January 20th and that the obligations and commitments had been undertaken before that time."[53] As for Laos, "US policy in that region had not always been wise," nor had he "been able to make a final judgment as to what the people's desires in that area are."[54] His concern was simply "to secure a cease fire in Laos and to establish a mechanism for its verification" in order to keep American and Soviet interests from colliding.[55]

U.S. support for Spain, a nation under the iron rule of General Francisco Franco, gave Khrushchev another opening to assail American hypocrisy for claiming to care about free elections. Rather than defend the Spanish dictator, Kennedy admitted that "if Franco should be replaced and if the new regime were to associate itself with the Soviet Union, the balance of power in Western Europe would radically change and this is, of course, a matter of great concern to us."[56]

When Khrushchev, untethered by facts, reduced U.S. African policy to "support for Colonialist powers,"[57] Kennedy offered a nuanced response better suited to a Ph.D. examination than an exchange between heads of the world's rival power blocs. According to records of the talks, "The President stated that in NATO the US is allied to a number of countries which are colonial powers. Yet in view of the great changes that have occurred in Africa, where some 25 countries have obtained their independence in a very short time, it is quite clear what the trend is." Briefly forgoing his bludgeon for a stiletto, Khrushchev retorted "that this was true but wondered what the reason for this trend was and whose effort had brought about the change."[58] Kennedy noted America's frequent support for African independence movements, then acknowledged, "Perhaps more could have been done, but we do have problems with our allies."[59]

Opportunities abounded during the summit for Kennedy to expose Khrushchev's claims as hyperbolic and at times absurd. Instead he contorted to avoid giving offense, even permitting the Soviet dictator to assert unopposed, "The Soviet Union does not sympathize with dictators or tyranny."[60] The president also politely passed over Khrushchev's contradictory boasts that the Soviet Union, as a Marxist nation, opposed war,[61] that it supported as "sacred" all "liberation wars,"[62] and that, had it been in Communist China's place, it would have attacked Taiwan a long time ago.[63]

Conflicts over the status of Berlin dominated the waning hours of the summit and further eroded the reserves of goodwill between Kennedy and Khrushchev. To many observers Berlin symbolized the cold war, straddling East Germany in the Soviet bloc and West Germany in the NATO alliance, but lying wholly within East German territory. Crises in Soviet-American relations had repeatedly flared over West Berlin, an outpost of Western democratic capitalism in the heart of the Soviet satellite states. The provocation cut more keenly because Russians harbored traumatic memories of German invasions as well as anxieties over West German rearmament and expressions of interest in nuclear weapons. Khrushchev called West Berlin "a bone in the throat" of the socialist world and considered its removal a prime test of his overtures to the West.

The immediate threat West Berlin posed to the Communist bloc was economic and political rather than military. Residents enjoyed a freedom and prosperity that acted like a magnet on businessmen and professionals from East Germany (the German Democratic Republic), draining an already bleak economy. According to the historian Vladislav Zubok, even Khrushchev's aides joked mordantly that "soon there will be nobody left in the GDR except for [Socialist party boss Walter] Ulbricht and his mistress."[64]

To ensure Ulbricht's survival, in November 1958 Khrushchev had demanded an end to the Western presence in Berlin. Otherwise he would sign a "peace" treaty with East Germany, ending its status as an occupied territory and, in effect, giving it control over access routes to West Berlin as a prelude to annexation. By early 1961 the unresolved tensions over Berlin had made it the primary flash point of the cold war. As Ulbricht became desperate to stem the flow of refugees, Khrushchev resolved to cajole, bluff, or threaten the new American president into concessions at Vienna.

Yet Kennedy held his ground, and the already floundering summit edged from disappointment to disaster. Khrushchev insisted that a treaty ending hostilities sixteen years after World War II was long overdue, and no power could afterward dispute East Germany's legal right to control access to West Berlin. Kennedy responded with his most forceful utterances of the summit:

> We are in Berlin not because of someone's sufferance. We fought our way there. . . . This is an area where every President of the US since World War II has been committed by treaty and other contractual rights and where every President has reaffirmed his faithfulness to his obligations. . . . US national security is involved in this matter because if we were to accept the Soviet proposal US commitments would be regarded as a mere scrap of paper.[65]

Kennedy then tried to mollify Khrushchev, saying that, like Eisenhower, "he recognized that the situation" in West Berlin was "abnormal" and unsatisfactory. "The US is not asking the USSR to change its position," but with so much instability in the world, "it should not seek to change our position and thus disturb the balance of power."[66]

Khrushchev's farewell to Kennedy included a threat of war. The Soviet Union intended to sign a peace treaty with East Germany by December unless the United States accepted an "interim agreement" to end West German rule over West Berlin. According to Vladislav Zubok and Constantine Pleshakov, the transcripts of the summit talks omitted the full horror of the chairman's valedictory remarks:

In the frenzy of brinkmanship Khrushchev said that the USSR would not start a war, but if the United States was going to unleash war, then let it be now, before the development of even more destructive weapons. This passage was so reckless that it was not included in either Soviet or American records of the conversation.[67]

Kennedy's reply was muted but resolute. If Khrushchev's threats were serious, "it would be a cold winter."[68]

Afterward the president brushed off criticisms that he had let Khrushchev off lightly. To his friend Dave Powers, Kennedy dryly pondered, "What was I supposed to do to show how tough I was? Take my shoe off and pound it on the table?"[69] Still, Khrushchev's irascible behavior was sobering. Robert Kennedy later reflected, "This was the first time the President had ever really come across somebody with whom he couldn't exchange ideas in a meaningful way and feel that there was some point to it. . . . It was a shock to him."[70]

Secretary of State Dean Rusk, a veteran diplomat, was also taken aback by Khrushchev's threats. "In diplomacy," Rusk explained, "you almost never use the word war. Kennedy was very upset. . . . He wasn't prepared for the brutality of Khrushchev's presentation. . . . Khrushchev was trying to act like a bully to this young President of the United States."[71] In his memoirs Khrushchev recalled almost wistfully how his words on Berlin had left Kennedy "not only anxious, but deeply upset. . . . Looking at him, I couldn't help feeling a bit sorry and somewhat upset myself. . . . I would have liked very much for us to part in a different mood." But "Politics," he said, "is a merciless business."[72]

"Roughest thing in my life," an exhausted Kennedy blurted to James Reston of the *New York Times* on returning to the American embassy in Vienna. In an unguarded, cathartic session with a leading member of the press, the president reflected on Khrushchev's virulent behavior and his ultimatum on Berlin:

> I've got two problems. First, to figure out why he did it, and in such a hostile way. And second, to figure out what we can do about it. I think the first part is pretty easy to explain. I think he did it because of the Bay of Pigs. I think he thought that anyone who was so young and inexperienced as to get into that mess could be taken. And anyone who got into it and didn't see it through had no guts. So he just beat hell out of me. . . . I've got a terrible problem. If he thinks I'm inexperienced and have no guts, until we remove those ideas we won't get anywhere with him. So we have to act.[73]

In his Inaugural Address, President Kennedy had asked Americans to "remember that civility is not a sign of weakness." But the Soviet chairman's belligerent swagger at Vienna showed the limitations of Kennedy's style. The president's one-sided restraint and confessions of fallibility were rare in the annals of cold war summitry. After the last chilling exchange he understood why.

Kennedy's sense that Khrushchev dismissed him as weak was later confirmed by Arkady Shevchenko, a Soviet defector who had served as special assistant to Foreign Minister Andrei Gromyko: "The impression in the Foreign Ministry was that . . . Kennedy failed to deal with Nikita. That was dangerous." The Kremlin leadership "remembered Truman, a cold warrior, and Eisenhower, who was all smiles, but who, they knew, was a tough man." But in Kennedy, a youthful, seemingly callow leader who had allowed the Bay of Pigs invasion to fail and had then tried soft reason with Khrushchev, "Nikita saw a weak man. He saw he could even intimidate him. Everyone was elated. It affected our inferiority complex about America.

To find that an American President can be bullied and won't react in a strong way. This psychological effect was very important."[74]

Khrushchev's dim view of Kennedy contributed to his decision in July 1961 to raise the temperature over West Berlin. Although Kennedy hoped to avoid a confrontation, he necessarily observed the twin imperatives of containment policy: to resist expansion of Communist influence and to face down Soviet demands. For more than a dozen years the U.S. government had rebuffed all threats to West Berlin, beginning with President Truman's airlift to thwart a Soviet blockade from June 1948 till May 1949. During his last years in office, Eisenhower disregarded Khrushchev's periodic ultimatums while vaguely hinting at a compromise. Kennedy too needed to demonstrate solidarity with leaders in NATO, above all the anxiously insistent Konrad Adenauer of West Germany.

As with the arms race, Cuba, and other foreign policy challenges, Khrushchev's ultimatum over Berlin spurred Americans to press Kennedy for bold action while balking at hints of compromise and conciliation. Kenneth Crawford of *Newsweek* found in July 1961 "no substantial disagreement" among politicians, who understood that "the people will go all the way on a firm line with Mr. Kennedy. . . . Pressure from the loyal Republican opposition is all on the side of toughness." As for Kennedy's public standing, Crawford later observed,

> He is criticized more for doing too little than for doing too much to counter Soviet pressure. Judging from opinion polls, editorial comment, and informal soundings, the "better dead than Red" stickers appearing on automobile bumpers . . . reflect something of the prevailing national mood. People are fed up with Khrushchev's hypocrisy and bluster. And this isn't because they lack understanding of

60

the consequences of atomic war. A recent Gallup poll reveals that most Americans accept the probability that they
would not survive such a conflict. . . . Its [the country's]
temper has not been whipped up by the President or anybody else. . . . The danger now is not that Americans will
panic but that they won't willingly accept an accommodation in Germany because they will regard any concession as
"appeasement."[75]

Americans tensed for a military apocalypse in Berlin yet
urged President Kennedy to act more forcefully. Householders
questioned local civil defense headquarters about underground
shelters, and men volunteered for enlistment or recall with the
reserves.[76] A woman in Seattle wrote, "I hope the President
knows that even mothers of small children are losing sleep over
this dread situation [Berlin]. But I can say that this mother
would rather lose all than raise her children under less than
freedom. Courage, JFK!"[77]

Through the summer of 1961 Khrushchev peppered the
media and visiting diplomats with word of an imminent Soviet
treaty with East Germany and threats of nuclear destruction
should the West then challenge East German control over all of
Berlin. Afraid that Khrushchev would catastrophically misread
Western resolve, Kennedy warned on July 25 that Soviet action
against West Berlin would mean war with the United States,
and he underscored this point by announcing varied military
preparations, including a call-up of reservists. His speech had a
tonic effect, dissuading Khrushchev from either signing a treaty
with East Germany or permitting Ulbricht to move against
West Berlin. But in early August, as East Germany's hemor-
rhaging population drain worsened, Khrushchev let Ulbricht
seal the border between East and West Berlin, first with barbed
wire, then with a concrete wall.

Americans were outraged. Former Secretary of State Dean Acheson privately expressed dismay that the president had not ordered the wall destroyed. But although Kennedy saw the building of the wall as a brutish act (and a propaganda windfall for the West), his prime concern remained to avert a wider conflict. National Security Adviser McGeorge Bundy later acknowledged that President Kennedy's deliberately narrow reference at a press conference on August 10 to defending "West" Berlin rather than simply Berlin "may have given advance encouragement to Khrushchev" to build the wall.[78] But as Michael Beschloss writes, "Unlike Eisenhower, Kennedy was not comfortable with ambiguity when the stakes were as high as they were over Berlin. He was always afraid of nuclear war by miscalculation."[79]

Beschloss makes a strong circumstantial case that Kennedy may have secretly assured Khrushchev he would acquiesce in the Berlin Wall "as the price of defusing the Berlin crisis."[80] Certainly Kennedy's public statements were as circumspect as American public opinion would tolerate. At his press conference just three days before East German police sealed off East Berlin, Kennedy pointedly refrained from disavowing a statement by Senator Fulbright in June that the Communists had a "right" to stop the exodus from East Berlin. Instead the president blandly observed that the United States would not either "encourage or discourage the movement of refugees."[81]

Although aides insisted that the president was "shocked and depressed" by the Berlin wall, his friend and appointments secretary Kenneth O'Donnell found the president relieved: "Actually, he saw the Wall as the turning point that would lead to the end of the Berlin crisis." Kennedy privately empathized with Khrushchev, saying, "This is his way out of his predicament. It's not a very nice solution, but a wall is a hell of a lot better than a war."[82]

Although Kennedy had finessed a showdown over Berlin, this did little to raise Khrushchev's estimate of the young president's mettle. A week before surprising the West—and his East European satellites—with the Berlin Wall, the Soviet leader told a meeting of visiting Communist party leaders in Moscow that Kennedy was well meaning but ineffectual. Trapped by warmongers, "he is rather an unknown quantity in politics. So I feel empathy with him in his situation, because he is too much of a light-weight both for the Republicans as well as for the Democrats." According to Khrushchev, Kennedy had admitted to his son-in-law Alexei Adzhubei that if he did as Khrushchev wanted on Berlin, the Congress would impeach him. "The situation is very grave there," Khrushchev concluded. "It looks as if I am a propagandist for Kennedy, to make you less stern about him. . . . You might turn on me for that, but I will survive."[83]

Kennedy's restraint could not avert a harsher confrontation in October 1961, springing not from his own or Khrushchev's design but from a random incident that ignited the tensions in Berlin. On October 22 East German police detained Allan Lightner, the ranking American diplomat in West Berlin, as he tried to enter the Eastern sector. Five days later General Lucius Clay, the president's personal representative in Berlin, decided on his own initiative to teach the Russians a lesson in American resolve. Without consulting or even informing his commander-in-chief, Clay sent a line of tanks to the edge of East Berlin, capable of bulldozing the newly built wall. An equal number of Russian tanks barred Clay's forces. Valentine Falin, then the Russian ambassador to West Germany, recalled:

> I would say that in October 1961 the world was closer to the third world war than ever. Our tanks were then positioned in Berlin, combat ready, two hundred meters from American tanks. And, as an immediate participant of these

events, let me assure you that if [the] Americans . . . [had tried] to destroy the Berlin Wall—our tanks would then open fire.[84]

Neither Kennedy nor Khrushchev was about to let his generals decide the future of Berlin. After a phone conversation in which Kennedy praised Clay for keeping his nerve—only to have Clay express doubts about the nerve of "you people in Washington"[85]—the president secretly conveyed through his brother Robert that if Khrushchev were to pull back the Soviet tanks, the American tanks would also withdraw. According to Falin, Kennedy also suggested that if the tanks "parted without damage to each other's prestige," he would show "certain flexibility" in a "productive, purely political exchange of opinions" on Berlin.[86] The outcome said much about foreign policy during this era, when both President Kennedy and Premier Khrushchev relied on secret maneuver to dampen the tinderbox of cold war confrontation.

3. The Web of Nuclear Terror

FEARS OF unchecked conflict over Berlin were bound up with a greater terror that loomed over virtually all cold war flash points. During the late 1950s and early 1960s the prospect of nuclear war appeared more vivid and imminent to Americans than is easy to imagine now. Nuclear weapons were proliferating along with their mushrooming destructive power. The resumption of nuclear tests by Russia in September 1961 and by America several months later aggravated anxieties. So did the two governments' readiness to brandish nuclear might—or bluff—in geopolitical conflicts from Laos to Berlin and, in the summer and fall of 1962, Cuba.

During these years nuclear war was far from "unthinkable." Rather it was the subject of intensive planning by academic strategists, military officers, and political leaders. Their common assumption was that although a nuclear exchange would be horrific, the country had nonetheless to prepare for it. Otherwise the risk of war could actually increase because Communist leaders would more readily commit acts of subversion and aggression. In one of the paradoxes of the nuclear age, the test of sound presidential leadership therefore included a resolve to risk mutual annihilation as the surest way to keep the peace.

The imperative for assertions of national will, even at great risk, had long been self-evident to the national security specialists grappling with how to wage a cold war in the shadow of nuclear destruction. In 1956 RAND's William Kaufmann forecast a period of "continuing competition" between the superpowers, ". . . as full of hairpin curves, of sudden rises and declines, of agreeable prospects and impending catastrophes, as the classic Alpine roads."[87] These ongoing crises would demand periodic displays of force by U.S. leaders to deter the Kremlin from making still greater mischief. Even wars, possibly involving nuclear exchanges as a "last resort,"[88] might prove necessary as "partial or token tests of strength" to clarify "relative power."[89]

Kennedy's presidency coincided with several other developments that added to the unique dangers of this age. The Soviet Union continued to build a long-range ballistic missile force that, though far inferior to the U.S. arsenal, would leave Americans vulnerable to devastating attack. Rapid breakthroughs in military technology also raised fears on both sides that the nuclear balance could suddenly shift. The diversity of views—or, as some saw it, the confusion—among strategic experts about whether a nuclear war could be fought, under what circumstances, and in what manner, showed such decision-making to be neither as predictable nor as rational as the theorists often implied.

Tensions and fears fed on each other, increasing the danger of escalation. Each country's limited, often distorted perceptions of the other's intentions made any policy statement or deployment involving nuclear weapons subject to intense suspicion and alarm. In this unstable atmosphere, even small incidents between the superpowers could acquire an apocalyptic aura as they became bound up in the deadly contingencies of nuclear deterrence.

At the highest levels of government, Kennedy and Khrushchev shared an unwavering conviction that nuclear war would be a catastrophe for their countries and the entire human race. Both men strove to ensure that such a war would never occur, whether by design or inadvertence. Yet, operating in a climate of fear, uncertainty, and unremitting rivalry, each became too entangled in the web of nuclear terror to free the other.

In a different era, free of cold war hatreds, the fear of war might have prompted Kennedy and Khrushchev to reduce their nuclear arsenals, as in fact occurred toward the end of the cold war in the late 1980s and early 1990s. But during the early 1960s the two leaders stepped up programs for new, more accurate, and more powerful strategic weapons as well as for civil defense measures such as the construction of fallout shelters. And, continuing a long, grim tradition of cold war brinkmanship, they proclaimed their determination to counter aggression with nuclear weapons.

As befitted his years of cold war bluster, Khrushchev spoke far more often, demonstratively, and crudely about his country's ability to inflict horrible damage with nuclear weapons. Remarkably he intended these verbal blasts about Soviet rocket power to promote peace. He aimed to use the illusion of Soviet nuclear supremacy as a shield behind which to secure the Soviet Union from attack[90] and to shift resources from the military to agriculture and consumer goods. Khrushchev further hoped that this aura of invincibility would pacify the Chinese Communists, who increasingly chafed at his overtures to the West.

The flaw in Khrushchev's approach, of course, was that his threats of nuclear destruction against a stronger but insecure adversary were not likely to foster peace. Even after Khrushchev's deceptive claims of missile superiority were discredited by satellites, U-2 flights, and defectors, no one could be sure that the chairman would respond reasonably in a crisis. Indeed, the Soviet defector Oleg Penkovsky, who passed classified microfilm to the West disproving the missile gap, claimed to have acted because Khrushchev's irrational behavior endangered the world.

Having entered office committed to closing a "missile gap," President Kennedy at first refused to publicize the United States' unexpected superiority for fear of alerting Republicans that his campaign rhetoric had been ill founded. He feared, as well, that exposing Soviet military inferiority might provoke Khrushchev into speeding Soviet missile construction. Yet in October 1961, as the president looked to dissuade Khrushchev from risking war over Berlin, he reluctantly entered the arena of verbal deterrence.

Recent CIA estimates had sharply reduced the number of operational Soviet intercontinental ballistic missiles to no more than twenty-five, compared with several hundred U.S. missiles and a much larger force of bombers equipped with nuclear weapons. On October 21, 1961, McNamara's Deputy Secretary of Defense Roswell Gilpatric revealed these disparities in a speech on October 21 to the Business Council in Hot Springs, Virginia.

Kennedy approved the announcement of U.S. nuclear superiority "only after much agonizing," according to Roger Hilsman of the State Department, "since everyone involved recognized that telling the Soviets what we knew entailed considerable risk. Forewarned, the Soviets would undoubtedly speed up their ICBM program." But if Khrushchev "were allowed to continue to assume that we still believed in the missile gap, he would very probably bring the world dangerously close to war."[91]

Kennedy preferred letting Gilpatric, a mid-level official, deliver this news because, he said, "When I get up and say those things it sounds too belligerent."[92] Nor would the president explain the facts of U.S. nuclear superiority to Khrushchev even privately, fearing that too might appear confrontational. As Carl Kaysen, a national security aide, explained, "John Kennedy isn't going to talk that way to Khrushchev."[93]

Gilpatric's speech had the desired effect of bursting Khrushchev's confidence that Washington harbored delusions of inferiority in nuclear power. Yet despite Kennedy's precautions to minimize confrontation, the speech had severe side effects. By undercutting Khrushchev's claims of Soviet might (and with it, his stature among hard-liners in the Kremlin and in Beijing), the speech seemed to confirm the chairman's nightmarish vision of the United States as run by a power-mad elite over which President Kennedy exerted little control. Khrushchev responded by redoubling his acts of bravado, including the detonation on October 30, 1961, of the largest explosion in history. That same day two Soviet officials involved in the project reported on the bomb's transcendent physical and psychological impact:

> The atmospheric disturbance generated by the explosion orbited the earth three times. The flash of light was so bright that it was visible at a distance of 1,000 kilometers, despite cloudy skies. . . .
>
> As one cameraman recalled: "The clouds beneath the aircraft and in the distance were lit up by the powerful flash. The sea of light spread under the hatch and even clouds began to glow and became transparent. At that moment, our aircraft emerged from between two cloud layers and down below in the gap a huge bright orange ball was emerging. The ball was powerful and arrogant like Jupiter. Slowly and silently it crept upwards. . . . Having broken through the thick layer of clouds it kept growing. It seemed to suck the whole earth into it. The spectacle was fantastic, unreal, supernatural." Another cameraman saw "a powerful white flash over the horizon and after a long period of time he heard a remote, indistinct and heavy blow, as if the earth has been killed!"
>
> "The ground surface of the island [at ground zero] has been levelled, swept and licked so that it looks like a skating rink," a witness reported. "The same goes for rocks. The snow has melted and their sides and edges are shiny. There is not a trace of unevenness in the ground. . . . Everything in this area has been swept clean, scoured, melted and blown away."

"In fact," the historians Viktor Adamsky and Yuri Smirnov write of the explosion, "its power was 10 times the total power of all explosives used during World War II, including the atomic bombs dropped on Japanese cities by the United States. It's hard to believe that a more powerful explosion will ever take place. . . ." According to the physicist Andrei Sakharov, "Nikita Khrushchev said: 'Let this device hang over the heads of the capitalists, like a sword of Damocles.' "[94]

As Khrushchev's threats over Berlin again increased early in 1962, President Kennedy resorted to another signal of U.S. nuclear readiness. In an interview reported by Stewart Alsop in the *Saturday Evening Post* on March 31, the president "quietly discarded" the doctrine "that the United States would never strike first with the nuclear weapon." Kennedy acknowledged that "in some circumstances we might have to take the initiative."[95] He intended this remark to assure West European leaders of an oft-stated U.S. position: that a Soviet attack on West Berlin risked a general war. Instead the president found that calibrating the optimal level of nuclear threat (or bluff) was a supremely taxing riddle, and that a single slip could wreak unintended havoc.

Khrushchev considered Kennedy's statements a deliberate provocation. "Is it wise to threaten someone who is at least your equal in strength?" the chairman commented in *Pravda*.[96] In fact, though, Khrushchev understood that his country was in no way the equal of the United States in nuclear strength, and he believed that the U.S. was flaunting its superiority in order to bully the Soviet Union. In his memoirs, Kennedy's National Security Adviser McGeorge Bundy acknowledged that Khrushchev was understandably alarmed, but at the time he and others in the administration

> believed that in the overall contest with the Soviet Union we were still on the defensive. It was not we who threatened destabilizing changes in Berlin or in Southeast Asia, or . . . in Cuba. Kennedy's remark to Alsop, however incautious, was limited to the context of what might become

necessary in response to major Soviet aggression. Finally, we did not suppose that nuclear superiority conferred on us the opportunity for political coercion that Khrushchev took for granted. Certainly we did not think it wrong for Khrushchev to know that we were undeceived about the real situation, but our main object in the Gilpatric speech had not been to terrify the Kremlin, but to give encouragement to our own people and to our allies.[97]

By the spring of 1962 Khrushchev was desperate to salvage his strategic offensive against the West despite the humiliating exposure of Soviet nuclear weakness. His concerns encompassed the young socialist regime in Cuba under Fidel Castro, whom the CIA had tried to destroy and continued to target. A covert interagency campaign of unprecedented scale was launched in November 1961 to weaken the Castro regime through acts of sabotage. Code-named Mongoose, the operation anticipated decisive U.S. military intervention were a civil war to erupt in Cuba. In addition, the CIA sponsored new attempts by the Mafia and Cuban dissidents to assassinate Castro and his brother Raul.

The impact of Operation Mongoose (and related CIA intrigues) was negligible despite the attorney general's insistence that "No time, money, effort—or manpower is to be spared."[98] But highly publicized U.S. military maneuvers in the Caribbean underscored the danger to Castro. In April 1962 U.S. Marines began a series of amphibious exercises that included a seven-thousand-man landing on Vieques Island near Puerto Rico. The dual aim was to refine contingency plans for an invasion of Cuba and to intimidate the Cuban leadership. A further landing at Vieques was scheduled for October 15, just one day before President Kennedy learned of the Soviet missiles in Cuba.[99]

The beleaguered Castro pressed his Soviet patrons for a bilateral defense treaty, believing that an eventual U.S. invasion was inevitable. Although Khrushchev would not commit formally to defend distant Cuba, he and everyone else in the Presidium agreed, as he later recounted, that

> We had an obligation to do everything in our power to protect Cuba's existence as a Socialist country and as a working example to the other countries of Latin America. It was clear to me that we might very well lose Cuba if we didn't take some decisive steps in her defense."[100]

On May 21, 1962, Khrushchev sprung a plan on his Kremlin colleagues that promised to save Castro while boosting Soviet nuclear strength. In a move far bolder than any earlier Soviet military gambit, the chairman proposed to station medium-range missiles in Cuba, within easy striking range of the United States.

To some members of the Defense Council, "the special standing body consisting of key Politburo members and government officials,"[101] the idea of sending nuclear weapons to Cuba was altogether too bold. Anastas Mikoyan, like Khrushchev a survivor of the Stalin era and the chairman's closest confidant, strongly opposed the risk."[102] Foreign Minister Andrei Gromyko also cautioned, "I must say frankly that putting our missiles in Cuba would cause a political explosion in the United States. I am absolutely certain of that, and this should be taken into account."[103] "The question of nuclear war was even raised" during the meeting.[104] But Khrushchev trusted that by shipping the missiles covertly he could announce their presence as an accomplished fact that President Kennedy would have no choice but to accept.

Questions also arose at the Defense Council sessions over whether oversized missile cargoes, even if camouflaged, would long escape U.S. surveillance. But when Major General A. A.

Dementyev, the Soviet Union's chief military representative in Cuba, objected that "It will be impossible to hide these missiles from American U-2s," the defense minister, Rodion Malinovsky, kicked the hapless officer under the table.[105] By the close of the council's deliberations, Khrushchev unsurprisingly prevailed and, for good measure, soon after required defenders, doubters, and dissidents alike to sign a directive to start the operation.[106]

Khrushchev later explained his motives in terms of ideology (providing comradely aid to socialist revolutionaries), strategy (offsetting America's dangerous edge in nuclear weaponry), and psychology (frightening Americans into a new sensitivity to Soviet concerns):

> In addition to protecting Cuba, our missiles would have equalized what the West likes to call "the balance of power." The Americans had surrounded our country with military bases and threatened us with nuclear weapons, and now they would learn just what it feels like to have enemy missiles pointing at you. . . .[107]

In July 1962 Soviet ships made the first of 185 deliveries to Cuba. The plan was to deploy 36 SS-4 medium-range ballistic missiles (MRBMs) that could reach American cities as far as Texas, and 24 SS-5 intermediate-range ballistic missiles (IRBMs) that could strike as far west as Seattle. By mid-September the medium-range missiles had arrived; a month later the intermediate-range missiles were en route. The island also bristled with 42,000 Soviet troops and, among other weaponry, 40 MiG-21 aircraft, batteries of surface-to-air missiles, 6 IL-28 bombers fitted to carry nuclear weapons, and, to deter or destroy an invading force, 12 army *Luna* missiles and 80 air force cruise missiles designed for short-range nuclear strikes.

"Never before in the history of the Soviet Armed Forces and

in the history of Russia had we transported so many troops to the other side of the ocean," recalled General Anatoli Gribkov, who commanded the operation. "We had to use eighty-five ships from our merchant marine, and to assemble in secrecy ships of various kinds scattered all over the seas."[108]

Gribkov's priority of "absolute secrecy"[109] with the strategic missiles withstood Western aerial surveillance for more than two months, though little aided by the Russian navy's often clumsy deceptions. On August 16 a Soviet crew, photographed by a NATO plane near Denmark, "tried to create the impression of a spontaneous deck party. They put out tables and invited the female nurses below to come above deck and dance. When the ship later passed the Azores the ruse was repeated, this time for the benefit of a curious U.S. reconnaissance plane."[110]

To divert suspicions from the Caribbean shipments, the operation was code-named Anadyr, after both a river and a strategic military base at the Pacific tip of Siberia. Many years later Anastas Mikoyan's son Sergo regaled a gathering of former U.S. and Soviet officials with tales of clandestine efforts run amuck: "The forty-two thousand people sent there by ships did not know where or why they were going. So they brought with them everything the detachments are supposed to have at their disposal. They had winter clothes, and skis." Robert McNamara drew a round of laughter by interjecting, "If we'd known that, it would *really* have upset us! We would have thought they were planning to invade Vermont."[111]

For all its comical frailties, Operation Anadyr's obsessive secrecy rested on a grim truth: shipping the missiles openly would have risked provoking a U.S. military reaction. Committed to his latest, gravest foreign policy gamble, Khrushchev simply brushed aside what Gromyko and Mikoyan understood all too well—the intensity of feeling in the United States about Cuba.

Even Americans who shared the president's reluctance to use force openly against Castro still believed, with James Reston of the *New York Times*, that there were obvious limits to nonintervention, chiefly the introduction of Soviet "missiles and missile bases which could threaten the security of the entire hemisphere."[112] Reston clarified the acceptable bounds of Soviet behavior—and U.S. restraint—saying, "President Kennedy is not in a belligerent mood, but he will not permit the creation of a major Communist military base in Cuba. There is a limit to his promise not to use the armed forces of the United States in Cuba."[113]

CHAPTER FOUR

"We Just Had to Get Them Out of There": Why Missiles in Cuba Triggered a Crisis

1. The Administration Under Siege

EVEN BEFORE rumors of Soviet missiles in Cuba sped from Miami to Washington in the late summer of 1962, President Kennedy had spent much of his presidency weathering criticisms for failing to stand up to Communist encroachments. A

"We Just Had to Get Them Out of There"

State Department study in November 1961 concluded, from "a comprehensive and representative sample of editorials and columns in newspapers and magazines" as well as congressional statements and public opinion polls, that while Americans felt great affection for the president, he "is charged with failure to take strong action. . . ." Few quarreled with Kennedy's foreign policy speeches, his creation of the Alliance for Progress to further relations with Latin America, and other initiatives, but a fervent minority warned that "While the Communists are defying world opinion and 'getting away with murder,' the U.S. does nothing."[1] The most sensitive nerve ending for these charges was Cuba, where Castro's arrogance and resilience, the failure at the Bay of Pigs, and a growing Soviet presence all mocked the administration's promise to show a new vigor in world affairs.

Despite pressures to move against the "Red outpost" in Cuba, Kennedy shied from overt intervention. The policies he had pursued—embargo, diplomatic isolation, and covert sabotage and subversion—all appeared low-risk actions that treated the Caribbean island as a cold war arena rather than a sovereign nation. But Kennedy's approach, however cynical, distinguished between skirmishes with a third world regime and the far greater risk of directly confronting Soviet military personnel. Although CIA director John McCone had warned the president in August 1962 that the presence of surface-to-air missiles in Cuba portended shipments of nuclear weapons, scarcely anyone else in government believed that Khrushchev would ever be so foolhardy. Kennedy therefore rebuffed both Republicans and Democrats who, abetted by feverish unconfirmed missile "sightings" by refugees newly arrived in Miami, proclaimed a Cuban crisis.

As Soviet military supplies to Cuba increased in the fall of 1962 and Kennedy minimized their significance, influential

journals disparaged him as less likely to unfurl the Monroe
Doctrine than to reach for a white flag. David Lawrence of *U.S.
News & World Report* deplored Kennedy's "retreat" from the
doctrine, and *Time* rebutted the administration's arguments
against using the military against Castro in an issue that featured an imposing cover portrait of the president—President
James Monroe. Clare Boothe Luce meanwhile pilloried Kennedy in *Time*'s sister publication *Life* for abandoning his tough
stand on Cuba in the 1960 campaign and warned, "Time is still
running out in Latin America and the cold war is still being lost
there." Armed intervention in Cuba was urgent not only for
"American prestige but . . . American survival." Even Arthur
Krock, a longtime friend of the Kennedy family, criticized the
president for narrowing the Monroe Doctrine.[2]

Pundits warned that Kennedy's restraint toward Castro
would invite rather than avert Communist aggression. For if the
president would not exert power in Cuba, how could the Russians respect American strength anywhere? "They are aware of
our military power," the *Wall Street Journal* counseled in September 1962, "but if they think we will never use it, they will go
on gaining. . . . Does the Government actually have a policy . . . ? Or is it wrapped in a Hamlet paralysis?"[3]

Media critics homed in on Kennedy's calm as itself cause for
alarm. The *San Diego Union* deplored the president's "dou-
bletalk" in conceding that Soviet "military technicians" were in
Cuba yet insisting there was "no evidence there are Russian
troops there." The powerful Scripps-Howard chain maintained
that "whether they are 'technicians' or 'troops' . . . a Soviet military stronghold in Cuba would greatly enhance Russia's bargaining position on U.S. overseas bases and on Berlin, and
therefore should be 'viewed with alarm,' not calmly."[4]

In a time when rumors of Soviet missiles in Cuba passed easily for fact, newspapers freely mixed alarms with calls for tough-ness. On September 8, 1962, a Nebraska paper wondered, "What Must Cuba and Russia Do to Wake Kennedy Up?" Cit-ing reports that Cuba was receiving Soviet rockets with a four-hundred-mile range that could "knock out Cape Canaveral, heart and soul of the U.S. space effort," the paper dismissed as "poppycock" claims that the Soviet weapons were "to discour-age Cuban rebels, and to make Cuba safe for Cubans." As for Kennedy's caution, "Such namby-pambyism cannot be under-stood by the Russians—or Castro, either. What is happening in Cuba is a serious breach of the Monroe Doctrine" that would leave the U.S. "with Communist guns at its back." The only remedy was "bold action to oust Khrushchev from Cuba. What is the greatest nation in the world waiting on [sic]?"[5]

Scattered administration advocates of a gentler policy to-ward Castro incurred savage media attacks on their judgment and manhood. In December 1961 William S. White saw "men" and "boys" vying to make policy on Cuba, with Kennedy nar-rowly gaining inclusion among the men for having "encouraged the patriots' invasion . . . though he gave far too little help." Raymond Moley of *Newsweek* found it "difficult to name any in-dividual other than [UN Ambassador] Adlai Stevenson" whose influence "would create more anxiety among" defenders "of long established and respected national policies" like the Mon-roe Doctrine. After Kennedy's roving ambassador and former Under Secretary of State Chester Bowles warned on September 16, 1962, against "hot-headed extremists," the *Wall Street Jour-nal* retorted "that advocacy of total inaction is a pretty extreme position. As a precedent, it would confer on the Soviet Union freedom of movement not only in Cuba but in the Western Hemisphere."[6]

Politicians on both sides of the aisle swelled the chorus of voices for firmer executive action against the Soviets in Cuba. The Republican senator Homer E. Capehart of Indiana was first off the mark with a speech on August 28 that asserted America's right "to land troops, take possession of Havana, and occupy the country" unless Cuba sent home all Soviet military personnel.[7]

Others in Congress soon began playing countless variations of Capehart's martial melody. Beginning on August 31, New York's Republican junior senator, Kenneth Keating, issued ten public warnings regarding the Soviet military buildup in Cuba.[8] On September 3 he urged the president to send an inter-American mission to Cuba to check on the possible construction of missile bases.[9]

In the weeks leading up to the missile crisis, Capitol Hill was awash in tirades against Castro, Khrushchev, and communism. The larger ideology of the cold war was fairly distilled by these speeches, in imagery as stylized as a Kabuki play. Among those demanding action was L. H. Fountain, a House Democrat from North Carolina, who mustered a motley array of images and insults to damn the Kremlin and its designs on Cuba:

> Surely no one doubts any longer that Russian rulers have no inner restraints. They recognize no God, indeed, they have formally abjured Him. They laugh at the word "honor." They hoot at truth. They sneer at the race which upholds honesty and dignity and kindliness. Theirs is a godless way of life, based upon a totalitarian dictatorship with unlimited power—power that rests on coercion and violence—not on law and morality; on terror, slavery, and methodical brutality; their cause thrives on hatred, prejudice, jealousy, and contempt for the dignity of man. . . . Do we not know that, like Satan and his followers in "Paradise Lost," they have lifted up their arms in defiance against the

Almighty who gave them life? . . . It is about time that we started calling the signals. Mr. Khrushchev has been the world's quarterback for too long.[10]

No policymaker in September and early October 1962 could ignore the insistent admonitions to view events in the Caribbean as serving a larger Communist conspiracy. Jack Miller, the Republican junior senator from Iowa, said of the tensions in Berlin, "We all know that the Communist-inspired crises around the world are a part of an integrated plan of aggression against the free world." Senator Winston L. Prouty, a Republican from Vermont, wondered, "When will we learn that Cuba, Laos, Vietnam, and Berlin are part and parcel of the one grand design of the Soviet Union—world conquest?"[11]

Instead of rallying around the president in this tense time, many Democrats and most Republicans deemed his measured approach to the Red presence in Cuba a liability in America's struggle for survival. A common concern was that Kennedy had let the Monroe Doctrine wither by his temporizing on Cuba. Republican Senate Minority Leader Everett Dirksen fairly summed up not only his party's stance but the prevalent feeling in Congress: "The Soviet Union has no business in the Western Hemisphere. I am one of those who will not confess that the Monroe Doctrine, adopted in 1823, is out of date."[12]

Republicans across a broad ideological spectrum hit at Kennedy's apparent passivity. Senator Barry Goldwater of Arizona, an extreme conservative and Kennedy's likely opponent in the 1964 presidential campaign, on September 14 attacked Kennedy's "weak" " 'do nothing' policy." Senator Strom Thurmond of South Carolina, the segregationist Democrat, charged that the president had "reinterpreted" the Monroe Doctrine with "major omissions" so that it was "no longer a bulwark of U.S. foreign policy which it was for over 100 years." The longer a

U.S. invasion was postponed, Thurmond warned, the more difficult it would become. The president received scarcely more comfort from liberal Republicans such as New York's Senator Jacob Javits, who saw that the Russians had chosen "to fly directly into the teeth of . . . the Monroe Doctrine" with their buildup in Cuba, thereby posing "a grave threat."[13]

To some in Congress, Kennedy's lax enforcement of the Monroe Doctrine exerted a poisonous ripple effect on U.S. interests in more distant lands. America's intervention in South Korea, Lebanon, the Dominican Republic, South Vietnam, Laos, and Thailand, "while we verbally sidestep the Soviet takeover of Cuba at our very doorstep," made for "a painful paradox," according to the junior Republican senator from Kansas, James B. Pearson. It had also made "of Cuba a Western Hemisphere Berlin Wall, a wall of shame, a symbol of uncertainty and indecision." And Democratic Senator Frank J. Lausche of Ohio asked, "How can we expect the Cambodians, the South Vietnamese, the Thai, and the many other people of the world to have confidence in us? It simply cannot be done."[14]

In the president's home state of Massachusetts, the Republican senate primary campaign saw a former senator, Henry Cabot Lodge, and a veteran congressman, Laurence Curtis, vying to show themselves tougher on Castro. In a televised debate, Lodge declared that the United States should have called for an economic boycott of Cuba—"a real boycott"—immediately after the discovery of Soviet troops there. Curtis countered with his own broadside at the president, calling the dispatch of Soviet troops to Cuba "a flagrant violation of the Monroe Doctrine" and insisting that Kennedy go immediately to the Organization of American States to see that "firm action" was taken.[15]

Kennedy's assurances of watchful waiting on Cuba did little

to assuage critics, who rightly believed the administration was avoiding a confrontation with the Russians. In reply to the administration's claims that the weapons coming into Cuba were defensive, Senator George Aiken of Vermont said dryly, "They are coming in by the boatload. That's a hell of a lot of defensive weapons." On September 6 Senator Thurmond declared, "This is no time to follow a 'watch and see' or 'let the dust settle' policy on Sino-Soviet intervention in the Western Hemisphere. . . . The dust which settled" in Cuba was "both red and active," and it was "contaminating the entire Western Hemisphere. The time has come for Cuba to be decontaminated," which could best be done "with the advice of our military leaders."[16]

These widespread calls to arms—or at least to urgency—often summoned the ghosts of recent history. Republican Senator John Tower of Texas branded Kennedy's approach toward Cuba and the Soviet Union "massive appeasement." "Our posture," Tower said, "makes that of [British Prime Minister Neville] Chamberlain at Munich seem lionlike." Senator Keating too invoked the lessons of Munich:

Remember, too, what happened before the outbreak of the Second World War. Had Hitler been stopped decisively when he marched into the Rhineland, into Austria, or even when he went into Czechoslovakia, the Second World War would probably never have occurred. Khrushchev cannot know where we will draw the line any more than Hitler knew where Britain or France would. He cannot know unless we tell him and show him that we mean business—not only in Cuba, not only Berlin, not only in South Vietnam, but everywhere freedom is endangered. . . . If we do not act decisively in Cuba, we will face more—not less—trouble in Berlin and elsewhere in the world. . . . In the long run, inaction and acceptance of the status quo in Cuba will amount to the greatest defeat this country has suffered since China was lost to the free world.[17]

Lending gravitas to such partisan barrages was Dwight D. Eisenhower, who, belying the later paeans to his calm restraint, criticized his successor for timidity. On October 16, 1962, the same day Kennedy learned of the Cuban missiles, he recoiled from a salvo closer to home, a front-page headline in the *New York Times*, "Eisenhower Calls President Weak on Foreign Policy." Speaking in Boston, Kennedy's political bastion, the seventy-three-year-old former president recalled that during his own years in office, "we lost no inch of ground to tyranny. We witnessed no abdication of responsibility. We accepted no compromise of [our] pledged word or withdrawal from principle. No walls were built. No threatening foreign bases were established."[18]

Kennedy's defenders among congressional Democrats insisted "This is no time for warhawks," deplored "emotionalism" as a poor basis for policymaking, and congratulated the president for having "kept his nerve as well as his head" despite "all the jingoistic speeches" that "would lead us down the way to war—thermonuclear war." Yet the president's advocates assured voters that their tolerance for Castro and Khrushchev had strict limits. Senator Clair Engle of California, after minimizing the importance of the arms already in Cuba, pledged that if the Soviets were ever to send "offensive armaments" such as nuclear missiles, "we must take action." And Senator Hubert Humphrey of Minnesota lived up to a reputation for loyalty and exuberant exaggeration by hailing the president's "modern application" of the Monroe Doctrine as so vigorous that it may well "become known as the Kennedy Doctrine."[19]

Some of Kennedy's allies on the Hill nervously nudged him to take stronger action. Congressman Armistead I. Seldon, Jr., of Alabama insisted that the president's patience was beyond second-guessing, but added, "The history of the cold war demonstrates that whenever the free world has faced up to the Communist threat, the Communists have backed down...."[20] Seldon's lesson ignored the deadly stalemate in Korea, the on-going war in Vietnam, and other blood-spattered landmarks of postwar foreign policy. But his words expressed a popular faith that, even in the nuclear age, America would remain indomitable so long as it faced down aggressors.

The most consistent opposition to intervention in Cuba came from a handful of congressmen who took similarly jaundiced—and unpopular—views of escalation in Vietnam. Democratic majority leader Mike Mansfield of Montana said on September 7 that the proposed Senate resolution endorsing armed force in Cuba was "an aggressive act, a warlike act" that would cost "thousands of Cuban and American lives." It was also empty bluster: "It is not the constitutional course, it is not the responsible course, to authorize the President to do by congressional resolution what he is already authorized to do—to command the Armed Forces of the United States and to conduct its foreign relations." A month later Oregon Senator Wayne Morse, foreshadowing his lonely opposition to a 1964 Senate resolution backing military action in Vietnam, cautioned "those who want our country to go to war over Cuba" that "world opinion is overwhelmingly against any such course ... and rightly so."[21]

Such dovish pronouncements were nonetheless seldom heard among congressmen of either party, who rightly gauged the public alarm over Cuba. Angry readers of *Time*, impatient with Kennedy's Cuban policy, questioned his fitness to defend the nation. A mother of two small children in Minneapolis lambasted "our President's indecision and hesitation," saying she had "good reasons for not wanting a war," but "if our leaders do not now tell the Russians to get out of the Western Hemisphere and back up the words with action, then God help the U.S.—no one else will be able to." A New Yorker pilloried Kennedy's neglect of lessons he had once seen plainly enough as a student, saying, "The Soviet buildup in Cuba suggests that it is time for a Harvard undergraduate thesis titled *Why Kennedy Slept*."[22]

Although a later generation of writers deemed President Kennedy's words alarmist and belligerent, *Time*'s readers in September and early October 1962 found his statements on Cuba a bland substitute for action. A San Francisco resident mocked the "big talk delivered in ethereal prose by a President with a decided verbal aptitude" but who "doesn't know a damn thing about the yearnings of millions of Americans. . . . The world waits—the American people are ready—and the President philosophizes about responsibility. Come on Hamlet—get Cuba!"[23] A man from Palo Alto suspected that Kennedy really "believes the American people can be lulled to inaction by a lot of grandiose verbiage, but this only shows how completely out of touch he is with the man on the street." As for the American people, the irate reader claimed,

> We are not going to be duped. . . . We definitely believe the Kennedy Administration was bluffed out of Laos, has bungled in Berlin, and is bewildered over Cuba. We want the line drawn on any further Communist expansion, and we want it drawn now. If Mr. Kennedy can't, two years from now the American people will put somebody in the White House who can . . . if it is not too late.[24]

While the hawkish publisher of *Time*, Henry Luce, might have accorded such citizens' indictments an especially prominent welcome, a deluge of letters on Capitol Hill conveyed identical frustration and derision. On September 10 Senator Thomas J. Dodd, a Democrat from Connecticut, found "the temper of the American people . . . demonstrated by the very heavy mail which Congress is now receiving on the subject of Cuba, urging a stronger policy toward the Castro regime. My own office alone has received literally hundreds of such letters and telegrams." They reflected "a growing feeling in our country . . . that cuts across party lines and political labels . . . that we cannot afford to delay much longer."[25]

On October 9, a week before the president first convened his Executive Committee (Ex Comm) to deal with the Cuban crisis, Senator Kenneth Keating readily shared credit for his vigilance on Cuba with the entire voting public:

> How can any Member of Congress fail to speak out, when we are bombarded daily with evidence of the deep concern of our people? It floods into our offices in mailbags, it dominates our television screens, and fills the news columns of our daily papers.

Keating told of a "solid, hard-working family man" in California "pointing to his neat little house and saying, 'The policy I favor might mean an A-bomb right there. But I'll risk that. It's worth it to win.'" The senator modestly concluded, "And so an obscure California householder, miles away from Washington, obviously is miles ahead of Washington in facing up to the meaning of Cuba. The American people, if not their leaders, have learned the lesson of Munich."[26]

Congressmen understood that although their manifestos on Cuba displayed more verbal muscle than the president, they still did not satisfy public cries for action. Republican Senator Alexander Wiley of Wisconsin believed his proposals for a pacific blockade paled before the angry letters of constituents asking, "Why don't we go in and knock the blazes out of Cuba?" Wiley admitted his unease over such demands because "we must use commonsense" and not "start a universal blaze."[27]

87

While Wiley, Dodd, and Keating each counseled against invading Cuba,[28] even such modest gestures of restraint faded with proximity to Cuba—and to Miami's Cuban-American community. A million refugees, 10 percent of the Cuban population, had arrived in the United States since Castro had seized power, settling mainly in southern Florida.[29] Florida's Senator George Smathers, weighing local Cuban-American sentiment more heavily than his friendship with John Kennedy, proposed on September 2 an invasion of Cuba by a U.S.-sponsored military organization formed of nations in the Western hemisphere. Kennedy was furious, but according to Dino Brugioni, "Smathers held his ground," telling the President: it's an election year.[30]

A *Congressional Quarterly* poll of editors and congressmen in mid-October 1962 confirmed Smathers's concerns, showing Cuba to be by far the leading election issue, ahead of medical care for the aged and federal spending. So did an official affirmation on October 16 by the Republican National Chairman William Miller that the "irresolution" of the Kennedy administration, prominently including its Cuban policy, would be the dominant election issue that November.[31]

In a private conversation with Khrushchev's son-in-law, Alexei Adzhubei, early in 1962, Kennedy analyzed the alarm over Cuba with remarkable detachment, implying it was an understandable overreaction but one that Soviet leaders should understand and accommodate:

The President emphasized that the strong reaction in the United States toward events in Cuba was due to the fact that over the past hundred and some odd years, the United States had had no hostile power close to its borders. Therefore, when a group which preached hostility toward the United States seized power in Cuba, the reaction in the United States was bound to be very strong. The US was psychologically unprepared for such a change. The President pointed out that the USSR would have the same reaction if a hostile group arose in the vicinity of its borders. In this connection, the President referred to the Soviet reaction to the Hungarian uprising.[32]

On the campaign circuit that fall the president personally faced the building clamor for action against Cuba. In Indiana he lashed out at "self-appointed generals." At a stop in New Haven, Yale students carried signs calling for "less profile, more courage" and taunting, "Castro loves Democrats."[33]

Kennedy understood that any further conciliation of the Soviets in Cuba would leave him bereft of support. He pointedly monitored public sentiment on this issue through his pollster Louis Harris, who warned him in early October that "the vast bulk of public opinion favors doing everything possible short of armed intervention." Theodore Sorensen meanwhile noted a *San Francisco Chronicle* poll that reported a 62 percent negative rating for the Kennedy administration's actions in Cuba.[34] This disapproval stemmed partly from fears that the president was abandoning the Monroe Doctrine. "Some observers think it has been outmoded by the subtle nuances of the cold war," *Newsweek* stated during the Soviet buildup in Cuba, "but for many Americans, it is invested with a special mystique and for them there is really no question but that the Monroe doctrine is being breached by the Soviet Union."[35]

The arguments of present-day historians that the Soviet military presence in Cuba was nonetheless justified by U.S. threats to Castro and by the many U.S. bases overseas would have impressed few Americans in the early 1960s as sensible, or even moral. The public overwhelmingly rejected the "so-called argument from morality," as the *Wall Street Journal* contemptuously termed it, because it "assumes that American purposes in the world are on a level with those of the international Communist conspiracy. The truth, of course, is that it is the Communist effort to enslave the world which requires us to resist" and "to keep Soviet forces as far away from our shores as possible." It was "silly to say our forward bases somehow 'entitle' the Soviets to a base in Cuba."[36]

The fact that the Cuban government had requested the Soviet weapons meant little to congressmen of either party, who saw their country in a mortal struggle against a ruthless enemy. The United States, Senator Dodd of Connecticut explained, could not waive the Monroe Doctrine whenever a hostile government seized power in Latin America, or it would scarcely apply at all. In any case, Iowa's Senator Miller declared, "Cuba is no longer an independent government, but a mere cog in the international Communist conspiracy."[37]

Anxieties over Soviet nuclear strength—and intentions—compounded the fears of Soviet intrusion in Cuba. Although the Kennedy administration early exposed the rumors of a "missile gap as unfounded," Khrushchev continued to shock and alarm the West with boasts of a hundred-megaton superbomb that could start fires over vast areas, rockets that made radar obsolete because they could not be shot down, and a missile so accurate it could hit "a fly in outer space."[38] The Soviet leader also compensated with chilling symbolism for the limits in his nation's nuclear technology: in September 1961 a series of Soviet atomic explosions raised U.S. fallout levels by 3,500 percent even while Kennedy was resisting pressures to resume American nuclear tests.[39]

The building tension over Cuba in the fall of 1962 unfolded against a backdrop of rival nuclear detonations. In August a 40-megaton blast in the Arctic led off a second series of Soviet explosions just as the United States was proposing a new test ban at Geneva. Headlines of competing nuclear blasts dotted news-

90

papers right through the missile crisis, including accounts of American detonations in the Pacific on October 18 and October 26, and a report on October 25 that "the Soviet Union has now tested nuclear weapons totaling more than twice the power of all United States tests to date" (305 megatons to 143).[40]

The political fallout from Soviet testing seeped into congressional speeches on Cuba. In his first warning of missiles in Cuba, on August 31, 1962, Senator Keating focused on the implications for the American space program, asking whether the Soviets might have caused several launch failures at Cape Canaveral. Outer space also seemed to Senator Howard W. Cannon of Nevada the final frontier of cold war perils, a deadly dimension of Soviet missile advances. "The Russians," he said, "have been speaking loudly while they are trying to get a bigger stick; that bigger stick may well be space superiority."[41]

In late September Congress responded to the frenzy over Soviet arms shipments to Cuba by authorizing the president "to prevent by whatever means may be necessary, including the use of arms, the Marxist-Leninist regime in Cuba from extending, by force or the threat of force, its aggressive or subversive activities to any part of this hemisphere" and especially "the creation or use of an externally supported military capability endangering the security of the United States." The resolution further implied continued efforts to oust Castro by working with the OAS "and with freedom-loving Cubans to support the aspirations of the Cuban people for self-determination." Although Kennedy himself did not push this initiative but merely endured it, the joint resolution passed by 86 to 1 in the Senate on September 20, and by 384 to 7 in the House six days later.[42]

The hawkish mood on Capitol Hill encompassed even the Senate's lone dissenter. Winston L. Prouty from Vermont rejected the joint resolution as too weak in warning the Soviet Union and sanctioning armed force. The resolution seemed to

Prouty as hollow as "the resolve from King Lear that goes: I will do such things—what they are I know not—But they shall be the wonders of the earth." Because the resolution lacked "fixed purpose," Prouty said, "I protest its every line."[43]

While the resolution formally supported the administration on Cuba, many of those who voted for it had aimed to confront President Kennedy with the force of public opinion. "Both Congress and the American people are far ahead of the President in their willingness and earnest desire for prompt, affirmative, and resolute action to meet the Communist military threat in Cuba," said Republican Senator Wallace F. Bennett from Utah. Now "he too will be compelled to take notice of the great concern. . . ."[44]

Kennedy himself evinced little fighting spirit over the doctrine that Congress had just honored as an inviolable shield around the Western Hemisphere. Disdaining its nebulous logic and dubious legal standing, he regarded the Monroe Doctrine as an embarrassing liability rather than a bulwark. When a Justice Department aide assured him that he could invoke this venerable document to justify to the UN any action against Cuba, the president snapped, "The Monroe Doctrine. What the hell is that?"[45]

Faced by pervasive demands for tough action in a cause he found doubtful, the president sought to shrink the Monroe Doctrine without publicly abandoning it. On September 4 Kennedy warned, through his press secretary, Pierre Salinger, that "the gravest issues would arise" if the Soviets were to place "offensive ground-to-ground missiles" in Cuba. But he found "no evidence" of this, and he preferred to treat the "Cuban question" in concert with other states in "the inter-American system.[46] Similarly Kennedy's renewed warning on September 13 against any Soviet attempts to deploy missiles in Cuba accompanied slaps at the talk of war over the existing Soviet presence.

Insisting that "unilateral military invervention . . . cannot currently be either required or justified," he trusted that the American people "will in this nuclear age, as they have in the past, keep both their nerve and their head."[47]

Kennedy's National Security Adviser, McGeorge Bundy, later explained that even the president's stern warning to the Soviets on September 4 was intended chiefly to defuse pressures at home for bolder leadership: "We did it because of the requirements of domestic politics, not because we seriously believed that the Soviets would do anything as crazy from our standpoint as placement of Soviet nuclear weapons in Cuba."[48] Several weeks later, confronted with the fact of Soviet missiles in Cuba, Kennedy lamented at an emergency meeting that he had not drawn the line of acceptable Soviet conduct still more cautiously: "Last month I should have said that we don't care."[49] But now Khrushchev's flagrant disregard of his warning had forced his hand.

2. An Inescapable Crisis

KENNEDY'S APPROACH to meeting the Soviet challenge in Cuba reflected a hard-wrought passage from early irresolution in foreign policy to full and formidable command. His maturation had been roughly speeded by the Bay of Pigs debacle in April 1961. Afterward the chastened president had rued how inertia could drive policy decisions through inadequate debate, reflexive support by military "experts" for military options, and scant calculation of consequences. Kennedy self-consciously applied these lessons in October 1962 when he convened the Executive Committee of the National Security Council, or "Ex Comm,"[50] of figures in and outside the government whose intellects—and egos—would assure vigorous debate. The president raised probing questions and at times deliberately absented himself to ensure that deference to his office would not stifle dissent, a move that "encouraged everyone to speak his mind" without regard for rank or protocol.[51]

Indeed, Robert Kennedy wrote later, "There was no rank, and, in fact, we did not even have a chairman" in the absence of the president. "During all these deliberations, we all spoke as equals."[52] Still, from the outset some were more equal than others, beginning with "Bobby" himself and the secretary of defense, Robert McNamara. "Bob" McNamara was an outsized force even among the Ex Comm's strong-willed talents. According to Under Secretary of State George Ball, one of the Ex Comm's fourteen regular participants, McNamara had "a natural flair for command and whenever he was in the room he tended to dominate the discussion" with his "unusually quick and incisive mind and supreme self-assurance," qualities Ball found "impressive and slightly exasperating—exasperating perhaps because he was so forceful." Of Robert Kennedy, Ball wrote, he "surprised me." Earlier "he had seemed to me—particularly in comparison with his brother—immature, far too emotional, and inclined to see everything in absolute terms." But during the missile crisis "he was a stabilizing influence," "a force for caution and good sense."[53]

Two brilliant intimates of the president, Special Counsel Theodore Sorensen and National Security Adviser McGeorge Bundy, wielded special authority. Sorensen seldom spoke at the formal meetings, but he conferred often with the president and crafted the cables and speeches that conveyed his decisions to Khrushchev and to the public. "Ted never ceased to amaze me," an Ex Comm member marveled of Sorensen's "capacity for producing apposite and dramatic prose."[54] As for Bundy, formerly dean of the faculty at Harvard University, his crisp logic more than once upended rapid moves toward consensus, reflecting his view that "the single most important lesson of our experience with crises . . . was that the president was ill-served if all reasonable options were not carefully explored."[55]

Others variously stood out for their expertise, their office, their constituency, or simply their ability to form concise and cogent arguments under pressure. Llewelyn Thompson, a once and future ambassador to the Soviet Union, gave "advice on the Russians and predictions as to what they would do," which Robert Kennedy deemed "uncannily accurate."[56] Ball's articulate, confident presentations at times eclipsed his formal superior, Dean Rusk, who later explained, "As secretary of state I felt that I should hold myself in reserve and hear all points of view before giving my recommendation to the president."[57] (One could scarcely imagine McNamara similarly upstaged by his own able deputy, Roswell Gilpatric, a Wall Street lawyer of whom Robert Kennedy wrote, his "ability, knowledge, and judgment" were sought by the president "in every serious crisis."[58]) Secretary of the Treasury C. Douglas Dillon, though a Republican partisan who had served in the Eisenhower cabinet, enjoyed President Kennedy's trust and radiated assurance in the Ex Comm debates. General Maxwell Taylor, chairman of the Joint Chiefs of Staff, was less sure-of-speech than many, but he commanded respect not only as a war hero, linguist, author, and the military's official spokesman but also as the sole officer whom the president found sensitive to his political concerns.

Some Ex Comm members made their most distinctive contributions behind the scenes. CIA director John McCone and his aides interpreted the high-altitude photographs revealing nuclear missiles in Cuba and tracked Soviet progress in readying the installations. Deputy Under Secretary of State for Political Affairs U. Alexis Johnson prepared an ambitious list of diplomatic tasks to build support in the UN, among allies, and with neutral countries.[59] Assistant Secretary of State for Latin America Edwin Martin made good his assurances of strong support for a blockade of Cuba, helping to secure a unanimous vote from the Organization of American States.

Kennedy's intent to view the crisis through many lenses led him to indulge pleas to conciliate the Kremlin even when, on occasion, these drew venomous criticism (not least, from his brother). "Hawks" were in greater supply in the Ex Comm, as in the country generally (General Taylor found even this term inadequate to his convictions as "a twofold hawk from start to finish"[60]), and the president permitted them, too, to fly with abandon. Kennedy also moved beyond his official circle to confer with several legends of Washington's foreign policy establishment. Preeminent was sixty-nine-year-old Dean Acheson, the urbane, imperious former secretary of state who, during the Berlin crisis in 1961, had impressed Robert Kennedy as more "lucid and convincing" than anyone he had ever heard.[61] A year later in the Ex Comm, Acheson still spoke with an acuity—and asperity—that age had not diminished.

The Ex Comm's spirited sessions have prompted more than a few accounts that liken them almost to ivory-tower seminars in which, amid ominous rumblings from Moscow and Havana, members explored "[t]he entire spectrum of possible American responses."[62] Yet those freewheeling exchanges should not obscure the cold war certitudes and sentiments that conditioned this august body as surely as they did all other levels of government and society. Far from serving as detached forums for reexamining first principles in foreign policy, the Ex Comm meetings reflected irresistible, if not always consistent, public pressures. Foremost was the necessity to remove the Cuban missiles without either compromising national security or, as

the president declared on October 22, "prematurely or unnec-
essarily risk[ing] a nuclear war in which even the fruits of victory would be ashes in our mouth."[63]

Kennedy's first crucial decision in the Ex Comm, to secure
removal of the missiles by any means necessary, followed inexorably from the nation's convictions about Cuba, Russia, and
the cold war. Whether John and Robert Kennedy fully believed
their speculation that a failure to act would have brought im-
peachment,[64] they surely feared that it would have fatally discredited the president's leadership—and with good reason. For
Khrushchev, whatever his aims, had so shockingly violated basic
U.S. interests that the inescapable logic of cold war politics at
home and abroad demanded strong countermeasures to uphold
the credibility of American power and commitments.[65]

Although the president's advisers all found the Kremlin's nuclear intrusion into the hemisphere intolerable, the actual military import of the Cuban missiles drew surprisingly little
comment—and still less agreement. To General Taylor, the deployment opened the way to further missile installations that
could become "a rather important, adjunct and reinforcement
to the strike capability of the Soviet Union. We have no idea
how far they will go." General Earle Wheeler, the army chief of
staff, warned that the missiles would pose "a sizable increase in
offensive Soviet strike capabilities against the United States,
which they do not now have. They do have ICBMs that are tar-
geted at us, but they are in limited numbers. . . . And this short-
range missile course gives them a sort of a quantum jump in
their capability to inflict damage on the United States." General
Curtis LeMay, the outspoken air force chief of staff, added that
stationing missiles so near the United States would "increase
their accuracy against the 50 targets that we know that they
could hit now."[66]

At the height of the crisis on October 27, Raymond Garthoff, a State Department specialist in Soviet affairs, prepared a top-secret memorandum on "The Military Significance of the Soviet Missile Bases in Cuba." Terming the bases "a significant accretion to Soviet strategic capabilities for striking the continental United States," Garthoff explained, "In view of the relatively limited numbers of Soviet operational ICBM launchers—at present an estimated 75—the missiles in the Caribbean will increase the first-strike missile salvo which the USSR could place on targets in the continental United States by over 40 percent." Worse still, Garthoff wrote, "There is no reason why the Soviets could not, if unimpeded by an effective quarantine, literally multiply the number of launchers to a force large enough to threaten the entire strategic balance of power. The Soviets have deployed over 500 MRBMs and IRBMs on their own territory, and the lesser cost compared to ICBMs would make a major expansion in Cuba very attractive."[67]

Yet Defense Secretary McNamara, conscious of a seventeen-to-one U.S. advantage in nuclear warheads (some five thousand to three hundred)[68] and convinced that, in any case, each side could already inflict unacceptable damage on the other, believed the transfer of a few dozen Soviet missiles to Cuba had no practical military impact. When Bundy asked on Tuesday, October 16, the first day of deliberations, "How gravely does this change the strategic balance?", McNamara replied, "Mac, I asked the Chiefs that this afternoon, in effect. And they said: 'Substantially.' My own personal view is: Not at all." Bundy agreed that the Cuban buildup "doesn't improve anything in the strategic balance."[69]

The president himself seemed resigned that the Russians would soon wield an effective missile force regardless of what happened in Cuba. "No matter what they put in there," he said, "we could live today under. If they don't have enough ICBMs today [in Russia], they're going to have them in a year." At a meeting in which General Taylor explained how the Cuban missiles could increase Soviet striking power, Kennedy asked rhetorically, "What difference does it make? They've got enough to blow us up now anyway."[70]

The divergence on whether missiles in Cuba would alter the military balance did not correspond simply to a clash between military and civilian perspectives. Secretary of State Dean Rusk, who became increasingly militant during the first week of discussions, observed on Monday, October 22, just before the president announced a blockade of Cuba,

> that missiles of this magnitude is not something that we can brush aside, simply because the Soviets have some other missiles that can also reach the United States. The fact is that, [just among us] here in this room, the number of missiles that launch in these sites would double the known missile strength the Soviet Union has to reach this country. And that, since we are the basic nuclear strength of all these alliances, . . . this is a matter we can't ignore.[71]

Disputes about the threat posed by the Cuban missiles nonetheless surfaced only sporadically, because all sides agreed that the danger could not be reduced to a question of imminent Soviet attack. Rather, the missiles imperiled all U.S. foreign policy because their presence, left unchallenged, would signal the Kremlin, Western allies, wavering neutrals, and the American people that the president would not uphold publicly stated vital interests at the country's doorstep.

Kennedy appeared genuinely puzzled that Khrushchev had so crossed the line of acceptable conduct—and risk—in superpower relations. At a meeting of the Ex Comm on Tuesday evening, October 16, he expressed dismay over the dangers in countering the chairman's secret nuclear shipments. "But he's initiated the danger, really, hasn't he?" Kennedy remarked.

"He's the one that's playing at God, not us." Later in the meeting the president confessed bewilderment over Khrushchev's motivations: "I don't think there's any record of the Soviets ever making this direct a challenge ever, really, since the Berlin blockade." Bundy, equally bemused, read aloud a statement by the Soviet news agency TASS on September 11 that appeared to rule out any offensive military base in Cuba.[72] Kennedy exclaimed,

> Well, it's a goddamn mystery to me. I don't know enough about the Soviet Union, but if anybody can tell me any other time since the Berlin blockade [of 1948–1949] where the Russians have given so clear a provocation, I don't know when it's been, because they've been awfully cautious, really.[73]

The perception that Khrushchev was testing Kennedy was not simply a collective chimera haunting the president and his advisers. According to Arkady Shevchenko, the former special assistant to Soviet Foreign Minister Gromyko:

> Nikita wouldn't have deployed missiles in Cuba unless he thought Kennedy wouldn't act. A few people warned him directly that the situation could lead to a blockade, and we would have no power to do anything. . . . Nikita ignored all this—because of his opinion of Kennedy. I once heard him myself in his office saying that Kennedy was a weak man. The Cuban crisis took him completely by surprise.[74]

Khrushchev, of course, had his own desperate reasons to place missiles in Cuba, including the safety of Castro's socialist regime and the chance to offset at least partly the lopsided American lead in nuclear weapons. He had not sought specifically to humiliate the president. Still, he had gambled in the belief that Kennedy could be bluffed and bullied. To reverse this dangerous dynamic before it produced new gambles in Berlin and other nerve centers of the cold war, Kennedy and his advisers perceived no alternative to firm action.

Bipartisan opinion within the Ex Comm overwhelmingly favored a military response to the Soviet missile gambit. Secretary of the Treasury Dillon warned on October 17 that accommodating the Soviet deployment would so discredit American credibility as to "lose all Latin America to Communism" and produce "similar reactions" in such countries as Iran, Thailand, and Pakistan.[75] Dean Acheson told Kennedy that Khrushchev was testing his will, and the sooner the showdown the better.[76]

In accepting the risk of war to prevent a Soviet missile base in Cuba, Kennedy implicitly honored his predecessor's policies. On June 16, 1959, President Eisenhower, explaining to the National Security Council his concerns about placing "provocative" intermediate range missiles in Greece, had drawn a cautionary parallel: "If Mexico or Cuba had been penetrated by the communists and then began getting arms and missiles, we would be bound to look on such developments with the gravest concern and in fact . . . it would be imperative for us [even] to take . . . offensive military action."[77] In January 1961 Eisenhower's director of the CIA, Allen Dulles, had privately warned senators that "Cuba might become a Sino-Soviet bloc missile base in this hemisphere." In that case, peaceful countermeasures might not be enough, for "we would be involved in a difficult bargaining position."[78]

Eisenhower never wavered on the "imperative" for military action against Cuban missiles. On October 21, 1962, after being briefed a second time on the Cuban missiles by CIA Director John McCone, he concurred that a blockade seemed a sound choice. The only other options the former president seriously considered were an air strike on the missile sites supported by an invasion of Cuba.[79]

Kennedy also heeded the CIA's Special National Intelligence Estimate of October 20, 1962, which concluded that acquiescence in the Soviet missile deployment would bring a "loss of confidence in US power and determination and a serious decline of US influence, particularly in Latin America," and encourage the Kremlin "in pressing the US hard in other confrontations, such as Berlin."[80]

The CIA report discounted the option of approaching Khrushchev privately to remove the missiles, because the Soviets were not likely to halt the deployment. Instead they would "probably link Cuba with the Berlin situation . . . implying that Berlin was held hostage to US actions in Cuba."[81] Even so, Kennedy initially considered possibilities for private diplomacy as a prelude to military action, until he found, as Sorensen reported, that "no one has been able to devise a satisfactory message to Khrushchev to which his reply could not outmaneuver us. . . ."[82]

During his first twenty-one months in office President Kennedy had indeed looked to behind-the-scenes cooperation with Khrushchev to prevent or defuse crises. His brother Robert had met regularly with a Soviet military intelligence officer, Georgi Bolshakov, to pass messages between the two heads of state. Throughout the summer and fall of 1961 this "back channel" had helped check tensions in Berlin despite posturing on both sides. The president also cultivated a secret correspondence with Khrushchev (aides dubbed these "the pen pal letters") to shield their exchanges—and assurances—from potential critics at home and abroad. But exposure of the deception cloaking Soviet missile shipments now militated against relying on private understandings with the Kremlin to secure their removal.

Khrushchev's falsehoods regarding the missiles struck Kennedy as especially brazen. On September 6, 1962, two days after assuring Robert Kennedy that Khrushchev would never place offensive weapons in Cuba, the new Soviet ambassador in

Washington, Anatoly Dobrynin, met with Kennedy's Special Counsel Theodore Sorensen. According to Sorensen's notes, Dobrynin related

> that (somewhat to his own surprise, I gathered) he had received a personal message from Chairman Khrushchev directing him to make known directly to me the following: 1. First, "nothing will be undertaken before the American congressional elections that could complicate the international situation or aggravate the tension in the relations between our two countries."[83]

Sorensen, who was then helping the president navigate past a battery of Republican attacks over his "soft" Cuban policy, was not mollified:

> I told the Ambassador that I appreciate his conveying the message to us; but that he should understand the President's feeling that the recent Soviet actions in Cuba had already caused considerable political turmoil—that this was a far more difficult problem for the Administration politically because of the frustration felt by many Americans over the Cuban situation—and that the Chairman's message therefore seemed both hollow and tardy. . . .
>
> With respect to Cuba, Dobrynin said that he would report this conversation in full to the Chairman and that he was aware himself of the political and press excitement regarding this matter. He repeated several times, however, that they had done nothing new or extraordinary in Cuba—that the events causing all the excitement had been taking place somewhat gradually and quietly over a long period of time—and that he stood by his assurances that all of these steps were defensive in nature and did not represent any threat to the security of the United States.[84]

The next evening Dobrynin told the U.S. ambassador to the UN, Adlai Stevenson "that only defensive weapons are being supplied" to Cuba.[85] (Twenty-seven years later, in 1989, Dobrynin attended a conference in Moscow that hosted Soviet and American scholars and former officials. He insisted he had conveyed his guarantees on the Cuban missiles in good faith, having been left in the dark by his Kremlin overseers. Andrei Gromyko, who as Khrushchev's foreign minister had known the strategy from the outset, exclaimed, "What, Anatoly Fyodorovich? Do you mean that I did not tell you, the ambassador, about the nuclear missiles in Cuba?" "No, you did not tell me." "That means," the normally taciturn Gromyko observed dryly, "it must have been a very big secret!"[86])

Gromyko was more recognizably in character on the afternoon of October 18, 1962, when President Kennedy, joined by Rusk and Llewelyn Thompson, spoke with him for several hours between sessions of the Ex Comm. Kennedy did not wish to disclose his knowledge of the missiles until he had decided how to respond, but he gave Gromyko a chance to admit to the deployment. Gromyko had begun the meeting by saying "he knew that the President appreciated frankness and therefore, with the President's permission, he wished to be frank too." But his response to Kennedy's questioning was, at best, evasive. "Soviet specialists," he said, "were training Cubans in handling certain types of armaments which were only defensive—and he wished to stress the word defensive—in character, and thus such training could not constitute a threat to the United States. He reiterated that if it were otherwise the Soviet Union would never have agreed to render such assistance."[87]

Kennedy silently marveled at Gromyko's hollow assurances. But "to be clear," according to minutes of their conversation, he restated U.S. policy toward the Soviet presence in Cuba:

Introduction last July of intensive armaments had compli-
cated the situation [in Cuba] and created grave danger. His
own actions have been to prevent, unless US security was
endangered, anything from being done that might provoke
the danger of war. The president then read a portion of his
September 4 statement on Cuba [warning that the presence
of a Russian offensive military base would create the gravest
issues]. Gromyko "had nothing to add to what he had already said."[88]

The colloquy with Gromyko did little to lift Kennedy's faith
that he could rely on private assurances from the Kremlin in
lieu of a military response to the Soviet challenge. After
Gromyko's departure, the president welcomed Bundy and
Robert Lovett, a former defense secretary in the Truman administration and a family friend. Lovett recalled:

[Kennedy] grinned and said, "I ought to [tell] you about
Gromyko, who, in this very room not over 10 minutes ago,
told more barefaced lies than I have ever heard in so short
a time. All during his denial that the Russians had any missiles or weapons, or anything else, in Cuba, I had the low-
level pictures in the center drawer of my desk, and it was an
enormous temptation to show them to him."[89]

Gromyko's evasions, which doubtless mirrored Khrushchev's instructions, weakened the prospects for accords not
only on Cuba but across the gamut of superpower negotiations.
That same evening, after a State Department dinner, Gromyko
and Rusk spoke at length about tensions in Berlin, with
Gromyko once more arguing that "the occupation regime in
West Berlin had outlived itself" and should be terminated.[90] A
day earlier William Foster, the head of the Arms Control and

Development Agency, had conferred with Gromyko on possible arrangements to prohibit the stationing of "weapons of mass destruction in outer space." Gromyko said that progress in this area would depend on developing a comprehensive disarmament plan.[91] But unknown to either Gromyko or Foster, discovery of missiles in Cuba—and Soviet denials—had unraveled the fragile skein of trust on which any agreements between the superpowers would rest.

In guarding their knowledge of the Cuban missiles from Gromyko and the rest of the Kremlin, the Ex Comm members necessarily kept the American public unwitting as well. Their exertions to avoid alerting the capital's hypersensitive media and political establishment could transform even a short car ride into a clandestine—and congested—mission. Late one evening, George Ball recalled,

> We were afraid too many black limousines would attract undue attention, so nine of us piled into my car, sitting two or three deep and instead of going directly to the White House, we went to the Treasury, then by a secret set of passages through the White House bomb shelter into the White House basement.

Paul Nitze, the assistant secretary of defense for international security affairs, appraised the subtlety of this cloak-and-dagger scheme: "We must have looked like the traditional twenty clowns in the circus climbing out of one small Volkswagen Beetle. . . ."[92] The Ex Comm's extraordinary secrecy (reinforced on October 21 by the president's calls to the *New York Times* and the *Washington Post*, urging them to defer stories on the crisis until he addressed the nation) provided a crucial breathing space from popular outcries. But no one expected this splendid insulation to endure more than a week.

"We Just Had to Get Them Out of There"

The Ex Comm sessions seldom focused explicitly on domestic politics, but they crackled with an awareness of public venom toward Soviet maneuvers in the Caribbean. At the opening meeting, on October 16, Vice President Lyndon Johnson favored a military strike against the missiles, saying that although these weapons would not change the military balance, the American people would never accept them: "I take the position . . . 'We ought to be living all these years [with missiles and not] get your blood pressure up.' But the fact is the country's blood pressure *is* up, and they are fearful, and they're insecure, and we're getting divided. . . ." The former Senate majority leader also clarified for the president the sentiment on Capitol Hill:

> I take this little *State Department Bulletin* that you sent out
> to all the congressmen. One of the points you make: that
> any time the buildup endangers or threatens our security in
> any way, we're going to do what must be done immediately
> to protect our own security. And when you say that, why,
> they give unanimous support.[93]

That Tuesday afternoon, Secretary of Defense Robert McNamara at first doubted the need for military measures because he did not see primarily a military problem but rather "a domestic political problem." Under Secretary of State George Ball disputed this distinction: "Yeah, well, as far as the American people are concerned, action means military action, period."[94]

The concern to sustain public support went far beyond crude calculations of electoral strength. Kennedy believed that, whatever policy he pursued, the episode would hurt his domestic standing. After a meeting with the Ex Comm on Saturday afternoon, October 20, the president, according to the historians Ernest May and Philip Zelikow, wandered out onto the "Truman" balcony outside the Mansion's Oval Room with his brother, Sorensen, and perhaps one or two others. Reflecting momentarily on domestic politics, he predicted that the crisis would damage the Democratic Party in the upcoming congressional elections. Some Democratic supporters might feel (like Stevenson) that they were being too warlike, while many voters would feel that Republican warnings about Cuba had been proved right. "Well," Sorensen clearly remembered him commenting ruefully (and perhaps sardonically), "I guess Homer Capehart is the Winston Churchill of our generation."[95]

Kennedy believed that a failure to act on the danger from Cuba would trigger such an outcry that extreme conservatives would exert far greater pressure on the administration's foreign policy. This fear was not simply a product of partisan prejudice. On October 18 Douglas Dillon, a Republican who had served President Eisenhower in the State Department, passed a note to Theodore Sorensen:

> Ted—Have you considered the very real possibility that if we allow Cuba to complete installation and operational readiness of missile bases, the next House of Representatives is likely to have a Republican majority? This would completely paralyze our ability to react sensibly and coherently to further Soviet advances.[96]

An equally unnerving scenario pondered by Ex Comm was that failure to act against Soviet missiles in nearby Cuba would so demoralize the American people as to erode the consensus for firm, responsible leadership throughout the world. Secretary of State Dean Rusk put the case squarely during the third morning of Ex Comm's deliberations. A weak response, he warned, would not only "undermine our alliances all over the world very promptly" and encourage the Soviets to "feel like they've got it made as far as intimidating the United States is concerned." It would also create

> an almost unmanageable problem in this country getting any support for a foreign policy that would assume we were going to sustain the cause of independence of states here and in all parts of the world. We have a million men in uniform outside the United States. We've got foreign-aid programs. We've got a major effort in the making in every continent. And it seems to me that inaction in this situation would undermine and undercut the long support that we need for the kind of foreign policy that will eventually ensure our survival.[97]

The convergence of foreign and domestic pressures for strong action proved irresistible. On October 18 the president canvassed the Ex Comm: "Is there anyone here who doesn't think that we ought to do something about this?"[98] According to notes that Kennedy dictated after a meeting late that evening, his National Security Adviser alone expressed doubts:

> Bundy continued to argue against any action, on the grounds that there would be, inevitably, a Soviet reprisal against Berlin and that this would divide our alliances and we would bear that responsibility. He felt we would be better off to merely take note of the existence of these missiles, and to wait until the crunch comes in Berlin, and not play what he thought might be the Soviet game.
>
> Everyone else felt that for us to fail to respond would throw into question our willingness to respond over Berlin, [and] would divide our allies and our country. [They felt] that we would be faced with a crunch over Berlin in 2 or 3

months and that by that time the Soviets would have a large missile arsenal in the Western Hemisphere which would weaken out whole position in this hemisphere and cause, face us with the same problems we're going to have in Berlin anyway.[99]

After a sleepless night, Bundy too found the logic of decisive action inescapable. Deciding that the stakes were too great to let the danger fester, he shifted the next morning to advocating an air strike on the missile sites without warning.

Kennedy's ambassador to the UN, Adlai Stevenson, was by all accounts the most pacific of Kennedy's advisers, as befitted a man charged with defending American conduct before the world. But although Stevenson was reviled by some Ex Comm members as an "appeaser" (and later defended by revisionist writers as a lone voice of reason), he too concurred that the Soviet deployment was intolerable. In a memo to the president on October 17, he cautioned against risking nuclear war through rash action but agreed that "the national security must come first," and, in any case, "we can't negotiate with a gun to our head."[100] "No politician could have missed the significance of Russian missiles in Cuba," Stevenson later told the newsman Elie Abel. "We just had to get them out of there."[101]

CHAPTER FIVE

The Decision to Blockade

1. Pressures to Act

THE PRESIDENT'S second key decision, to blockade Cuba, has been widely portrayed as the fruit of Ex Comm's feverish brainstorming and Kennedy's uniquely resourceful, nuanced leadership. It is nonetheless helpful to note that the "quarantine" had a far longer and more complex evolution than the debates in the Ex Comm. It was the most commonly prescribed, best publicized, most widely endorsed action to counter Soviet arms shipments to Cuba even before discovery of the missiles themselves.

The quarantine was, on one level, a military extension of the policy pursued by both Eisenhower and Kennedy, progressively to isolate Castro's Cuba by means short of outright invasion. The initial targets of this policy were economic, the means diplomatic. On July 8, 1960, Eisenhower had suspended the Cuban sugar quota, in effect ending 80 percent of Cuba's subsidized exports to the United States. On October 18 Vice President Nixon, speaking before the American Legion's annual convention in Tampa, Florida, had proposed still stricter economic sanctions to curb Castro's influence; he called his policy a defensive "quarantine."[1] The next day the State Department further curtailed trade with Cuba, barring all exports to the island except medicine, medical supplies, and some food products.

The Kennedy administration tightened the restrictions imposed by its predecessor. On March 31, 1961, the president ended Cuba's small remaining quota of sugar exports to the United States. On January 28, 1962, Dean Rusk urged a conference of the Organization of American States in Punta del Este, Uruguay, to adopt immediate economic and other sanctions on Cuba. Three days later a bare two-thirds majority of the attending ministers partly accommodated American pressure, voting to exclude Cuba "from participation in organs of the inter-American system" and prohibit OAS members from selling arms to Cuba. On February 3, 1962, Kennedy ordered a ban on imports of Cuban tobacco, industrial molasses, and vegetable products, a move aimed at depriving Castro's regime of some $35 million annually. The administration claimed that the expanded trade embargo, though still exempting exports of medical supplies and certain foodstuffs on humanitarian grounds, would reduce Castro's threat to other nations in the hemisphere.[2]

In the weeks before the missile crisis the Kennedy administration expanded the Cuban embargo. On October 4 the government set tough penalties, including loss of all U.S. cargoes and U.S. port privileges, for foreign ships engaged in trade between Cuba and the Soviet bloc, and barred all U.S. ships from carrying goods to Cuba.[3]

The *New York Times* lauded Kennedy's initiative for its prudence. The president, "refusing to be stampeded by advocates of direct action against Cuba" and instead strengthening a policy "long ago adopted," "has now produced a program that might materially reduce the Soviet bloc's military and economic support without risking an armed collision or violation of international law."[4]

As the Soviet presence in Cuba grew, so too did calls to extend the embargo by force. The Kennedy administration had sporadically considered just such a naval blockade for nearly eighteen months before the missile crisis. On April 19, 1961, Robert Kennedy had written to his brother after the failure of the Bay of Pigs invasion, "If we don't want Russia to set up missile bases in Cuba, we had better decide now what we are willing to do to stop it."[5]

The attorney general had offered three options for dealing with missiles in Cuba, of which a blockade occupied a middle ground in his thinking. One was an invasion with U.S. troops, but this was a proposal "you [the president] have rejected . . . for good and sufficient reasons (although this might have to be reconsidered)." A strict blockade around Cuba was a second option, though as an act of war and "a drawn-out affair" it "would lead to a good deal of world-wide bitterness." Finally, as a purely diplomatic route, Washington could press the Organization of American States to ban arms shipments to Cuba while guaranteeing Cuba's territorial integrity. This, however, seemed a pallid answer to the need for "something forceful and determined" in a "showdown" between America and Russia.[6]

In May 1961 Secretary of State Rusk had raised the prospect of a blockade in testifying before the Senate Committee on Foreign Relations on possible dangers from the Soviets. Rusk noted that the Soviets had only small numbers of submarines and intercontinental ballistic missiles, but if they could transfer some of these to Cuba it would "impose a degree of blackmail upon the United States in dealing with our problems in all parts of the world." Only if the United States discovered missile bases, though, might it have to blockade.[7]

The idea of using the navy to tighten the ring around Castro held strong appeal in an era when the U.S. government shied from directly invading the island but periodically dispatched warships to counter suspected Cuban threats to hemispheric security. In November 1960 Eisenhower had sent warships to Guatemala and Nicaragua to thwart Cuban aid to a rumored Guatemalan rebellion. During the Bay of Pigs operation the following April, Kennedy had afforded discreet naval aid—but not U.S. troops—to land Cuban rebels. In March 1962 he had ordered ships to patrol the sea lanes between Guatemala and Cuba when Guatemalan president Miguel Ydigoras labeled student-led protests Castro-inspired.[8]

In the fall of 1962 Kennedy encouraged ambitious naval and amphibious exercises in the Caribbean to intimidate Castro and sharpen contingency plans ranging from blockade to full-scale assault. An operation involving 20,000 soldiers and support personnel, including 7,500 marines, with four aircraft carriers, some twenty destroyers, and fifteen troop carriers, was set for mid-October to conduct a mock invasion on the coral beaches of Vieques Island near Puerto Rico. Their stated mission was to liberate the mythical Republic of Vieques from a mythical tyrant named "Ortsac"—Castro spelled backward.[9]

Perceptions of both military convenience and military necessity increased the momentum favoring a decision to blockade. The political scientist Elizabeth Cohn details how, even before U-2 planes had spotted missiles in Cuba, the U.S. Navy was rehearsing for a blockade of the island. On October 1, 1962, McNamara and the Joint Chiefs of Staff reviewed evidence of possible Soviet missile deployment in Cuba and decided "to alert Admiral Dennison, Commander-in-Chief of the Atlantic Fleet, to be prepared to institute a blockade." Cohn argues that these preparations, which began October 3, may well have inclined the president toward the blockade option: ". . . He knew that a naval operation was feasible because the Navy had already determined how many ships they needed, and had even begun to make the ships available by reconfiguring the Atlantic Fleet." (By contrast, air force commanders who later pressed for strikes on the Cuban bases were unable to assure Kennedy that any amount of bombing would destroy all the nuclear missiles.) Indeed, Cohn notes, even at the first Ex Comm meeting on October 16 the president "was exploring the details of a blockade when others present focused on an air strike or invasion."[10]

Scattered calls for a blockade had appeared in the news media long before the Russians dared place missiles in Cuba. In January 1961, while Eisenhower was still president, the *Houston Chronicle* recommended that the Organization of American States impose economic sanctions against Cuba that might include "an inter-American naval force to halt suspect ships entering the Caribbean, to search them for arms and to confiscate where such weapons are discovered." If, however, the OAS failed to act, the *Chronicle* added, "we could take this action ourselves" to enforce the Monroe Doctrine.[11]

As Soviet arms shipments to Cuba quickened in the late summer and fall of 1962, the media increasingly circulated the idea of a blockade as a practical alternative to inaction or attack. Arthur Krock of the *New York Times* chided both Kennedy and his critics for ignoring the option of a "naval patrol, which is the most effective means of keeping Cuba from acquiring Communist missiles and other offensive-war weaponry, and does not involve military invasion at all." *Life* magazine called in September for an immediate blockade, admitting that "it may mean war" but insisting it would be "less warlike than Khrushchev's massive arming of Castro." The *Wall Street Journal*, aiming to dispel the president's perception of his options as limited between "inaction and a precipitate plunge into Cuba," mentioned the possibility of "a blockade as far as military shipments to or from Cuba are concerned. Now a blockade is a military act but it is not of itself war. . . . We would have neutralized the threat to our security."[12]

Congressmen typically shied from recommending specific measures against Castro and his Soviet arms caches, instead preferring airier calls to uphold the Monroe Doctrine.[13] But "blockade" was the most frequent proposed countermeasure to the Soviet presence. Republicans led the clamor for action. On September 5, 1962, Steven B. Derounian of New York's Second Congressional District compressed nearly every major cold war axiom and image into a call for the president to blockade Cuba:

> Since you assumed the Presidency, not only has Castro pushed us around but he has kicked us in the teeth and is now spitting in our faces. . . . The Monroe Doctrine has been violated and we have done absolutely nothing heretofore. . . . I, therefore, recommend that the United States institute a blockade of Cuba preventing any further military shipments to or from Cuba. Our national security is in danger. I am sure you realize that appeasement of Hitler led to war and further appeasement of the demented, bearded dictator of Cuba will certainly eventually lead to war. We must stop this Communist cancer now, with or without the cooperation of our sister states in this hemisphere. . . . The

American people are sick and tired of cowering before the Communist thug. They know that knuckling under to Hitler brought war; that weakness brings war and strength assures peace."[14]

Calls to blockade enlisted other Republicans eager to stagger Castro, stun Khrushchev, and scold Kennedy.[15] On September 9 the prominent senator Karl Mundt of South Dakota urged an immediate air and naval blockade of Cuba. Senators Barry Goldwater of Arizona, John Tower of Texas, and Strom Thurmond of South Carolina all leaned at one point or other toward a blockade.[16]

Adding to the appeal of a blockade was the hope that it would do what the president had not: enable Cuban exiles to undermine Castro's regime. Representative Bob Dole of Kansas linked the two aims because "the very presence of thousands of Soviet technicians lessens the chance for a successful revolution to overthrow Castro from within Cuba."[16] Senator Prescott Bush of Connecticut, undiscouraged by the fate of the Bay of Pigs landing, asserted that Cuban exiles themselves could conduct "their own blockade of Cuba" with minimal supply by the U.S. Navy. "It would not require many PT boats for these Cubans to be able to stop ships. They would not have to stop more than one or two ships . . . to convince the Russians that it would be very dangerous for them to proceed with the military buildup in Cuba."[17]

Democrats were more wary of criticizing the president, but some did join the growing clamor for naval action. As early as September 10, Senator Thomas Dodd of Connecticut invoked the Monroe Doctrine in calling for a total embargo on Communist military shipments to Cuba and a possible "total blockade on [all] shipments to Cuba" except food and consumer goods. A month later the senator referred on a television talk show, *Open End*, to the problem posed by "Khrushchev's Cuba," saying, "I suggest we start with a partial blockade. If it isn't adequate, we move to a total one."[18]

Foreshadowing the approach by President Kennedy and others in the Ex Comm, the early proponents of a blockade emphasized its defensive character. Republican Senator Hugh Scott of Pennsylvania insisted, "I am not advocating an invasion" but simply a blockade "whereby, preferably with the help of the other American states, we all join in an economic and a military blockade against the importation of Communism." Richard Nixon, then running for governor of California, preferred a softer term than "blockade," saying, "The Castro-Soviet regime must be quarantined" to halt the flow of Soviet arms. Nixon stopped short of endorsing a naval blockade outright but said he would back President Kennedy if the latter deemed encirclement of Cuba necessary.[19]

The senior Republican Senator from Wisconsin, Alexander Wiley, offered the most elegant euphemism for a blockade by suggesting on September 4 that an inter-American "peace fleet," or "flotilla of peace" patrol the Western Hemisphere. Two days later Craig Hosmer of California caught the spirit by recommending that the United States "declare the Western Hemisphere a peace zone, and tell the world we mean to keep it that way through use of national power, if necessary." Echoing a resolution introduced a year earlier by Republican congressman Glenn Cunningham of Nebraska, Hosmer proposed that the United States treat "all Communist war material, including fuel, as contraband and prohibit its shipment into the peace zone of the Americas." Hosmer aimed further to promote peace through "the ousting of Castro's Communist dictatorship from Cuba."[20]

Senator John Stennis of Mississippi, a key member of the Senate Armed Services Committee, explained that America's

right to act against Cuba was so clear that normal definitions of
international law, war and peace, even "blockade" itself did not
apply. On October 9 Stennis dismissed fears that a blockade
might offend world opinion: "The entire world knows that we
are not the aggressor. . . . We did not create this powder keg in
the Caribbean." Nor was this all. "A blockade is not a blockade," he reasoned, "when a nation acts prudently in its own interest and in self-defense, choosing not to wait until it is too
late."[21]

In recasting a technical act of war as a gesture of restraint
under duress, congressmen were responding, in part, to the
public's strong aversion to firing the first shot in what could
prove the world's final conflict. In late September 1962 only 10
percent of respondents to a Gallup survey thought the United
States should bomb, invade, or take "belligerent action" against
Cuba, though a slim majority of those who expressed an opinion favored some pressure, whether a trade embargo or other
action "short of actual war." Asked whether the United States
should "send our armed forces into Cuba to help overthrow
Castro," only 24 percent agreed and 63 percent disagreed, with
51 percent fearing it would lead to all-out war between the
United States and the Soviet Union.[22] A blockade of Cuba appeared more attractive, less cataclysmic.

Congressmen otherwise free with bold words understood
that an assault on Cuba risked tearing apart the Organization of
American States. They recognized too that pitting U.S. troops
against defenders likely to include armed and uniformed Soviet
"technicians" would heat the cold war unacceptably. Even most
critics of the president's "vacillating" policies therefore disclaimed interest in any measure beyond a blockade.

Kennedy's most insistent gadfly, Senator Keating, took pains
to deny any warlike aims. When on September 6 a colleague
hearing him call for stronger action "wondered if the Senator

was going so far at this moment to suggest that U.S. troops be used to storm the shores of Cuba," Keating replied, "I am not, and I never have. . . . I do not advocate, I do not favor at this time, an invasion of Cuba by American forces. . . ." Nearly a month later, even as his criticisms of the president sharpened, Keating indignantly complained, "A determined effort is being made to make it appear that anyone who favors a stronger and more vigorous policy with regard to Cuba" must want "an immediate U.S. invasion of Cuba or some other warlike action. . . . Of course that is not true. . . ." Representative James E. Van Zandt of Pennsylvania and Senator Stennis displayed similar reserve amidst the bravado.[23]

Mounting alarm over Soviet weapons during October 1962 raised public approval for a blockade but not an invasion. The pollster Louis Harris alerted the president on October 4, "In Michigan, within the past week, a majority of 82–18 percent wanted a blockade of Cuba, although a majority of 68–32 percent oppose going to war there." Nationwide the fear of precipitous action was even more pronounced; about 90 percent of two thousand Americans interviewed by *Newsweek* disapproved of invading Cuba. Senator Homer Capehart of Indiana, whose reelection campaign had featured demands for an invasion, by mid-October saw public revulsion coming at a Gallup and amended his position to favor a blockade.[24]

By the time the Ex Comm began its deliberations on the morning of October 16, the idea of blockading Cuba was already standard discourse in the Capitol and in myriad opinion columns. That option, rather than an air strike or invasion, best accorded with the thrust of U.S. policy toward Cuba since 1960 and the unbroken policy imperative to avoid killing Russians. It also best fit the public's own decisive preference, of which the president was keenly aware.

2. Moving Toward a Quarantine

THE CIA'S REVELATION of medium-range missiles in Cuba of course transformed the political setting in which officials pondered the option of a blockade. Until mid-October proponents of a blockade had not aimed to undo a particular weapons system but rather to halt ongoing Soviet arms shipments, discomfort the Kremlin, and tighten the siege of Castro's regime. No one in the Ex Comm, however, contended that a blockade alone could end the threat of nuclear weapons already on the island. Only air strikes or invasion could destroy the missiles targeting American cities. The idea of a blockade therefore changed literally overnight from the most militant step with broad public support to the mildest initiative that offered a chance both to sway the Kremlin and to placate the American people.

Filtered through the imperatives of repelling a Soviet nuclear challenge and sustaining domestic support, President Kennedy's impact on the decision-making process becomes apparent. The reckless buccaneer of so many "revisionist" portraits is almost nowhere to be found in the transcripts of secret committee meetings, correspondence with Khrushchev, executive orders, or the recollections of Soviet and American officials. Instead one finds a leader familiar from the partisan but perceptive histories by Sorensen, Schlesinger, and other veterans of the New Frontier: a controlled, intellectually curious and alert chief executive straining to fathom Soviet motivations, foresee pitfalls, and refrain from needless provocations.

It nonetheless required a day's reflection before President Kennedy and others in the Ex Comm moved beyond their immediate shock and alarm. On the first day of deliberations, most advisers felt it urgent to bomb the missile sites and perhaps other Cuban military bases, even to invade the island, before the nuclear missiles could become operational. After that, they feared, an attack would risk retaliation by surviving missiles against American cities.[25] The president assumed that "At least we're going to do number one," meaning an air strike on the sites. Among the military options seriously debated, it was a temperate course, though the president himself later expressed relief that there had been time to reconsider. "If we had had to act in the first twenty-four hours," he said, "I don't think . . . we would have chosen as prudently as we finally did."[26]

Robert Kennedy seriously considered an invasion. At the afternoon meeting he drew inspiration from the sinking of an American ship in Havana harbor in 1898 that helped trigger war with Spain, and asked "whether there is some other way we can get involved in this through [the U.S. naval base in] Guantanamo Bay or something. Or whether there's some ship, you know . . . sink the *Maine* again—or something."[27] When he scribbled his now famous wry and rueful remark, "I now know how Tojo felt when he was planning Pearl Harbor,"[28] his meaning was both ironic and literal.

Within the Ex Comm, on October 17 Under Secretary of State George Ball became the first sustained advocate of a blockade.[29] Anticipating Robert Kennedy's now celebrated stand, Ball opposed a surprise air strike on Cuba as no worthier than the Japanese sneak attack on Pearl Harbor. He broached his concerns during the first evening of Ex Comm's deliberations, invoking hardheaded considerations of likely Soviet reprisals:

> This coming in there, a Pearl Harbor, just frightens the hell out of me as to what goes beyond. . . . You go in there with

a surprise attack. You put out all the missiles. This isn't the end. This is the *beginning*, I think.[30]

The next day Ball revealed a moral core to his objections, saying, "It's the kind of conduct that one might expect of the Soviet Union. It is not conduct that one expects of the United States." To Ball's satisfaction and amazement, Robert Kennedy belied his image as an inflexible anti-Communist hard-liner and, in Ball's words, "restated my argument in much more vivid and compelling terms." With impassioned reference to the Japanese leader who ordered the surprise attack on Pearl Harbor just over two decades earlier, he exclaimed, "My brother is not going to be the Tojo of the 1960s."[31]

The Ex Comm spent "more time on this moral question during the first five days than on any other single matter," Robert Kennedy recalled, and he more than any other member transformed the debate. Speaking with quiet intensity, he asked "what kind of a country we are. . . . We've fought for 15 years with Russia to prevent a first strike against us. . . . Now, in the interest of time, we do that to a small country. I think it's a hell of a burden to carry."[32]

On Friday, October 19, after Acheson renewed his call to bomb the missile sites, Robert Kennedy insisted, "A sneak attack was not in our traditions. Thousands of Cubans would be killed without warning, and a lot of Russians too." He favored action but of a kind that "should allow the Soviets some room for maneuver. . . ." At a point when Bundy, General Taylor, and other key advisers had supported a surprise air strike, the attorney general's words exerted a critical impact. Douglas Dillon was among several participants who later credited this speech with leading them to rethink their hard-line views: "Frankly, these [moral] considerations had not occurred to me until Bobby raised them so eloquently."[33]

Robert Kennedy's bid to temper strategy with scruples merely offended Dean Acheson, the Ex Comm's formidable senior statesman and a man who, as Arthur Schlesinger writes, "detested moral anguish."[34] Acheson persistently rejected Robert Kennedy's "false and pejorative analogy,"[35] with Pearl Harbor, observing that the president had given fair warning and that destroying the missiles was a legitimate act of self-defense. His argument was characteristically brisk, magisterial, and a touch caustic. It also showed how far the spectrum of cold war militancy extended in mainstream politics, as Theodore Sorensen recounts:

> I will always remember Dean Acheson . . . saying that he felt that we should knock out Soviet missiles in Cuba by air strike. Someone asked him, "If we do that, what do you think the Soviet Union will do?" He said, "I think—I know the Soviet Union well. I know what they are required to do in the light of their history and their posture around the world. I think they will knock out our missiles in Turkey." And then the question came again, "Well, then what do we do?" "Well," he said, "I believe under our NATO treaty with which I was associated, we would be required to respond by knocking out a missile base inside the Soviet Union." "Well, then what do they do?" "Well," he said, "then that's when we hope cooler heads will prevail, and they'll stop and talk." Well, that was a rather chilling conversation for all of us.[36]

Although Acheson never wavered in his view, most Ex Comm members repeatedly shifted during the first week. Rusk and Bundy registered the sharpest policy swings. On October 16, as the Ex Comm began its deliberations, Rusk tried to brake the momentum toward what he considered rash action, but on October 17, while many colleagues were becoming more circumspect, he proposed a surprise air strike. Over the next several days Rusk became so elusive in his recommendations that few on the committee knew where he stood. Bundy at first leaned toward an air strike, then on the evening of October 18, alone among Ex Comm members, he opposed any action that could give the Russians an excuse to seize Berlin. But by the next morning he pronounced the danger in Cuba too great to let fester, and called for an air strike without warning.

Such dizzying policy peregrinations reflected the fact that every option had severe drawbacks. Even if the administration were prepared to risk killing thousands of Russians and Cubans, no amount of bombing could be sure to destroy all the nuclear missiles, a fact the Joint Chiefs acknowledged and that led them to press for a follow-up invasion. Yet an invasion would likely cost tens of thousands of American lives as well as untold Russian and Cuban casualties, virtually compelling a sharp Soviet response. Even toppling Castro, however keenly desired, would entail problems by requiring an open-ended occupation of Cuba to impose a semblance of political stability.

A blockade was also fraught with risk. Challenges by Soviet ships might bring war on the high seas; or Khrushchev could counter by blockading West Berlin, a prospect that had long haunted the administration. Then too, even an airtight naval surveillance would have no effect on missiles already in Cuba. A blockade might therefore drag on for months—"a very slow death," Robert Kennedy called it,[37] requiring further military action or diplomatic concessions or both.

President Kennedy's search for the right balance between force and prudence led him, like most of his advisers, on an unsparing but also uncertain journey among these imperfect alternatives. Among those who shaped his thinking was Robert Lovett, a former under secretary of state and then secretary of defense under President Truman. After Kennedy's victory in

1960, ill health had led Lovett to decline a cabinet post of his choice, but both McNamara and Rusk had gained their appointments on his recommendation. According to Bundy, "The president and Lovett liked and respected each other. They were much alike; both had charm and wit; both knew that 'life is unfair,' and each understood and enjoyed the unusual grace of the other." Compared with Acheson's crackling presence in the Ex Comm, Lovett traveled softly but surely through the corridors of the Kennedy White House. During the first week of the crisis he was "a particularly impressive and influential advocate of the blockade," but his "role is often neglected because his advice was given in a very small group."[38]

By Thursday, October 18 the president leaned toward a blockade because, unlike an air strike, it would not immediately kill Cubans and Russians and therefore would give Khrushchev time to reconsider. As his brother Robert explained to the like-minded Lovett, "we could always blow the place up if necessary but that might be unnecessary and we would then be in the position of having used too much force."[39] In the Ex Comm earlier that day, the president had cautioned that an air strike would confirm fears harbored even by allied nations that his administration was dangerously obsessed with Cuba. When McNamara asserted that the presence of Soviet missiles there posed "a political problem . . . of holding the alliance together" that "requires action," Kennedy was unimpressed, saying:

> Which one would strain the alliance more: this [proposed] attack by us on Cuba, which most allies regard as a fixation of the United States and not a serious military threat? . . . Because they think that we're slightly demented on this subject. So there isn't any doubt that, whatever action we take against Cuba . . . a lot of people would regard this as a mad act by the United States, which is due to a loss of nerve

because they will argue that taken at its worst, the presence of these missiles really doesn't change the [military] balance.[40]

Recent scholars have punctured the once-common claim that Kennedy exerted flawless control over the armed forces during the missile crisis. In reality the administration had limited or no knowledge of the informal steps taken by military commanders to raise the alert status of NATO forces, of the false nuclear alert (ostensibly from Cuba) on a Florida radar screen, of the "routine" U-2 flight (to gather air samples from Soviet nuclear tests near the North Pole) that strayed into Siberia, and of diverse other military maneuvers and miscues. Kennedy's strivings to limit risks were nonetheless prodigious and at times pitted him against officers and advisers who objected to his exacting precautions.

Even in considering an air strike, Kennedy dismayed the Joint Chiefs with his preference to attack only the nuclear missiles. The chiefs wanted also to hit the Russian surface-to-air missiles that could target U.S. planes; the Russian IL-28 bombers that might conceivably infiltrate thin U.S. air defenses in the South with nuclear payloads; and other military units and installations that could resist a subsequent U.S. invasion. General Maxwell Taylor, chairman of the Joint Chiefs, told the president that his colleagues "feel so strongly about the dangers inherent in the limited strike that they would prefer taking *no* military action. . . ."[41]

Kennedy appreciated his military officers' professional judgments, but, as he explained to Taylor, the risks of failure in Cuba seemed preferable to those of unchecked escalation:

I think the only thing is, the chances of it becoming a much broader struggle are increased as you step up the [number of targets]. . . . I mean, you're running a much more major operation, therefore the dangers of the worldwide effects are substantial to the United States, [they] are increased. That's the only argument for it [the limited strike].

I quite agree that, if you're just thinking about Cuba, the best thing to do is to be bold, if you're thinking about trying to get this thing under some degree of control.[42]

But the president refused to think about Cuba alone. His overriding concern remained the spectre of nuclear war, which seemed to lie in wait for a leader who would lose his moral compass or simply his patience amid calls for action. At a meeting on October 18 in which his advisers, including Taylor, speculated on possible Soviet responses, the president clarified their main goal: "Now, the question really is to what action we take which lessens the chances of a nuclear exchange, which obviously is the final failure—that's obvious to us—and at the same time, maintain some degree of solidarity with our allies."[43]

On Friday, October 19, Kennedy had his sole meeting during the crisis with the assembled Joint Chiefs of Staff: Admiral George Anderson of the navy, General Earle Wheeler of the army, David Shoup of the Marine Corps, General Curtis LeMay of the air force, and the chairman, General Taylor. It was scarcely a meeting of minds. The chiefs again pressed for a massive air strike without warning, and most of them favored an invasion to destroy any remaining missiles. The president instead invited them to consider the risks:

First, I think we ought to think of why the Russians did this. . . . If we attack Cuban missiles, or Cuba, in any way, it gives them a clear line to take Berlin. . . . We would be regarded as the trigger-happy Americans who lost Berlin. We would have no support among our allies. We would affect the West Germans' attitude toward us. And [people would believe] that we let Berlin go because we didn't have the guts to endure a situation in Cuba.[44]

A quick strike, Kennedy conceded, would "neutralize the chance of danger to the United States of these missiles being used," but: "On the other hand, we increase the chance greatly" of the Soviets' "just going in and taking Berlin by force. Which leaves me only one alternative, which is to fire nuclear weapons—which is a hell of an alternative—and begin a nuclear exchange. . . ."[45]

Kennedy's admonition that discretion would be the better part of military valor grated on officers already chafing at their commander-in-chief's seeming irresolution. The generals believed that overwhelming force was the only antidote to Soviet aggression, whereas, in General LeMay's words, "This blockade and political action, I see leading into war. I don't see any other solution. It will lead right into war. This is almost as bad as the appeasement at Munich."[46]

Weathering the barely contained resentments of his top officers, the president showed equal energy in readying the blockade and limiting or forbidding other actions that could spark a wider conflict. On October 22, hours before addressing the nation, Kennedy asked about the status of his request a day earlier that the Joint Chiefs specially instruct U.S. missile base commanders in Turkey not to fire—even in the event of a Soviet attack—without specific presidential authorization. Roswell Gilpatric in the Defense Department replied, ". . . The Chiefs came back with a paper saying that those instructions are already out," meaning that such standard procedures needed no repetition. Kennedy persisted: "Well, why don't we reinforce them because, as I say, we may be attacking the Cubans, and a reprisal may come. We don't want these nuclear warheads firing without our knowing about it." That did not sit well with Paul

Nitze, the assistant secretary of defense for international security affairs, who believed that U.S. nuclear superiority would permit bolder action in Cuba without fear of Soviet retaliation. The president heard out Nitze but left no room to set aside his request:

> PRESIDENT KENNEDY: They [the Joint Chiefs] object to sending a new [set of instructions] out?
>
> NITZE: They object to sending it out because it, to their view, compromises their standing instructions. . . . They said the orders are [already] that nothing can go without the presidential order. Which—
>
> PRESIDENT KENNEDY: But they don't know in Greece and Turkey—ah, Turkey and Italy—what we know. And therefore they don't realize there is a chance there will be a spot reprisal.
>
> And what we've got to do is make sure these fellows *do* know, so that they don't fire them off and put the United States under attack. I don't think we ought to accept the Chiefs' word on that one, Paul.
>
> NITZE: All right. . . .
>
> RUSK: They might think a nuclear war is already on.
>
> NITZE: I'm sure that these fellows are. . . . Surely they're indoctrinated not to fire. This is what Secretary McNamara and I went over, looked into, and they really are—
>
> PRESIDENT KENNEDY: Well, let's do it again, Paul.
>
> NITZE: I've got your point and we're going to get that.[47]

At this point the Ex Comm erupted in unaccustomed laughter, stemming, as Ernest May and Philip Zelikow surmise, from "Kennedy's insistent refusal to take it on faith that military standing orders would be observed, and Nitze's discomfort at giving in to him."[48]

Kennedy's efforts to avoid miscalculation encompassed the very word "miscalculation." In Vienna Khrushchev had bristled at this term, which seemed to him a code word by the West to blame Russia and communism for all international conflicts. At the close of the Ex Comm's late-morning conference on October 22, the president "asked that the word 'miscalculate' be taken out of a letter prepared for him" to inform Khrushchev of imminent U.S. steps regarding Cuba. Kennedy "recalled that in Vienna Khrushchev had revealed a misunderstanding of this word when translated into Russian."[49] The version Kennedy approved expressed the country's determination "that this threat to the security of this hemisphere be removed," assured the Soviet leader "that the action we are taking is the minimum necessary," and cautioned against any "misjudgment" or action that "could widen or deepen this already grave crisis."[50]

The administration also trimmed its verbal sails to emphasize the defensive character of its naval action. The inspiration for using the term "quarantine" instead of "blockade" has been attributed variously to the State Department's deputy legal adviser, Leonard Meeker (by his superior, Abram Chayes), to Dean Acheson (by Paul Nitze), and to others. The word self-consciously recalled President Franklin Roosevelt's exhortation in 1937 for "peace-loving nations" to "quarantine the aggressors." The term later resurfaced among politicians and newspapers advising first Eisenhower and then Kennedy on policy toward Castro. White House aides also repeatedly used the word "quarantine"—up until the time the missiles were discovered—to connote simply a tightening of economic restrictions on Cuba.

On Monday, October 15, 1962, an unidentified "informed U.S. official" had told reporters that the government expected imminently to enlist European allies for a "quarantine" on ships serving Cuba's trade, in arms or other goods, with Soviet bloc countries:

> With Cuba already costing the Soviet Union a million dol-
> lars a day, the proposed quarantine looked to make aid to
> Cuba "as expensive as possible" to the Communist bloc.
> According to Edwin M. Martin, Assistant Secretary of State
> for Inter-American Affairs, the Administration planned to
> "close all U.S. ports to ships of any country whose vessels
> carry war materials to Cuba;" deny government cargoes to
> ships of any company that aided commerce "between Cuba
> and the Communist bloc;" and bar U.S. ships from trading
> with Cuba.[51]

Over the following week the Ex Comm appropriated the word "quarantine" as a velvet wrap to cushion global reaction to the U.S. show of sea power. This gained importance when Meeker and Assistant Attorney General Nicholas Katzenbach reported that a blockade need not involve a declaration of war if it had the formal support of a regional security organization. By connoting a defensive interdiction of weapons rather than an indiscriminate hostile act, the term "quarantine" helped U.S. diplomats gain a needed two-thirds mandate within the OAS.

The final Ex Comm gathering before Kennedy's televised address on October 22 considered what his advisers could say if questioned by members of the Congress. No one worried that the blockade would appear an overreaction, but, in Rusk's words, "If any of our colleagues think that this is, in any sense, a weak action, I think we can be quite sure that in a number of hours we'll have a flaming crisis on our hands." Surprisingly, Kennedy declined to impose on his aides a uniform public line on why there had been no air strike or invasion, and whether his response had been strong enough. "Everybody has to follow their own judgment in these matters," he said. "It just seems to me to be the appropriate answer."[52]

3. "United and Firm": Americans Respond to the Blockade

YEARS AFTER the missile crisis the iconoclastic journalist I. F. Stone asked mockingly "how many Americans, consulted in a swift electronic plebiscite, would have cared to risk destruction to let John F. Kennedy prove himself."[53] The results of such a plebescite might have surprised Stone; they would surely have dismayed him. The evidence is substantial that most Americans accepted the risks of strong executive action because they, at least as much as President Kennedy, found the pawing of the Russian bear near their doorstep an intolerable sign of graver dangers to come.

An early and invaluable supporter of Kennedy's course was Dwight Eisenhower. Briefed twice during the Ex Comm's early deliberations by CIA director McCone, the immensely popular former president agreed that either a blockade or an air strike was essential. He refrained from favoring either option because of his limited familiarity with the evidence.[54]

On Sunday, October 21, Eisenhower breathed new life into the adage "Politics stops at the water's edge" by admonishing fellow Republicans to place Cuba off limits as a subject of campaign rhetoric. He acknowledged that on his trips for GOP candidates most people wanted to talk about Cuba, but "this I just refuse to talk about" because it was no time to be "badgering

President Kennedy about the Cuban situation." Eisenhower's forbearance extended even to the Bay of Pigs failure, which he noted had occurred when Kennedy had been in office for only three months. He added protectively, "At this point, no matter how bad a mistake of the past might be gauged by someone else, I think it is not the time to be badgering the Administration on what it is going to do next."[55]

At five o'clock in the afternoon of October 22, two hours before going on national television, President Kennedy briefed a bipartisan congressional delegation on the missiles in Cuba. The most influential senator, Democrat Richard Russell of Georgia, chairman of the Armed Services Committee, acerbically dismissed Kennedy's preference for a blockade as a sign of weakness:

> We're either a first-class power or we're not. You have warned these people time and again. . . . I don't know whether Khrushchev will launch a nuclear war over Cuba or not. I don't believe he will. But I think that the more that we temporize, the more surely he is to convince himself that we are afraid to make any real movement and to really fight.

Russell urged an immediate invasion of Cuba, warning Kennedy against any delay at this "crossroads": "And you are only making sure that when . . . they do use these MiGs to attack our shipping or drop a few bombs around Miami or some other place, and we do go in there, that we'll lose a great many more men than we would right now."[56]

Kennedy had counted on the restraining influence of J. William Fulbright of Arkansas, chairman of the Senate Foreign Relations Committee, known for his opposition to military intervention in Latin America. In March 1961 Fulbright had privately opposed the Bay of Pigs operation, and he declared on the Senate floor in June that even if the Soviets were to deploy missiles in Cuba, "I am not sure that our national existence would be in substantially in greater danger." Only "precipitate action" that might alienate Latin America would hurt American power.[57] But on the afternoon of October 22, 1962, Fulbright's dovish sentiments melted under the glare of CIA aerial surveillance revealing Soviet missile bases in Cuba. Terming a blockade too pale and protracted an answer, he urged instead "an invasion, and an all-out one, and as quickly as possible."[58]

Fulbright argued that "a blockade seems to me the worst alternative" because it would openly confront Russian ships, whereas the Soviets could look away from an invasion of Cuba, which "isn't a member of the Warsaw Pact" and therefore did not directly challenge the Kremlin. When President Kennedy asked how there wouldn't be "more confrontation [with] an invasion of Cuba," Fulbright replied, "But they're Cuban [missile] sites. They're not Russian sites." In any case, the senator added, "It seems to me that the time has now come, under your statement of the 13th of September, for an invasion. You said, if it changes and it's offensive, we'll take what's necessary for our defense. And if I understand it correctly, that means nothing but an invasion."[59]

Although the militant mood pervading the congressional gathering left Kennedy on edge, his conduct remained controlled, as Dino Brugioni recounts, even gallant:

[CIA analyst Arthur] Lundahl noted that Senator [Alexander] Wiley, at the advanced age of seventy-eight, was having great difficulty understanding the intelligence evidence and the policy being enunciated. Finally getting the president's attention, he said, almost naively, "Now, I think we ought to tell the Russians that they should not do a thing like that." The president paused momentarily and looked patiently at this fine old gentleman who had served his country so well. Instead of being brusque, he answered in a slow, understanding fashion: "We've told them all these things, but they ignored us. And now we must do something else." It was an admirable trait of the president to be brittle, crisp, and full of spontaneous humor in one instance but equally gentle and considerate to age and infirmity in another. Patting Senator Wiley on the hand, President Kennedy announced that he had to leave to get ready for his speech to the nation.[60]

Despite the private criticisms of the president's caution by Senators Russell and Fulbright, the blockade triggered relief nationwide that Kennedy was at last moving against a critical threat. Opinion polls during the height of the crisis showed that one in five Americans believed the quarantine would lead to World War III, and three in five believed " 'some shooting' was inevitable." Yet a Gallup poll conducted immediately after Kennedy's address on Monday evening, October 22, showed that 84 percent of Americans favored the blockade; only 4 per cent opposed it. According to the historian David Detzer, even this may have understated the militancy among Americans, for some who backed the blockade would have preferred still stronger action against Castro and the missiles.[61]

The four thousand telegrams to the White House following the president's speech ran twelve to one in favor of his actions. A New York City taxi driver bluntly expressed the readiness for a clash with the Communists: "It had to come. That slob, Castro, sold out his people. Like the President said, the Cubans aren't running that country."[62]

A Los Angeles realtor, L. M. Williams feared for his son in the National Guard but insisted that "the country should do what's necessary to stop communism even if it puts us in war."

A Milwaukee, Wisconsin, National Guardsman, Raymond Metiva, affirmed, "This is something we have to do. . . . I'm in favor of moving in and cleaning up." He added, "And this could mean my life!" When a Detroit woman, staying in New York with her husband, expressed alarm, saying, "I hope this doesn't mean Jim has to go to war," her husband interjected, "Well, if I have to, I will." In Topeka, Kansas, Mrs. Steven Roper, aunt of a sailor at the U.S. naval base at Guantanamo, Cuba, admitted concern that the blockade "could lead to a sticky situation," but said she was "glad the president has finally decided he should do something. We've been lackadaisical long enough."[63]

Having helplessly lived through a nuclear war of nerves for years, Americans made a virtue of fatalism about the risks of superpower confrontation. A Denver architect wrote warmly at the height of the crisis, "The calm attitude of my fellow citizens toward the prospect of thermo-nuclear war has restored my faith in Americans."[64]

According to regional correspondents for the *New York Times*, sentiment across the country was virtually unanimous in support of the blockade despite isolated demurrers and expressions of apprehension. Southerners "displayed an almost monolithic unity" behind the president. Senator Sam Ervin of North Carolina, whose "country lawyer's" barbed folk wisdom would later captivate the nation during the Watergate hearings, hailed Kennedy's "eloquent speech" as proof that "free men can preserve their freedom only if they keep their hearts and courage and lift up their hands in strength." A small-town paper in the Tar Heel state, the *Shelby Daily Star*, meanwhile exulted, "It's great to feel like an American again. . . ."[65]

In the Midwest there was "general approval." Although a substantial number of people admitted worry, more expressed the sense that "It's about time." David Heffernan, a Chicago school official, said after listening to the president's speech in a crowded hotel lobby, "When it was over, you could feel the lifting of a great national frustration. Suddenly you could hold your head up."[66]

Columnist Joseph Alsop confirmed that "the long strain and frequent frustrations of the Cold War seem to have wrought an astonishing transformation" in the Midwest, forging "a new belligerence" in what had been the "heartland of American isolationism." Two days of intensive door-to-door polling by Alsop and a member of the Louis Harris agency revealed a "remarkably uniform" pattern, "whether in the Republican, small-town semi-suburbs of Columbus [Indiana], or in Democratic, labor union neighborhoods" in Indianapolis. Of seventy-three respondents, nearly all "had clear and frequently impassioned views" on Cuba. "Only 16 men and women, or just a hair more than one-fifth of our total sample, did not favor any form of military action to humble Fidel Castro, because they 'did not want a war.'" Twenty-four voters, about a third of the sample, "positively favored going the whole hog, with an armed invasion of Cuba." The largest group, twenty-seven respondents, "were ready or even eager for more limited military action, in the form of a naval blockade of Cuba," most seeing it "as a way of avoiding the need for an invasion." Alsop thought "the most striking point" was that more than two-thirds "were ready for military action of some sort."[67]

In the plains states the blockade "won virtually unanimous approval from government officials as well as from the man in the street." Leaders in industry and labor rallied quickly to the president while "Ordinary citizens, for the most part, also expressed approval, but showed some fear about the possible consequences." Residents of Los Angeles were "solidly in favor," though many worried about "war and its consequences." In Kennedy's home region of New England, people "overwhelmingly stood behind the President," agreeing with the *Boston Herald Traveler* that "What has to be done is better done now."[68]

Although the 1960s are remembered as a time when young people became alienated from their leaders and their nation's foreign policy, teenagers in October 1962 largely shared the cold war fervor—or fatalism—of their parents. A New Jersey student exulted that Kennedy's speech had spurred students at Roxbury High School and other schools to take an interest in the crisis: more even than in "our overwhelming football victory over our archrival Dover three weeks ago." Overall the crisis revealed little to distinguish the generations. "I think it's about time the president made his move," said a New Haven, Connecticut, high school student, Joseph Patton. "They have been pushing us around too much. The situation is getting out of hand."[69]

Colleges experienced greater dissent, spearheaded by leftist and pacifist groups like the Socialist Club and Students for Peace and Disarmament at the University of Wisconsin. Members passed out handbills the day after the president's speech, branding the blockade a "bellicose, unilateral act." Yet compared with the powerful student movement against the war in Vietnam just a few years later, campus protests against the blockade were far fewer, milder, and often smaller than counterprotests by students and others. At the University of California campuses at Berkeley and Los Angeles, at Wayne State University in Detroit, at Indiana University, Boston University, Wesleyan University in Middletown, Connecticut, and Sarah Lawrence College in New York, students who opposed Kennedy's action found themselves decisively outnumbered—and sometimes outshouted—by supporters of the blockade. Joan Rosenstein, editor of the school paper at Long Island University, explained the general feeling in words that could as easily have come from a Texas town or a Midwestern farm: "President Kennedy couldn't do anything else. This country has procrastinated too long in its decision to take action against the intimidation of the Soviet Union."[70]

Even student protesters disclaimed any sympathy for communism. Instead they focused on the dangers of war and the seeming symmetry between the missile sites in Cuba and those in Turkey. The fifteen-thousand-strong Student Peace Union, which staged a march on the White House, the State Department, and the Capitol on October 27, and encouraged "sympathy demonstrations" in Berkeley and other cities, pointedly claimed to be "an anti-Communist 'third camp' organization that avoids supporting the Castro regime as such." National secretary Gail Paradise, a twenty-two-year-old history graduate student at the University of Chicago, said the Student Peace Union shared the alarm over missiles in Cuba as a threat to peace, but said this was also true of American bases in Greece and Turkey.[71]

Nowhere in the country were critics of the blockade a majority, but their often articulate dissent exposed misgivings about how best to answer Communist probes. "I'm sympathetic with President Kennedy's motive," wrote a resident of Jersey City, New Jersey, "but I think his method is too risky." The United States should first have let the UN mediate, because "Cuba is not worth going to war over. For us to sink a Russian ship would justify their sinking any of our ships supplying our overseas bases which Russia could claim are pointed at them."[72]

Like other mainstream newspapers, the *Philadelphia Inquirer* indulged dissenting letters but feted the conventional wisdom that the threat from Cuba made the blockade imperative.[73] "How many of these people who are protesting our blockade of Cuba would raise their voices if the Nazis had built a missile base there?" a woman in Springfield, Pennsylvania, asked. "We all know the evil of Nazism but some people do not seem to realize that Communism is just as great an evil and menace to us."[74]

Stray doubters of America's moral superiority risked scoldings for failings of character as well as policy. When a woman from Adel, Iowa, lamented ". . . but we are not in the right,'" she drew a prompt rebuke that questioned her patriotism as much as her prudence: "[Her letter] sounded a little too much like un-Americanism to me. . . . I'm a Republican; we have a fine president. Let's back him up."[75]

With several decades' hindsight, Kennedy's grim televised statement that the risks of a nuclear war were preferable to surrender struck even stalwarts such as Theodore Sorensen and Arthur Schlesinger, Jr., as excessive.[76] But if so, these were the excesses of an entire age, when the norms of healthy thinking included a reasonable willingness to sacrifice all in the struggle against the Soviet menace. Frazier Cheston, president of the National Association of Mental Health, did not question the president's allusions to imminent nuclear Armageddon but rather saw an opportunity to teach children a valuable lesson: "It is possible for the adult to paint a picture of freedom and right versus slavery and wrong, and to point out that no effort is too great to protect the way of freedom."[77]

In just a few more years, such eminent religious figures as Martin Luther King, Jr., William Sloan Coffin, and Abraham Heschel would proclaim it a central test of faith to oppose as immoral the war in Vietnam and America's whole "militaristic" foreign policy. But in October 1962, at the height of cold war fervor, clerical pronouncements on the missile crisis revealed little to separate church and state. The Rev. Dr. Nathaniel M. Guptill, minister of the Connecticut Conference of Congregational Christian Churches, acknowledged that the president's policy risked nuclear war but denied that this was contrary to

Christian values. The supreme ethical concern of a Christian, Guptill explained, was for the welfare of his fellow man, and the President could better express this through decisive action than through acquiescence. "To allow installation of nuclear missiles in Cuba would be the more dangerous of the two risks and could not be an effective expression of respect for life, because it would endanger life," Guptill said.[78]

The liberal World Council of Churches briefly flirted with pacifist idealism, questioning the president's "unilateral" action and calling for "restraint." But thunderous approval of the blockade by parishioners of every denomination sent these clerics scurrying. They hastily explained that their seeming reproach had been issued before support by the Organization of American States and other international developments cast the president's naval action in a more favorable light.[79]

The blockade's cathartic effect on the public led to a media outpouring of faith in the president greater than at any time since his Inaugural Address. He had acted "magnificently," "with wisdom, with courage and with reason," "wisely and unemotionally," with "forthright courage," in a manner "properly tough and forthright," "bold but necessary." These paeans were mingled with fatalistic comments that the president "could not have done much less than he now has done," "had no [other] recourse," and "has made the inevitable response."[80] The *Pittsburgh Post-Gazette* candidly asserted the national mood:

> When the legalisms and sophistry have been stripped from the arguments over our weapons quarantine of Cuba, the fact remains that we simply cannot permit this hemisphere to become an armed camp for communism. . . . We are interested not so much in sophisticated distinctions between offensive and defensive weapons (if, indeed, any such distinction can be made), or in arguments over which country

took counteraction in response to the moves of an ideological foe, as we are in our own security and that of our hemispheric allies. That is the crux of this crisis and no amount of debate over right or wrong can wash it away. . . .

Like it or not, the burden of free world leadership has devolved upon us and there are occasions, such as this one, upon which unilateral action may be the only timely and effective way to protect our interests.[81]

While Americans loathed Castro, most believed that Cuba was not really a sovereign nation but merely a tentacle in "a world conspiracy centered in the Kremlin." Whatever risks lay in Kennedy's "minimal program for the defense of the Americas" were surely "less than the danger of condoning the presence of a time bomb in this hemisphere, ninety miles from our own coast—a time bomb whose mechanism can be triggered by a ruthless foe in a distant continent." Nor was this crisis simply a tragic aberration, for "The Communists are everywhere the destroyers, we are the defenders of civilization. In Cuba . . . we use force only because others have forced it."[82]

Ralph McGill, editor of the *Atlanta Constitution* and the South's most respected liberal journalist, insisted that the greatest evil even in the atomic age would be the triumph of communism:

> If the decision [blockade] leads to war, it will be . . . horrible beyond compare. But, the alternative was to sit and wait for the enemy to make world victory and enslavement inevitable. Only that is worse than nuclear war.[83]

James Reston thought the blockade a favor to Khrushchev, who badly needed a reality check on the limits of American forbearance: "[Kennedy] has reduced the dangers of miscalculation in

Moscow by demonstrating his willingness to fight for the vital interests of the United States."[84]

Looming over support for Kennedy's armed response was the shadow of Munich. Americans old enough to remember World War II proffered analogies to the dangers of a generation earlier. A Detroit car salesman, Jack Young, said, "We let Japan slap us, kick us and tear up our flag. We shouldn't let Russia and Cuba do the same thing." The *Hartford Courant* warned Khrushchev not to "misread the mood of America or misjudge her, as Kaiser Wilhelm and Adolf Hitler did, to let loose two world wars." "Soviet missiles in Cuba are today's equivalent of Hitler's march into the Rhineland," Chalmers M. Roberts declared in his nationally syndicated column. The difference was that "America today will not sit idly by, as did the West a quarter century ago, to see tyranny make its aggression unopposed. The threat will be met now; to avoid war, war will be risked."[85]

"Across the nation," George Gallup reported, "interviewers encountered an odd mixture of tension and relief in the comments they heard from voters—tension stemming from a somber realization of the fateful risks involved in the action, relief that finally we had taken a stand and cleared some of the fog which enshrouded the Cuban situation. . . . Kennedy's decision eased many frustrations that had been building up for months— the frustration of wanting to "do something" about Cuba, but not wanting to go to war."[86]

Although some in the press found it "to Mr. Kennedy's credit that he had first investigated carefully and thoroughly," others asked "why it was so long in coming" and insisted, "The tragedy of United States foreign policy is that Mr. Kennedy waited so perilously long before acting against the baldly obvious threat Red Castro posed as a willing stooge of the Kremlin's aggressive intrusion into the Western Hemisphere." The President would not have to lead public opinion, for "the will of the people was probably in advance of events. . . ." The *Chattanooga Daily Times* approvingly saw the American people rather than government officials as scripting a newly dynamic national policy:

> There is indeed a tide in the affairs of men, and this is one of them. Instinctively and, as it happened, intuitively the American people reacted with dread and anger to the first major Soviet moves of equipment and men to the Antilles. In the end, they forced and assured the global moves in which virtually every instrument of American policy has had a hand.[87]

Few Americans considered that the president might have acted for political advantage—and fewer still doubted the necessity of his action. In a San Francisco bar, a young man watching Kennedy's blockade speech on television said wryly, "He wants a war before election, doesn't he?" An older man next to him replied, "If there's a war, there won't be any election. There won't be any world."[88]

However tardy Kennedy's actions may have appeared, they still positioned him unassailably in the heart of public opinion from coast to coast and from the corn belt to the beltway. His speech naturally heartened Democrats, whose party had been attacked throughout the 1962 election campaign for weakness, if not cowardice, over Cuba. The two ranking members of Congress, House Speaker John W. McCormack of Massachusetts and Senate Majority Leader Mike Mansfield of Montana, approved Kennedy's actions unreservedly. Senator George A. Smathers of Florida, the state where Castro cast the longest political shadow, credited the American people for pushing the administration to act. Even Mississippi's Governor Ross Barnett, who just weeks earlier had inflamed a racist mob against federal marshals helping to desegregate the state university, now boasted of his solidarity with the president on Cuba.[89]

Republican spokesmen, realizing that the president's blockade order had wrested from them the political center, dutifully pledged support. A day after Kennedy's announcement, seven ranking Republicans, including Senate Minority Leader Everett Dirksen of Illinois and House GOP leader Charles Halleck of Indiana, issued a blanket—albeit bland—patriotic assurance that "Americans will support the President on the decision or decisions he makes for the security of our country." Senator Keating, a prophet now obliged to honor the leader he had long declaimed against, pledged the day after Kennedy's speech that "the firm stand of the President will have the 100% backing of every American regardless of party. It is what the American people have been waiting for."[90]

Some Republicans continued to chafe. William Miller, the Republican National Chairman, called Kennedy's action "long-delayed." From the far right of the party, Senator Barry Goldwater grudgingly saluted the commander-in-chief but stressed that Kennedy was merely following a trail long since blazed by Republicans and traversed by most Americans. Goldwater added, "All Americans are waiting to see if he [the President] carries through with his intentions."[91]

Such sour sniping, however, amounted to little more than a last-ditch bid by Republicans to salvage credit for the president's decision to act. Senate Deputy Minority Leader Thomas H. Kuchel, a former critic of the president who had flown back to the capital for bipartisan conferences on the blockade, summed up the new electoral realities. "Foreign policy is no longer an issue in the campaign," Kuchel declared. "So far as American policy is concerned, politics has adjourned."[92]

4. "Defense, Diplomacy, and Dialogue"

IN THE TENSE DAYS that followed his speech of October 22, Kennedy pursued, in Sorensen's words, "a carefully measured combination of defense, diplomacy and dialogue."[93] Diplomacy early secured Latin American and NATO support for the quarantine, while on Thursday, October 25, a dramatic UN presentation by U.S. Ambassador Adlai Stevenson, employing photographs from CIA reconnaissance flights, dismantled Soviet denials of missile sites in Cuba. Dialogue ranged from secret correspondence with Khrushchev (twenty-two letters bearing on Cuba exchanged from October 23 through December 14) to ongoing back-channel contacts, often after midnight, between Robert Kennedy and Soviet Ambassador Anatoly Dobrynin.

Defense centered on the quarantine, which the president directed with self-conscious prudence. He appealed to world opinion by exempting medical supplies, food, and oil; drew in American vessels to give Soviet ships heading toward Cuba more time to reconsider; and imposed special caution in treating foreign ships that did not clearly carry military equipment. "What would you do then," the president asked at an Ex Comm meeting on Tuesday, October 23, "if we go through all of this effort and then find out there's baby food on it?"[94]

To ensure compliance with Kennedy's strictures against needless force, Robert McNamara personally supervised the U.S. Navy's 180-ship blockade. Admiral George Anderson, chief of naval operations, bridled at McNamara's curt questioning, which he saw as ignorant civilian intrusion in a matter best left to military professionals. In the first of several charged encounters in the Pentagon, Anderson acerbically assured the defense secretary, on Wednesday, October 24, that blockades had been standard naval procedure since the days of John Paul Jones. But McNamara retorted with equal venom and greater authority, "I don't give a damn what John Paul Jones would have done," explaining the president's intent not to humiliate the Russians militarily but rather to send a political signal to Khrushchev. He walked out of the room, insisting that "no force would be applied without my permission; and that would not be given without discussion with the President."[95]

Disregarding advice from military and some civilian advisers to board all ships approaching the quarantine line, the president decided on Thursday, October 25, to clear a Soviet tanker that radioed it carried only petroleum. He also cleared an East German liner rather than risk harm to fifteen hundred civilian passengers. Waiting an extra day, Kennedy designated a Russian-operated and -chartered but Panamanian-owned tanker of Lebanese registry as the first vessel to be boarded, so as to project resolve without directly confronting a Soviet ship. In such ways Kennedy steadily ratcheted up pressure on the Soviets without ever slipping into a vortex of uncontrolled escalation. For all this, as Robert Kennedy recounted, there was little rejoicing in the Ex Comm:

> ... privately the President was not sanguine about the results of even those efforts. ... Both "hawks" and "doves" sensed that our combination of limited force and diplomatic efforts had been unsuccessful. If the Russians continued to be adamant and continued to build up their missile strength, military force would be the only alternative.[96]

CHAPTER SIX

Kennedy's Hidden Concession –to Public Opinion

"THE OTHER MISSILES OF OCTOBER," as the historian Philip Nash calls the U.S. Jupiters in Turkey,[1] figured crucially in President Kennedy's efforts to end the crisis over Cuba. Some writers have seen in Kennedy's shifting stance on the Jupiters a unique resourcefulness, others an irrational prolongation of the danger or a deceptive diplomacy that mainly misled allies and the American people. In fact the president's actions, culminating in a secret pledge to remove the Jupiters, once again followed the most careful path consistent with foreign policy precedent and political constraints. These pressures were becoming ever more complex and contradictory as the crisis intensified. Kennedy responded with a growing willingness to make concessions and a growing urgency to conceal them.

Most Americans who welcomed the blockade as an overdue assertion of national will nonetheless hoped for a peaceful diplomatic resolution. The *Des Moines Register* expressed the anxious faith that a show of naval force need not lead to war: "We hope the carrying out of this defensive policy of blockade will proceed with caution, with the utmost discretion, and without undue provocations." The *Milwaukee Journal* hailed Kennedy's "prudent" decision to quarantine Cuba and stressed that "Our own will to peace is shown in the quick submission of our case to the United Nations. . . ."[2]

In the South, traditionally a bastion of support for military toughness, the wisdom of negotiation wove through coverage of the crisis. The *Chattanooga Daily Times*, while conceding that "direct measures" to remove the missiles might become necessary, deplored "Sen. Goldwater's typically extreme view that an invasion is 'inevitable'" as "far out of line at this point." The *Raleigh News and Observer* balanced calls to brave the "hazards and dangers which a free people must face" with a plea that Kennedy receive "full support, too, in any subsequent efforts and actions to achieve a meaningful peace." Days of living on the edge of war led the paper to caution that beyond the current crisis "the even larger problem of 'real peace' remains," but "From the forge of current fears there may yet come the chance to achieve that goal."[3]

The popular appeal of a negotiated settlement grew as the crisis awaited resolution. Senator J. William Fulbright, who had urged the president on Monday, October 22, to invade Cuba, told a Democratic rally at Fort Smith, Arkansas, three days later that U.S. policy toward Cuba should be to negotiate whenever it could. "It's better to talk than to destroy each other," Fulbright said, though noting, "Whether or not the Russians will be reasonable nobody knows." That weekend an editorial in the *New York Times* insisted that "Violence is not the way to settle this or any other argument." The *Times* approvingly quoted Adlai Stevenson's admonition, "This is a time for diplomacy," and added, "It is not a time for mutual annihilation."[4]

But what could the president trade? The status of West Berlin, though a certain lure for Khrushchev, had long been deemed non-negotiable by the United States and its European allies. Most NATO outposts, including nuclear missile sites, were similarly viewed as beyond the scope of bilateral barter. The salient exception, which Ex Comm members privately broached and the media increasingly blared, involved fifteen U.S. nuclear missiles in Turkey that prompted uncomfortable analogies with the Russian presence in Cuba.

1. The Other Missiles

THE HISTORY of the Turkish bases from the late fifties until mid-October 1962 consistently pointed to their expendability, to parallels with Cuba, and to the desirability of including the missiles in some larger diplomatic gambit. These considerations had languished in the recesses of the White House, confined there by the political costs of straining the NATO alliance and appearing lax toward the Kremlin. But the discovery of Soviet missiles in Cuba thrust the issue of comparable U.S. weapons in Turkey into the high-stakes negotiations between the superpowers. It remained for President Kennedy to manage the consequences while containing the political fallout at home and in NATO.

Virtually all the contours—and ambiguities—of Kennedy's policy toward the Jupiters were foreshadowed during the Eisenhower presidency. In 1955, when the U.S. military appeared years away from perfecting long-range missiles, it embarked on a crash program to produce intermediate-range ballistic missiles (IRBMs) that, if deployed in Europe, could reach the Soviet Union. In March 1957 the Eisenhower administration promised a squadron of such weapons to its closest ally, Great Britain, and between March and October 1959 it made similar pacts with two other NATO members, Italy and Turkey.

Eisenhower decided to deploy the IRBMs despite sharp misgivings. These weapons were by all accounts primitive, vulnerable, slow to launch, and inaccurate. Worse still, their limited range (seventeen hundred miles) encouraged placement provocatively near the Soviet Union. Still, the Departments of State and Defense, the Joint Chiefs, officials completing a study of U.S. overseas bases, and the authors of the prestigious Gaither Report on upgrading strategic deterrents all supported the deployment of IRBMs in Europe as a stopgap measure until more advanced weapons became available. Eisenhower himself cited the "tremendous psychological importance" of these missiles for Americans (more than Europeans), although even at this early stage he doubted their actual "military significance."[5]

At a NATO summit in December 1957 the administration pledged to send IRBMs—still in development—to any receptive ally. Yet most NATO governments squirmed over this doubtful gift, fearing to provoke the Soviet Union and realizing the limited deterrent value of the missiles themselves. Turkey alone showed unqualified enthusiasm, moved by a history of thirteen wars with the Russians in three hundred years, a fierce nationalist resistance to Soviet demands for territory and access to Turkish port facilities, and Khrushchev's threat in the wake of Sputnik, "If war breaks out, Turkey would not last one day."[6]

The prospect of converting intermediate-range missiles into the equivalent of long-range missiles simply by installing them overseas stirred an early flurry of support amid anxieties over the U.S. strategic deterrent. *Time* magazine, the nation's leading news weekly, and a prestigious Rockefeller Panel study group both lauded the air force's Jupiter missile (and the army's virtually identical twin, the Thor) for offsetting a dangerous imbalance in nuclear forces. But U.S. officials and strategic analysts soon began probing whether bases so near Russia would truly enhance American security.

In November 1959, delays in producing Jupiters and Thors, combined with accelerated development of intercontinental missiles, led *Time*'s defense correspondent Charles Murphy to observe wistfully that the IRBMs attested to "the unprecedentedly swift onset of obsolescence." By then the Rockefeller Panel too had ceased to advocate "the most rapid development and procurement" of both IRBMs and ICBMs," admitting that the value of these bases might "diminish in the future." And in 1960 Henry Kissinger, the Harvard professor who chaired the Rockefeller Panel, renounced his claim three years earlier that IRBMs might help NATO "to withstand Soviet atomic blackmail." Instead he termed these missiles so vulnerable as to have no purpose even as interim weapons.[7]

Apart from Kissinger's fleeting endorsement, the country's leading strategic thinkers early on agreed that intermediate-range missiles would have little impact, and even this would be negative. Albert Wohlstetter of the RAND Corporation warned that deploying IRBMs would actually undermine deterrence because their proximity to the Soviet Union and their vulnerability would tempt a preemptive Soviet strike. In his book *Strategy in the Missile Age* (1959), Bernard Brodie concluded that the value of advanced bases was "overrated" and that "the missiles themselves were exceedingly vulnerable" and "could have no dependable retaliatory value." In 1960 Herman Kahn cautioned, in his tome *On Thermonuclear War*, that IRBMs could at best "play an ambiguous role in deterrence" because it would be "relatively easy for the Soviets to destroy them" in a first strike.[8]

George Kennan, whose writings had crystallized America's "containment" strategy during the first years of the cold war, lectured a decade later on the folly of deploying nuclear weapons in NATO countries. It would, he warned, needlessly alarm the Russians, complicate efforts to free Central Europe of cold war alignments, and make governments so reliant on missiles and the treaties sanctioning them that "it becomes difficult to consider their withdrawal or to make them the subject of negotiation."[9]

Two influential works on U.S. strategic planning by retired generals added to the crushing weight of critical opinion about IRBM bases. Both James M. Gavin, the army's chief of research and development until 1958, and Maxwell Taylor, the army chief of staff from 1955 to 1959, credited the IRBMs with limited deterrent value but deplored the actual plans for deploying them. Gavin wrote in *War and Peace in the Space Age* (1958) that these "Model T's of the missile age" had to be made "entirely mobile" or they would simply offer the Russians additional targets. The following year Taylor concurred in *The Uncertain Trumpet* that IRBMs placed on fixed, unhardened sites would be a "sterile asset," mere "stationary bull's-eyes . . . which would invite atomic attack in case of general war."[10]

Support for overseas missile bases also eroded within the White House. Eisenhower foresaw that these missiles "would be prime targets for an enemy attack." He later remarked with dour candor, "It would have been better to dump them in the ocean instead of trying to dump them on our allies."[11]

Several years before President Kennedy thought to remove the Jupiters as a way to end the Cuban missile crisis, the Eisenhower administration considered trading away rather than deploying such weapons. In March 1958 the director of the State Department's Policy Planning Staff, Gerard Smith, wrote to Secretary of State John Foster Dulles that the IRBMs had no security value and that they might best "be viewed as a bargaining counter" to promote arms control. His recommendation meshed with pleas made in December 1957 by the West German Foreign Office and by British Prime Minister Harold Macmillan. And Christian Herter, who succeeded the ailing Dulles in 1959, thought about offering to cancel deployment at the foreign ministers conference in Geneva in May 1959, in response to complaints by the Russian foreign minister, Andrei Gromyko.[12] None of these initiatives went beyond in-house memoranda and discussions, but they reflected a widespread suspicion among Western officials that the Jupiters would have more value as diplomatic currency than as military fixtures.

On June 16, 1959, Eisenhower confided to members of his National Security Council that while short-range Redstone, Corporal, or Honest John missiles in Europe made sense to thwart a Soviet ground offensive, he wondered whether placing longer-range missiles in Greece was not simply being "provocative." The next day he told Under Secretary of State Douglas Dillon and his chief of staff, Andrew Goodpaster, that deploying missiles "so far forward, in exposed areas" was of questionable value, nor would it "serve to reduce tensions" with the Soviets. The president recommended that the State Department and the Joint Chiefs thoroughly review whether deployment of such missiles justified the political costs.[13]

Second thoughts about the Jupiters persisted through Eisenhower's final week in office. On January 13, 1961, the director of the Atomic Energy Commission, John R. McCone, urged reconsideration. Secretary of Defense Thomas Gates conceded that the Jupiter deployments were "actually more symbolic than useful." But he warned against alienating the Turks, saying, "To reverse our agreements regarding JUPITER would cause political difficulties which would exceed the difficulty of maintaining the missiles on site." Eisenhower reluctantly backed Gates's view that the weaknesses of these bases could not determine policy; the need for harmony within NATO and firmness toward the Kremlin appeared overriding.[14]

Philip Nash finds that the failure to reverse a policy no one considered militarily helpful fit the iron logic of cold war politics and strategy: "[A] solid case against the IRBMs came easily" to Eisenhower as it had to his subordinates, "but when presented with the costs of reversal—the appearance of giving in to Soviet threats, the wrath of allies double-crossed, the accumulation of expensive missiles—he too found it easier to step aside and let the IRBM deployment proceed at its torpid pace." "Shackled like other Cold War presidents by the chains of 'credibility,' Eisenhower worried about the effects of accommodation: if he withdrew the IRBM offer in response to the Soviets' opposition, what would they do next?"[15]

The transition from Eisenhower to Kennedy did nothing to raise estimates of the proposed Jupiter bases in Turkey and Italy. Secretary of Defense McNamara, who prodded the Pentagon with ferocious energy to separate vital arms programs from merely venal ones, dismissed the Jupiters as "a pile of junk." National Security Adviser McGeorge Bundy termed them "worse than useless." Secretary of State Dean Rusk recalled, "We joked about which way those missiles would go if they were fired." Everyone, including the president, acknowledged that the Jupiters were not a real security asset but rather a military problem without a clear political solution.[16]

Kennedy's doubts about the Jupiters fed on expert evaluations that greeted him almost from the moment he entered the White House. A joint congressional subcommittee, formed in

1960 to review control over nuclear weapons, flatly urged in its February 1961 report, "The Study of United States and NATO Nuclear Weapons Arrangements," that deployment of missiles in Turkey be canceled. The report formed Kennedy's introduction to the subject of overseas IRBMs and made clear that such bases did not strengthen the national security:

> Instead of placing 15 obsolete liquid-fueled JUPITERS in Turkey, an alternative system such as a POLARIS submarine with 16 IRBM's operated and controlled by U.S. personnel could be assigned to NATO in lieu [thereof]. Such an assignment could be made before 1962 when the JUPITER system would be coming into operation. The POLARIS submarine system would be mobile and thus a much better retaliatory force.[17]

The following month a presidential task force on NATO chaired by Dean Acheson, a venerable architect of containment policy during the Truman years, observed that the U.S.

> should consider suggesting to the Turks that their resources would be better used and their interests better served by the projected deployment and commitment of Polaris submarines in place of the first generation IRBM squadron now scheduled for Turkey.

Acheson's report, known as the "Green Book," allowed that "If the Turks feel otherwise . . . we should not press the point," but expressed hope that cancellation "would free the Turkish and MAP [Military Assistance Program] resources involved for other purposes, and it would avoid the deployment of 'strike-first' weapons in a politically volatile country on the Soviet border."[18] Swayed by these bleak findings, Kennedy's Secretary of Defense, Robert McNamara, recommended canceling the deployment in Turkey.[19]

Congress and the media added to misgivings about the Jupiters by probing whether U.S. actions in Turkey might not spur or excuse Soviet military moves in Cuba. On February 28, 1961, before an executive session of the Senate Foreign Relations Committee, Democratic Senator Albert Gore told Secretary of State Dean Rusk that the Jupiter deployment "is the kind of provocation which needs to be considered very carefully. I wonder what our attitude would be if warheads should be attached to missiles in Cuba."[20]

In May 1961, in the wake of the failed Bay of Pigs invasion, as Castro drew closer to his Soviet patrons, Senator Claiborne Pell of Rhode Island wrote to President Kennedy about the "inconsistency" of declaring allied missiles in Turkey acceptable yet Soviet missiles near the United States unacceptable. That same month the *New York Times* columnist Arthur Krock, a friend of the Kennedy family, privately cautioned the president about the weakness in Washington's statements that the United States, which had "ringed Russia around with military bases, could not accept a pro-Communist base" in Cuba.[21]

Kennedy considered aborting plans for the Turkish bases but held off after renewed exposure to European fears about the strength of the U.S. commitment to NATO. On May 29, 1961, Thomas Finletter, chief of the U.S. mission to NATO, informed the president that the Turks especially objected to the administration's "new emphasis on conventional weapons":

> Being exposed and away from the bulk of NATO military power, they fear the new U.S. thinking will be a temptation to the Russians to walk over them with conventional forces. They would like to see our policy be to use tactical nuclear weapons from the beginning—for this would make for the minimum of temptation to the Russians to attack them.[22]

On June 16, 1961, Dirk Stikker, the Dutch secretary general of NATO, injected a further dose of political reality when Kennedy met with him to press for an upgrading of non-nuclear forces. Kennedy's agenda accorded with the administration's overall strategy of reducing the U.S. military's increasingly dubious reliance on the threat of "massive retaliation" with nuclear weapons to deter Communist encroachments. But Stikker "said that it would be hard to get Continental acceptance of the proposed improvement of non-nuclear forces (with which he agreed) unless the Continental countries felt that adequate nuclear power was being deployed on the Continent."

Faced with Stikker's strong request for a modernization of NATO's nuclear missiles, Kennedy abandoned any immediate hopes of support for canceling the deployment of medium-range missiles in Turkey and Italy. Instead he "indicated that the question of MRBM's was for the fairly distant future and that, for the present, the alliance should face up to immediate tasks, e.g., improving existing forces. . . . The President stressed that the proposed improvement in conventional forces did not imply any weakening of the nuclear deterrent."[23]

Kennedy's wobbling resolve to cancel deployment of the medium-range missiles took another damaging blow when George McGhee, a recent ambassador to Turkey, warned him on June 22 that the Turks would not agree. The president instead ordered the offending passage in the "Green Book" deleted.[24] He also formed a task force headed by McGhee to review plans to send missiles to Turkey; but, while it pondered, construction on the bases continued.

Political inertia lumbered over the last objections to building the Turkish bases. The Joint Chiefs, the Bureau of European Affairs at the State Department, and the American supreme commander of NATO forces, General Lauris Norstad, all argued that the Jupiters had political and psychological value for NATO members, particularly Turkey. When Secretary of State Rusk and Paul Nitze of the Defense Department sounded out the Turkish foreign minister, Selim Sarper, in April 1961, about substituting Polaris submarines for the Jupiters, Sarper was "outraged." His government had staked its prestige on a commitment to these bases. Missiles on Turkish soil would symbolize U.S. support for Turkey's security in a way that underwater Polaris missiles could not. On June 22, 1961, McGhee further swayed the president by urging him to go ahead with building the bases in Turkey "based primarily on the view that, in the aftermath of Khrushchev's hard posture at Vienna, cancellation of the IRBM deployment might seem a sign of weakness."[25]

In displaying grudging but persistent support for the Turkish bases, Kennedy stumbled along the path blazed—or backed into—by Eisenhower. Both chief executives had wished to scrap the venture as unsound but decided that NATO's expectations as well as Soviet bravado precluded an American retreat. Kennedy in particular glumly rode the momentum of policies already in motion when he entered the White House. Philip Nash writes of his acquiescence in both the Bay of Pigs operation and the building of Turkish bases, "Changing course in midstream is always more difficult than avoiding a particular course at the outset, even if someone else began the journey and even if it seems increasingly dubious."[26]

In another echo of the Eisenhower presidency, Kennedy's experts privately suggested trading intermediate-range missile bases in England, Italy, and Turkey for concessions by the Russians. In September 1961 a study of weapons systems by representatives of the State and Defense Departments and the CIA declared, "It is conceivable that [the Soviets] might be prepared to offer something in return for the liquidation of such forward bases . . . since there is some evidence that such bases, in their eyes, appear to have utility primarily if used in a first strike capacity."[27] Like similar proposals during the late fifties, this recommendation was ill timed to dissuade the president from commitments to buoy NATO's morale. The idea to trade bases would not bear fruit until October 1962, at a point when concerns to soothe NATO allies suddenly contended with other, still more urgent diplomatic needs.

By early March 1962 the Turkish launch sites had become fully operational, though under U.S. crews while the Turks completed their training. The missiles were imposing, if only as towering tributes to technological obsolescence:

> On fixed, unprotected sites above the ground . . . [they] stood ready, pointed at the sky. Nine feet in diameter and sixty feet long, with a large metal skirt shielding the engine, each was rather conspicuous, gleaming white, resembling an enormous crayon or the "Washington Monument," as a U.S. congressman would later recall. On the side of each Turkish Jupiter was painted a Turkish flag and an insignia consisting of a large arrow and, in a none-too-subtle indication of what this thing was for, a mushroom cloud.[28]

The administration's fears that sending missiles to Turkey might provoke the Kremlin proved understated. Khrushchev routinely asked guests at his Black Sea retreat at Sochi to look through binoculars across the water. Unable to see anything, they then asked Khrushchev what he saw when he took his turn. "US missiles in Turkey," he said, "aimed at my *dacha*." In April 1962 Soviet Defense Minister Rodion Malinovsky rekindled Khrushchev's obsession by reminding him that the Jupiters "could in a short time destroy" all cities in the southern USSR. Khrushchev became angry and then exclaimed that he would place missiles in Cuba and give Americans a taste of the terror they had long forced on the Soviet Union.[29]

The similarities between rival overseas bases were not lost on President Kennedy. In the spring and summer of 1962 he asked the State Department to renew inquiries with the Turks about yielding the Jupiters, still to no avail. Then, at a meeting on August 23, 1962, to consider policy toward Castro, Kennedy expressed concern whether transferring U.S. nuclear warheads to Turkey might seem to justify growing Soviet arms shipments to Cuba. John R. McCone, the new director of Central Intelligence and an old critic of the Jupiters under President Eisenhower, again cited the weapon's weaknesses. Defense Secretary McNamara "agreed they were useless," but that made them no less "difficult politically to remove." Kennedy insisted on another test, directing the Department of Defense to ask, "What action can be taken to get Jupiter missiles out of Turkey?"[30] But fears of alienating the Turks drained this last initiative before discovery of Russian missiles in Cuba cast a powerful, unwelcome spotlight on the Jupiters.

A last omen of the coming confrontation over the Turkish missiles came on October 14, 1962, when President Kennedy's special ambassador Chester Bowles met at length with Soviet Ambassador Dobrynin. Bowles presciently wrote that "Dobrynin's comments on the Cuban situation may be of special interest." Dobrynin early on "protested that the Soviet presence in Cuba was no greater provocation than the U.S. presence in Turkey." Bowles countered that the U.S. presence in Turkey "had become part of a *status quo* which in all its complexity could safely be changed only by negotiation," whereas "in Cuba the U.S.S.R. had unilaterally altered this *status quo* by introducing a wholly new element."[31] Although neither Bowles nor Dobrynin yet knew of the Soviet nuclear deployment, their remarks pointed to the insistent link between Cuba and Turkey that the U.S. disparaged yet could not dispel.

2. The Ex Comm and the Turkish Missile Crisis

THE CONVENTIONAL WISDOM after the missile crisis, spread by administration insiders, was that Kennedy's ambassador to the UN, Adlai Stevenson, had been the lone advocate of withdrawing the Jupiters; in contrast to Kennedy and other firm anti-Communists in the Ex Comm, Stevenson "wanted a Munich."[32] The UN ambassador had indeed early on advised Kennedy to entertain a range of concessions to the Soviet Union. On October 17, 1962, before leaving Washington for a UN Security Council session, Stevenson privately urged Kennedy to show restraint, and explained in a memorandum:

> To start or risk starting a nuclear war is bound to be divisive at best and the judgments of history seldom coincide with the tempers of the moment. . . . We must be prepared for the widespread reaction that if we have a missile base in Turkey and other places around the Soviet Union surely they have a right to one in Cuba. If we attack Cuba, an ally of the USSR, isn't an attack on NATO bases equally justified? One could go on and on. While the explanation of our action may be clear to us it won't be clear to many others. . . . *I feel you should have made it clear that the existence of nuclear missile bases anywhere is NEGOTIABLE before we start anything.*[33]

On Saturday, October 20, Stevenson, already suspect among Ex Comm members, compounded their misgivings on returning from New York. Unfamiliar with the long discussions just now gelling into a consensus for a blockade, Stevenson was the guest painfully out of step. He spoke of the need to win over world opinion and "urged that we offer the Russians a settlement involving the withdrawal of our missiles from Turkey and our evacuation of Guantanamo base."[34]

According to George Ball, a friend of Stevenson's who had worked on both his presidential campaigns, these proposals set off a chain reaction of abuse:

> Though the President was courteous but firm [in rejecting Stevenson's ideas], some of the others present were outraged and shrill. Dillon, [former Secretary of Defense Robert] Lovett, and McCone violated the calm and objectivity we had tried to maintain in our ExCom meetings when they intemperately upbraided Stevenson. The attack was, I felt, quite unfair, indicating more the state of anxiety and emotional exhaustion pervading the discussion than any reasoned reaction. . . . I felt protective of Adlai, embarrassed for him, and exceedingly annoyed with my colleagues.[35]

President Kennedy himself was protective of Stevenson's dissent in the Ex Comm. According to the White House appointments secretary, Kenneth O'Donnell, who silently monitored the Ex Comm's rhetorical melees, Robert Kennedy privately urged replacing Stevenson with a more tough-minded emissary to the UN. But the president defended Stevenson to his "furious" brother, saying,

> I think Adlai showed plenty of strength and courage, presenting that viewpoint at the risk of being called an appeaser. It was an argument that needed to be stated, but nobody else had the guts to do it. Maybe he went too far when he suggested giving up Guantanamo, but remember we're in a situation here that may cost us millions of lives, and we should be considering every side of it and every way to get out of it. I admire him for saying what he said.[36]

The historian Jeff Broadwater finds that Stevenson was in fact ideologically in tune with President Kennedy and his inner circle and that "the soft and hard nomenclature" of doves and hawks "does not go to the heart of Stevenson's differences with his ExComm colleagues":

> A memorandum [Stevenson] composed on Sunday [October 21] . . . demonstrated his commitment to the process of diplomacy, his own orthodox anticommunism, and . . . a tendency to address large issues, not specific problems. Stevenson sought the "neutralization" of Cuba, the withdrawal of Soviet aid and advisers as well as of nuclear weapons. Thus, he hoped to solve the administration's Cuban problem; ending Russian support for the Castro regime, he predicted, "would probably result in its early overthrow."

By October 21, moreover, Stevenson had dropped his proposal to trade American missiles in Turkey and Italy. Now he merely looked to include them in future disarmament talks.[37]

Despite Stevenson's later notoriety for urging the president to declare all bases negotiable, his conciliatory approach repeatedly echoed in the White House from many points on the political spectrum. A strategy brief prepared during the first week by "air-strike 'hard-liners,'" Theodore Sorensen wrote, included "a pledge that the United States was prepared to promptly withdraw all nuclear forces based in Turkey, including aircraft as well as missiles."[38] Robert Kennedy, who harshly criticized Stevenson as weak, objected mainly to the timing rather than the substance of the ambassador's suggestion. "We will have to make a deal at the end," Kennedy told Arthur Schlesinger, "but we must stand absolutely firm now. Concessions must come at the end of negotiation, not at the beginning."[39]

During the first Ex Comm meeting, on Tuesday morning,

October 16, parallels between the bases in Cuba and Turkey repeatedly surfaced. Rusk said of the Soviet deployment in Cuba, "One thing Mr. Khrushchev may have in mind is that he knows that we have a substantial nuclear superiority, but he also knows that we don't really live under fear of his nuclear weapons to the extent that he has to live under fear of ours. Also, we have nuclear weapons nearby, in Turkey and places like that." President Kennedy's response, belying his usual precise recall, confirmed the marginal place these weapons held in his concerns: "How many weapons do we have in Turkey?"[40]

The president's memory lapses about the Turkish missiles included his own role, however reluctant, in deploying them. Expressing dismay at the Soviet gamble, he said, "It's just as if we suddenly began to put a major number of MRBMs in Turkey. Now that'd be goddamn dangerous, I would think." Bundy gently pointed out, "Well, we did, Mr. President." "Yeah, but that was 5 years ago," replied Kennedy, still convinced that this unpalatable decision had been Eisenhower's alone.[41]

During an Ex Comm meeting on Thursday, October 18, no one could envision a scenario that preserved the U.S. missile bases in Turkey. Bundy commented that an overture to Khrushchev would mention "that we understand this base problem," and that if the Russians "scrub" their missiles in Cuba, "then we do expect to dismantle our Turkish base." Rusk worried that a "disadvantage to the blockade" was that then "the Soviets get the Turkish missile sites," though he left unclear whether this would be through a retaliatory strike or an eventual trade. McNamara replied that "the minimum price you pay" after attacking the Cuban sites "is missiles out of Turkey and Italy," possibly "because of the Russians moving against them."[42]

In the discussions leading to the decision to blockade, McNamara repeatedly insisted that withdrawal of the Jupiters was unavoidable. On Friday, October 19, according to a record by the State Department's deputy legal representative, Leonard Meeker, McNamara "more than once . . . voiced the opinion that the US would have to pay a price to get the Soviet missiles out of Cuba. He thought we would at least have to give up our missile bases in Italy and Turkey and would probably have to pay more besides." And on Saturday afternoon, October 20, McNamara reiterated that "we could obtain the removal of the missiles from Cuba only if we were prepared to offer something in return. . . ." The Jupiters headed his list of likely concessions, which now expanded to include shortening America's use of the Guantanamo naval base in Cuba "to a specified limited time."[43]

During that Saturday meeting, President Kennedy ruled out surrender of Guantanamo but "was not opposed to discussing withdrawal of our missiles from Turkey and Greece [sic]," though "we should only make such a proposal in the future." The president allowed, though, that the United Nations could force his timetable for negotiations, saying, "Only if we were asked would we respond that we were prepared to talk about the withdrawal of missiles from Italy and Turkey. In such an eventuality, the President pointed out that we would have to make clear to the Italians and the Turks that withdrawing strategic missiles was not a retreat and that we would be prepared to replace these missiles by providing a more effective deterrent. . . ." Kennedy directed Paul Nitze, the assistant secretary of defense for international security affairs, "to study the problems arising out of the withdrawal of missiles," especially "complications which would arise in NATO."[44]

Nitze, who later recalled being "outraged" by Stevenson's "attempt at total appeasement," seemed not to view President Kennedy's approach to the Jupiters as notably tougher. Nitze wrote that Kennedy had been receptive to Stevenson's pleas, leaving implicit that only the ensuing firestorm of protest by Nitze and others led him to reconsider: "The President at first accepted and then courteously rejected Stevenson's last-minute appeal, although he recognized that the missiles in Turkey and Italy eventually would have to be removed."[45]

On Sunday, October 21, the Defense Department circulated a memorandum that losing the Turkish bases would not damage national security. A State Department group, chaired by Stevenson and attended by Rusk, also discussed a missile trade. That evening Robert Kennedy convened a meeting in the Situation Room at the White House that, according to legal adviser Abram Chayes, "almost unanimously" accepted the necessity of a missile trade: "McNamara had said we would be lucky to get out of the crisis with only a trade of the Turkish missiles. In response to Robert Kennedy's direct question to every person at the table, there was no disagreement with McNamara's evaluation."[46]

In his notes for drafting the president's televised address on October 22, his longtime aide Theodore Sorensen revealed bewilderment over a single pitfall: ". . . that the Soviets will probably be able to point to one or more US statements in the past that our base structure, including missile bases, was clearly defensive in purpose." The usually incisive Sorensen sketched a tentative reply that reflected the administration's inconsistency on the distinction between offensive and defensive weapons. "Don't see how to deal with this in the statement," Sorensen acknowledged.[47]

Interest among officials in bartering the missiles remained intense, though top secret, as the president prepared to address the nation about the Cuban missiles. On October 22 Averell Harriman, the assistant secretary of state for Far Eastern affairs and a veteran negotiator with Moscow, implied in a memo to the president that a missile trade might help Khrushchev save face.[48] And Sorensen's alternate draft of the president's speech, in the event of an air strike on the bases, announced amid otherwise apocalyptic musings, a readiness to "withdraw all nuclear forces presently based in Turkey."[49]

Kennedy's belief that the Turkish bases were peripheral to national security glared through a directive that McNamara issued to the Joint Chiefs on October 22: "The President has ordered me to make certain that the Jupiters [in Italy and Turkey] will not be fired without his further authorization, even in the event of a selective nuclear or non-nuclear attack on these units by the Soviet Union in response to actions we may be taking elsewhere." The administration, in effect, would let the Soviets retaliate with impunity for the blockade of Cuba, so long as they confined their attacks to bases in Turkey that the United States wished to liquidate anyway.[50]

In the days following his speech to the nation, President Kennedy pursued a dual track on the Turkish missiles, devising strategies to justify publicly their presence in contrast to the "offensive" and offending missiles in Cuba, yet also dwelling on the inevitability of a trade. In a National Security Council meeting the afternoon of October 22, Kennedy said, "I want to get it clear to the American press and others as to why" the deployments did not "match" in light of the Soviets' secrecy and deception. But Kennedy mused to British ambassador David Ormsby-Gore that the IRBMs "had become more or less worthless," though it "was hard to tell" whether trading them would be politically feasible.[51]

Once again the president looked vainly to the Turks to extricate him from commitments that could thwart his efforts to avoid war. On October 24 Kennedy had Rusk "urgently" request his ambassadors to Turkey and NATO to assess the "political consequences" of surrendering the Jupiters as part of a "negotiated solution" to the missile crisis.[52] Building on the same logic that had moved the president, the nation's most venerated columnist meanwhile floated the idea of a trade of missile bases, easing Kennedy's task of signaling the Russians while preparing public opinion.

At seventy-three, Walter Lippmann of the *Washington Post* had been shaping both liberalism and journalism for half a century when he turned, in columns scrutinized by U.S.—and Soviet—leaders, to the "liability" of American bases in Turkey. On Tuesday, October 23, Lippmann disparaged their value, declaring, "These advance bases of ours . . . are more hostage than ally" because of the fear that intervention in Cuba could bring Soviet retaliation in Turkey. Two days later he made the case for a trade of bases, arguing that the blockade of Cuba alone could not secure removal of the Soviet missiles, that the missiles in Cuba and Turkey were comparably provocative and ineffectual, and that they "could be dismantled without altering the world balance of power."[53]

Few voices in the media carried nearly as far as Lippmann's, but others also wrote that trading the Turkish bases offered a sensible solution to the Cuban crisis. A day after Lippmann's first column appeared, William H. Stringer, the Washington bureau chief of the *Christian Science Monitor*, discerned a "missing ingredient" in Washington's strategy: a "way out" for Premier Khrushchev. As a "face-saving" gesture, Stringer suggested, "a Western ally—or a neutral nation—could propose at the United Nations that, in return for Moscow's abandonment of its missile bases in Cuba, the United States might begin phasing out its missile installations in Turkey or elsewhere." Stringer feared only that Khrushchev might spurn such paltry compensation when "he was after bigger game than IRBMs in Turkey," namely, "the deal—his deal—on Berlin."[54]

Khrushchev and others in the Kremlin, accustomed to controlling their own country's media, believed Lippmann's syndicated column was a key to decrypting the mood of official Washington. In this instance they may not have been far wrong.

Lippmann had visited George Ball at the State Department to tell him about his second column the day before it ran, and Ball had not tried to dissuade him.[55]

Soviet leaders would have found in the *New York Times* even clearer prospects of a deal involving Cuba and Turkey. Editor Max Frankel reported in a page-one story on October 24 that while the Kennedy administration rejected the Cuba-Turkey analogy, officials acknowledged "the appeal of this argument" and said "it was conceivable that the United States might be willing to dismantle one of the obsolescent American bases near Soviet territory." The next day Frankel recorded "unofficially" interest in a trade among leading U.S. officials.[56]

Kennedy's doubts about whether a trade would be "politically feasible" nonetheless remained. While Lippmann had publicized the strategic logic of removing obsolete missiles from Turkey, he simply ignored the prohibitive political costs of making such explicit concessions to Soviet power. Americans may have known little and cared less about Jupiter missiles apart from the current crisis, but the imperatives of cold war politics still held sway: to contain the Russians at all points, keep commitments to allies, and never yield to Communist pressure. To the average American—and many pundits, Lippmann's call to withdraw the Jupiters failed these basic tests.

As the crisis worsened, the *Philadelphia Inquirer* reduced debate over American missiles in Turkey to the distinction between good and evil alliances: "The Soviet Premier conveniently ignores the totally different U.S.-Turkey relationship as compared with the Soviet-Cuba relationship. Turkey is an equal partner of the United States in NATO. Cuba has become a Soviet satellite slave state."[57] This, more than Lippmann's view of a symmetry between Cuban and Turkish bases, became a standard media refrain.

C. L. Sulzberger, the leading foreign affairs columnist for

the *New York Times*, wrote soon after the crisis ended that Kennedy had had no choice but to reject Soviet demands: "For it would have been lunatic at this time to barter a Soviet withdrawal from Caribbean bases against a concurrent United States withdrawal from bases in Turkey, the link between NATO and CENTO [Central Treaty Organization]." To Sulzberger, Turkey was a vital partner of the West against "Soviet aggression," whereas Cuba was "not even Russia's ally" and so had no sound claim to nuclear missiles.[58]

Newspapers and magazines pounced on the "false analogies" between Turkey and Cuba, insisting that "the West can honorably and fearlessly deny to the Communists bases whose motive is assault, while invoking the full strength of its own military forces whose motive is to preserve and protect."[59] The *Philadelphia Inquirer* elaborated, in the wake of Kennedy's speech:

> The Soviets, by Khrushchev's own admission, are out to conquer the world. Soviet missile bases are for that purpose. They are for aggression and enslavement. United States missile bases at home and abroad are for the defense of freedom. They are to protect mankind against the menacing evil of Communist tyranny. Let not the arguments of those who deal in finely drawn legalisms obscure these basic truths.[60]

The *Chicago Tribune* declared that history had shown conclusively "Why Cuba Isn't Like Turkey" because "the aggressive designs of the Communists are well established . . . while for 60 years the United States has shown that it has no desire to subvert the Cuban government." (The Bay of Pigs invasion then seemed to most Americans an attempt to *restore* decent government.) As for the claim that Cuba had a right to request missiles, there was "no evidence that the Cuban people want Soviet bases on their island," and, in any case, the Castro regime lacked democratic legitimacy and so "cannot claim to represent the Cuban people according to the principles which govern the civilized world." The *Tribune* elegantly understated that "the art of representative government is not fully developed" in Turkey either, but it was progressing, and in any case, all four major parties were "staunchly pro-western."[61]

Even as Kennedy pondered withdrawing the Jupiters from Turkey, newspapers that had endorsed negotiations in general terms stiffened at the thought of actual cutbacks in American forces. Richard Wilson wrote in the *Des Moines Register* that Americans would back Kennedy no matter the danger—"unless he listens to counsel urging compromise and backing away":

> We might, for example, take our missiles out of Turkey . . . in a deal with the Soviet Union which would bring the confrontation to an end, save face on both sides, and avoid nuclear war. Unfortunately, counsel of this kind has been all too persuasive in the Kennedy administration since the beginning, and was responsible for the retarded action in Cuba. . . . There is no accommodation that can be made with Russia on this issue. Nor is there any deal the President can wisely make.[62]

Such media sniping compounded the difficulty in finding common ground with the Russians firm enough to support the administration's credibility at home and with NATO. Whether NATO would have agreed to removal of missiles from Turkey (and possibly Italy) to end the crisis was uncertain, in part because NATO governments themselves divided and at times shifted on the issue. The historian Barton Bernstein concludes, "A formal trade, especially a public one, would have unnerved some governments, particularly the German, possibly the British, and probably the Dutch; it would have confirmed the analysis of President Charles de Gaulle of France [that an independent French nuclear deterrent was necessary], delighted Canada, and probably pleased the Italian, Greek, Danish, and Norwegian governments." On balance, Bernstein finds, Kennedy might with difficulty have limited the damage from a trade of bases because the fear of war would have outweighed all other concerns:

> America's complex alliance system did rest partly upon faith in its credibility, but many governments also feared that efforts to affirm credibility could be rash and dangerous. They did not usually expect the United States to maintain blind allegiance, and, as the history of recent American foreign relations demonstrated, discretion, tempered force, and the willingness to compromise were also essential to operating the far-flung alliances.[63]

Yet much rested on the Turks, who were hardly inclined to salvage Kennedy's position.[64] Confident of U.S. backing, Premier Ismet Inonu ignored Washington's nudges and defied Soviet bullying to surrender the Jupiters. On October 25 Inonu rejected a Russian ultimatum to dismantle the missiles or face a concerted Soviet nuclear attack in case of war. The Soviet ambassador to Turkey, Nikita Ryzhov, warned, "If you don't think we are ready to make war over Cuba, you are mistaken." Inonu replied, "Don't make me laugh."[65]

Inonu's defiance led the U.S. ambassador to Ankara, Raymond Hare, to discourage any deal involving the Jupiters. In response to an inquiry from Secretary of State Rusk,[66] Hare cabled on October 26 that the Turks would resent "that Turkish relationship with US can be equated with stooge status of Cuba with USSR" and "that their interests as an ally were being *traded off* in order to appease an enemy."[67] The ambassador nonetheless dutifully broached the possibility of a pact "on [a] strictly

secret basis" with the Kremlin, followed by a prompt dismantling of the Turkish missiles.[68] Although Hare doubted such a
secret could be kept, the president soon afterward trusted that a
back-channel agreement on the Jupiters, without informing the
host government, might discreetly defuse the Cuban crisis.

On Friday, October 26, Khrushchev cabled to Kennedy a
long, emotion-laden message on the horrors of war, hinting at a
settlement involving Cuba alone. The Soviets, Khrushchev implied, would remove the missiles from Cuba if the United States
would end the blockade and pledge not to invade the island. Ex
Comm members briefly relaxed their focus on the Turkish bases
as they scrutinized Khrushchev's hopeful message. But the next
morning a terse second cable from Khrushchev, bearing the
hallmarks of a carefully vetted committee document, made removal of the Jupiters a central bargaining point. This unexpected hardening of the Kremlin's position, broadcast on
Moscow radio in contrast to Friday's message for Kennedy's
eyes only, renewed the administration's urgency either to win
Turkish acceptance of a trade or face the likelihood of an esca-
lating conflict.

Solidarity with NATO remained the president's official
watchword. On October 27 he alerted British Prime Minister
Macmillan to Khrushchev's proposal for a "reciprocal removal
of missiles from Cuba and Turkey" but assured him, "I do not
feel that this country should allow itself to become engaged in
negotiations affecting the individual security interests of our
NATO allies. Any initiatives in this respect, it seems to me,
should appropriately come from Europe."[69] Within the recesses
of Ex Comm, however, Kennedy's priorities drifted back to the
necessity of withdrawing the Jupiters by whatever means.

Among Ex Comm members on Saturday morning who
adopted or at least articulated the Turkish government's hard
line, Paul Nitze feared that the Turks would resist a trade and,

still worse, that the Soviets would next demand denuclearization of the entire NATO area. Ball reported, to no one's surprise, that Italy, which had thirty Jupiter missiles, would make negotiations "relatively easy" but "Turkey creates more of a problem." Rusk believed the Jupiter issue should be kept separate from the Soviet "intrusion into the Western Hemisphere" and dealt with in the context of NATO and Warsaw Pact forces. Bundy also opposed accepting the Soviet proposal on Turkish bases because the Soviet missiles were not out of Cuba. He feared a problem of credibility because "all of NATO" would suspect "we were trying to sell our allies for our interests. . . . Now, it's irrational and it's crazy, but it's a *terribly* powerful fact."[70]

President Kennedy still inclined to a trade of bases as necessary to preserve peace and the appearance of justice. "We're going to be in an insupportable position on this matter," he said in the Ex Comm's morning meeting, "if this becomes his [Khrushchev's] proposal. . . . To any man at the United Nations or any other rational man it will look like a very fair trade." When Ball objected that "if we talked to the Turks, I mean, this would be an extremely unsettling business," Kennedy replied, "Well *this* is unsettling *now* George, because . . . most people would regard this as not an unreasonable proposal. . . ."[71]

The discussion uncovered further obstacles to a quick diplomatic fix involving the Jupiters. McNamara said that the missiles actually belonged to Turkey; only the nuclear warheads were under U.S. control, and this was merely in a custodial role for the Turks. While Kennedy left to take a call from Ambassador Stevenson at the United Nations, Alexis Johnson reported that the Turkish government had just publicly denounced the Russian proposal. Robert Kennedy added his influential voice to separate the issue of Turkish missiles from negotiations over Cuba. And McNamara's deputy, Roswell Gilpatric, said the

Russians must be convinced that until they stopped work on the missiles in Cuba, there would be no negotiations.[72]

Just before noon on Saturday, President Kennedy faced yet another expression of public militancy when he welcomed members of the Civil Defense Committee of the Governors' Conference then convening in Washington. According to Dino Brugioni, "There was a consensus among the governors that the president might not have been forceful enough with Khrushchev." California's Democratic governor Edmund Brown asked, to the discomfort of some other members, "Mr. President, many people wonder why you changed you mind about the Bay of Pigs and aborted the attack. Will you change your mind again?" Kennedy paused before replying, "I chose the quarantine because I wondered if our people are ready for the bomb."[73]

The president returned to the Ex Comm that afternoon, and returned as well to the necessity of a mutual dismantling of missile bases. Amid dissents by Bundy, Nitze, and others, Kennedy's conciliatory voice seemed to echo—though with decisively greater stature—Stevenson's lonely leanings a week earlier. According to minutes of the meeting, the president

> recalled that over a year ago we wanted to get the Jupiter missiles out of Turkey because they had become obsolete and of little military value. . . . But we are now in the position of risking war in Cuba and in Berlin over missiles in Turkey which are of little military value. . . . We are in a bad position if we appear to be attacking Cuba for the purpose of keeping useless missiles in Turkey. We cannot propose to withdraw the missiles from Turkey, but the Turks could offer to do so. The Turks must be informed of the great danger in which they will live during the next week

and we have to face up to the possibility of some kind of a trade over missiles.[74]

During a discussion that stretched from 4 p.m. on Saturday for nearly three and a half hours, Kennedy tacked toward a consensus to trade the Turkish bases but met spirited warnings that NATO might well founder on such a deal. Bundy said, "If we sound as if we wanted to make this trade, to our NATO people and to all the people who are tied to us by alliance, we are in real trouble." Kennedy replied that rash action could also shake the alliance: "If we reject it out of hand, and then have to take military action against Cuba, then we'll also face a decline."[75]

Estimates of NATO's likely response to a proposal to remove the Jupiter missiles from Turkey were grim. Ball, a seasoned negotiator with NATO governments, said, "If you have a NATO Council meeting in the morning, I think you are going to get a flat rejection of this. . . ." Kennedy replied that the key was to educate NATO on the harsh consequences of a failure to compromise:

> You see, they haven't had the alternatives presented to them. They'll say: "Well, God, we don't want to trade them off!" They don't realize that in 2 or 3 days we may have a military strike which would bring perhaps the seizure of Berlin or a strike on Turkey. And then they'll say: "My God, we should have taken it!"[76]

Llewelyn Thompson, Kennedy's chief Kremlinologist at the meeting, persisted in discouraging a trade because "the Soviets [would] still [be] in Cuba with planes and technicians and so on, even though the missiles are out. And that would surely be unacceptable and put you in a worse position." Kennedy defended the basic fairness of a trade, reminding Thompson that U.S. "technicians and planes and guarantees would still exist for

Turkey." It would be tragic, the president said, to order military action against Cuba, "and possibly an invasion, all because we wouldn't take the missiles out of Turkey. We all know how quickly everybody's courage goes when the blood starts to flow," especially if the Soviets "grab Berlin." "Today it sounds great to reject it [a trade of missile bases], but it's not going to, after we do something."[77]

Yet Kennedy, like his advisers, shrank from offering concessions on behalf of NATO that the member governments had not yet discussed, let alone sanctioned. When Bundy, moved by the president's insistence that a trade would be better than a "very bloody" conflict, said, "If you have that conviction . . . then I would say that an immediate personal telegram of acceptance [of Khrushchev's public offer] was the best thing to do," Kennedy demurred. Rather than accept a trade of bases "over [Turkish] opposition and NATO opposition," he said, ". . . I'd rather go the total blockade route [adding petroleum, oil, and lubricants to the supplies to be interdicted], which is a lesser step than military action. What I'd like to do is have the Turks and NATO equally feel that this is the wise move."[78]

This circle of doubt about risking either war with the Russians or an implosion within NATO allowed Thompson, Sorensen, Bundy, and others[79] to champion a third route: a letter to Khrushchev accepting the terms hinted at in his private cable of Friday evening, which had made no mention of the Turkish missiles. Robert Kennedy pressed to delete any references to Turkey in the president's reply, even assertions that the Jupiters should not be part of the settlement. "[Just] say you're accepting his offer," the attorney general urged, because anything more "sounds slightly defensive. . . ."[80] President Kennedy remained skeptical that Khrushchev would so easily drop his public demand to withdraw the Jupiters. But as an interim tactic, he approved a letter drafted by Sorensen and Robert Kennedy that "accepted" Khrushchev's implicit proposal involving Cuba alone.

The Ex Comm's marathon talks at the White House unfolded on Saturday afternoon in an atmosphere of growing pressure to strike at Cuba. Around noon a surface-to-air (SAM) missile, fired by a local Soviet commander without approval from Moscow, had fatally downed a U-2 pilot over Cuba, Major Rudolph Anderson. Khrushchev was incensed and appalled, rightly fearing that American leaders would hold him responsible. Robert Kennedy later recalled the spasm of belligerence that surged through the Ex Comm, and the lone voice that tamed it:

> At first, there was almost unanimous agreement that we had to attack early the next morning with bombers and fighters and destroy the SAM sites. But again the President pulled everyone back. "It isn't the first step that concerns me," he said, "but both sides escalating to the fourth and fifth step—and we don't go to the sixth because there is no one around to do so. We must remind ourselves we are embarking on a very hazardous course."[81]

The Joint Chiefs pressed hardest for that "first step" in the wake of Major Anderson's death. They drafted a formal recommendation to destroy the SAM site responsible, and added that unless the Russians promptly defused their nuclear missiles in Cuba, the U.S. Air Force should conduct massive bombings on Monday, followed a week later by an invasion. "Well, that was a surprise," Robert Kennedy quipped amid general laughter,[82] expressing the Kennedy brothers' unease with the leanings of military commanders toward military solutions.

As war loomed, some in the Ex Comm insisted that a trade of bases fit well within the bounds of sound national security strategy. In an informal session following the formal meeting,

Vice President Johnson emerged from near silence to share his legendary deal-making savvy, honed by years as Senate majority leader. "Why don't you . . . make the trade," Johnson asked, ". . . [and] save all the invasion, lives, and everything else?" As for the Turks, someone should explain to them, "Now, you've got these Jupiters, and they're lighted up there [as targets for the Russians]. The searchlights are on them, and everybody knows about them. They're not worth a damn. And we'll take that old Model T out, and we'll give you a Polaris, a much better job."[83]

Ball also set aside his worries about NATO in pressing for a trade: "We were going to *let* him [Khrushchev] have his [air] strike in Turkey, as I understood it last week." Everyone then believed that to save Berlin, giving up only the Jupiters "would be an easy trade and a very advantageous deal." When Bundy pressed, "And what's left of NATO?" Ball replied, "I don't think NATO is going to be wrecked. If NATO isn't any better than that, it isn't that good to us."[84]

For Kennedy, as for most of his advisers, the Jupiter missiles posed no crucial test of presidential will but only a political conundrum, as the scholar James G. Blight observed: "This isn't a debate between a dove and several hawks, but a discussion about which particular political problem is central: that arising from the U.N. because the U.S. does not trade, or that deriving from NATO if it does."[85]

Of primary concern to Kennedy, though, was the imperative to avoid war. Shortly before the afternoon Ex Comm meeting adjourned, he told Thompson and others unreconciled to yielding on the Jupiter missiles:

> We can't very well invade Cuba, with all the toil and blood
> it's going to be, when we could have gotten them [the So-
> viet missiles] out by making a deal on the same missiles in

Turkey. If that's part of the record, then I don't see how we'll have a very good war.

As the president had earlier exhorted, "It seems to me . . . we ought to—to be reasonable."[86]

The full weight of American (and Soviet) foreign policy throughout the cold war reinforced Kennedy's restraint. No matter the tensions and threats, the crises and recriminations, Presidents Truman and Eisenhower had in practice recognized an impassable line between military readiness and recklessness, and had invariably refrained from attacks on the Russians. Soviet subversion in Eastern Europe, the Berlin blockade in 1948 and subsequent Berlin crises, aggression by the Soviet client-state of North Korea in 1950,[87] the Soviet invasion of Hungary in 1956, the downing of an American U-2 pilot over Russia in 1960: each episode had underscored the U.S. government's resolve—or resignation—that the cold war remain cold.

The taboo on direct combat with the Russians was in force years before the Soviet Union developed nuclear weapons and long-range missiles; by October 1962 the dictates of sanity had long since enshrined this unbroken if unspoken rule never to fire first. President Kennedy thus maneuvered within a highly circumscribed setting that permitted, even encouraged military displays yet barred actions that might kill so much as a single Soviet soldier.

Kennedy understood as well that the political tides impelling him toward a firm stand on the Cuban missiles might well ebb and strand him were he to aggravate the conflict without compelling need. Even the congressional war hawks, to all appearances solidly behind his firm stand, had enlisted for uncertain duration. The embers of the last Democratic president's prolonged ordeal with Republican congressmen in wartime were still white hot, as a State Department official, Roger Hilsman, later observed: "No one could forget that Senator Robert A. Taft, leader of the opposition during the Korean War, had praised President Truman's decision to fight in Korea in the twenty-four hours after it was made, but within weeks had begun to call it 'Truman's War.'"[88]

Around 7:20 p.m. on Saturday the president briefly convened a smaller group, including Robert Kennedy, Rusk, McNamara, Bundy, Ball, Gilpatric, Thompson, and Sorensen, to consider what the attorney general should tell Ambassador Dobrynin later that evening. To everyone's rapid agreement, Rusk proposed sweetening the administration's official offer with a private assurance that the president planned to remove the Jupiter missiles from Turkey and would do so as soon the crisis ended. In his memoirs Bundy wrote that when he asked Rusk, a staunch defender of NATO's interests, "why he had been the one to make the proposal, he replied simply that the Turkish missiles were always 'a phony issue.' To him it was never a concession to tell Khrushchev that we were going to do what we had wanted to do for so long."[89]

3. Kennedy's Trade

THE PRESIDENT'S PENCHANT for secrecy now enveloped most of the Ex Comm, as Bundy recalled:

Concerned as we all were by the cost of a public bargain struck under pressure at the apparent expense of the Turks, and aware as we were from the day's discussion that for some, even in our own closest councils, even this unilateral private assurance might appear to betray an ally, we agreed without hesitation that no one not in the room was to be informed of this additional message. Robert Kennedy was instructed to make it plain to Dobrynin that the same secrecy must be observed on the other side, and that any Soviet reference to our assurance would simply make it null and void.[90]

Few even in this small circle fully learned that Robert Kennedy planned to offer an explicit deal on the Turkish missiles rather than simply a loose assurance of the president's intent.[91] Others in the Ex Comm remained wholly in the dark, including Republican stalwarts McCone and Dillon, the veteran hardliner Nitze, and others whose political loyalties were deemed suspect, notably Vice President Johnson.

The attorney general welcomed Dobrynin at the Justice Department at 7:45 p.m. and conveyed the administration's proposal, embedded in warnings that time was outstripping their countries' ability to control events. If the Soviet Union halted work on the missiles and, under international control, rendered the weapons inoperable, the United States would end the quarantine and pledge not to invade Cuba. According to Dobrynin's cable to the Kremlin following this meeting, the Soviet ambassador raised one more point—for which Robert Kennedy had been fully prepared:

"And what about Turkey?" I asked R. Kennedy.

"If that is the only obstacle to achieving the regulation I mentioned earlier, then the president doesn't see any unsurmountable difficulties in resolving this issue," replied R. Kennedy. "The greatest difficulty for the president is the public discussion of the issue of Turkey. Formally the deployment of missile bases in Turkey was done by a special decision of the NATO council. To announce now a unilateral decision by the president of the USA to withdraw missile bases from Turkey—this would damage the entire structure of NATO and the US position as the leader of NATO, where, as the Soviet government knows very well, there are many arguments. In short, if such a decision were announced now it would seriously tear apart NATO."

"However, President Kennedy is ready to come to agree on that question with N. S. Khrushchev, too. I think that in order to withdraw these bases from Turkey," R. Kennedy said, "we need 4–5 months. This is the minimal amount of time necessary for the US government to do this, taking into account the procedures that exist within the NATO framework. . . . However, the president can't say anything public in this regard about Turkey," R. Kennedy said again. R. Kennedy then warned that his comments about Turkey are extremely confidential; besides him and his brother, only 2–3 people know about it in Washington.[92]

In his memoir of the crisis, *Thirteen Days*, Robert Kennedy recalled that while denying he was issuing an ultimatum, he told Dobrynin that unless the Soviet Union promptly agreed to remove the missiles, the United States would do so, clearly implying an imminent military strike. Dobrynin's cable to Moscow casts the attorney general's words in a milder light. Kennedy merely conveyed the president's request to Khrushchev

to give him an answer . . . "if possible within the next day (Sunday) on these thoughts in order to have a businesslike, clear answer in principle. [He asked him] not to get into a wordy discussion, which might drag things out. The current serious situation, unfortunately, is such that there is very little time to resolve this whole issue. Unfortunately, events are developing too quickly. The request for a reply tomorrow," stressed R. Kennedy, "is just that—a request, and not an ultimatum. The president hopes that the head of the Soviet government will understand him correctly." Kennedy gave Dobrynin a direct telephone line to the White House to expedite communication.[93]

Robert Kennedy seemed to Dobrynin "very upset" rather than militant, as if the urgency of the situation had drained his usual combativeness. "In any case," Dobrynin reported, "I've never seen him like this before":

> True, about twice he tried to return to the topic of "deception" (that he talked about so persistently during our previous meeting) [on October 23], but he did so in passing and without any edge to it. He didn't even try to get into fights on various subjects, as he usually does, and only persistently returned to one topic: time is of the essence and we shouldn't miss the chance.[94]

Robert Kennedy proved firmer in negotiating secrecy than substance. On October 28, the day Khrushchev broadcast acceptance of a deal involving only a Soviet pledge to withdraw missiles from Cuba and a U.S. promise not to invade the island, Dobrynin reported on a follow-up talk with the president's brother:

> In parting, R. Kennedy once again requested that strict secrecy be maintained about the agreement with Turkey. "Especially so that the correspondents don't find out. At our place for the time being even [Pierre] Salinger [the president's press secretary] does not know about it" (It was not entirely clear why he considered it necessary to mention his name, but he did it). I responded that in the Embassy no one besides me knows about the conversation with him yesterday. R. Kennedy said that in addition to the current correspondence and future exchange of opinions via diplo-

matic channels, on important questions he will maintain contact with me directly, avoiding any intermediaries.[95]

On October 29 Robert Kennedy received a letter from Khrushchev confirming the agreement, but the next day he refused to retain, let alone ratify, the document. Dobrynin cabled his superiors on Kennedy's reasons for this abrupt behavior:

> The President, Robert Kennedy said, confirms the understanding with N. S. Khrushchev on the elimination of the American missile bases in Turkey. Corresponding measures will be taken towards fulfilling this understanding within the period of time indicated earlier, in confidential observance of NATO guidelines, but of course without any mention that this is connected to the Cuban events.
>
> We, however, said Robert Kennedy, are not prepared to formulate such an understanding in the form of letters, even the most confidential letters, between the President and the head of the Soviet government when it concerns such a highly delicate issue. Speaking in all candor, I myself, for example, do not want to risk getting involved in the transmission of this sort of letter, since who knows where and when such letters can surface or be somehow published—not now, but in the future—and any changes in the course of events are possible. The appearance of such a document could cause irreparable harm to my political career in the future. This is why we request that you take this letter back.[96]

That neither superpower thought the Jupiters a critical issue surely helped them, first to strike a deal, then to leave it unratified and indeed unreported beyond a few top-level officials. A sign that the Soviet Union viewed these missiles as a vexing but not vital threat had emerged on Friday afternoon, October 26, during a meeting initiated by KGB officer Alexander Feklisov (under the cover name Fomin) with an acquaintance at ABC news, John Scali. Unaware of breaking Soviet actions but familiar with the Kremlin's priorities, Feklisov broached with Scali a possible settlement of the crisis based on withdrawal of the Cuban missiles in exchange for an end to the blockade and a promise by U.S. officials not to invade Cuba. Although Feklisov had not cleared his proposal with the Kremlin, Ex Comm members took Scali's report as confirming that Khrushchev's winding message later that same day looked to a compromise centered exclusively on Cuba. Despite their flawed logic they had the larger picture right, for Khrushchev was then urgently seeking to end the crisis and safeguard Cuba. Only later did he feel it expedient to add the Jupiters to his core demands.[97]

4. Aftermath: Living Down the Victory

WORD OF the settlement lifted Kennedy's stature to almost Lincolnesque heights. An editorial by the *New York Herald Tribune* might as easily have followed reports from Gettysburg or Appomattox: "And at the center of this great aggregation of moral and physical force was the President of the United States. This country, and free peoples everywhere, may well be grateful for the firmness and skill he has displayed in this crisis, aware of the risks, under pressure from the fainthearted and the impatient, yet holding to the course he had set."[98] Richard Rovere declared in the *New Yorker* in November 1962, "[Kennedy] has won what is perhaps the greatest personal diplomatic triumph of any President in our history."[99]

The president's apparent victory still could not extinguish criticisms from the Pentagon and Capitol Hill that he had been entirely too conciliatory toward Khrushchev and Castro. Military leaders fumed over the president's refusal to bomb or invade Cuba, and even the censored version of the final accord did not mollify them. Admiral Anderson said of the news, "We have been had," and General LeMay, hoping to make the best of a bad situation, urged the president, "Why don't we go in and make a strike on Monday anyway." Kennedy politely declined the advice and afterward remarked to Arthur Schlesinger, "The military are mad."[100]

At least the White House could count on the military to mutter only in private about alleged presidential dereliction. The Republican opposition, having thirsted for partisan openings throughout the crisis, did not remain so forbearing. Instead the fading of danger appeared to dissolve any rhetorical inhibitions. George Bush, a Republican party leader in Houston, urged Kennedy to "muster the courage" to attack Cuba. Barry Goldwater demanded that the president "do anything . . . to get rid of that cancer. If it means war, let it mean war."[101]

The president discouraged such hawkish posturing in an interview broadcast on national television on December 17. Instead of blaming the Russians, he found most troubling

that both governments were so far out of contact, really. I don't think that we expected that he [Khrushchev] would put the missiles in Cuba, because it would have seemed such an imprudent action for him to take, as it was later proved. Now, he obviously must have thought that he could do it in secret and that the United States would accept it. So that he did not judge our intentions accurately.

Such "misjudgments of the intentions of others," Kennedy added, had pulled nations into wars throughout the century. Add to that "the Soviet Union and the United States so far separated in their beliefs . . . and you put the nuclear equation into that struggle, that is what makes this . . . such a dangerous time," when "one mistake can make this whole thing blow up. . . . That is why it is much easier to make speeches about some of the things we ought to be doing, but I think that anybody who looks at the fatality lists on atomic weapons, and realizes that the Communists have a completely twisted view of the United States, and that we don't comprehend them, that is what makes life in the sixties hazardous."[102]

Partisan demands for tougher action against Castro and his Soviet patrons continued throughout Kennedy's tenure in the White House. Some urged armed action to rid Cuba of Soviet troops, others focused on ways to hasten Castro's downfall. Two days after Kennedy announced a deal ending the missile crisis, right-wing Americans backed by some Republican congressmen formed a Committee for the Monroe Doctrine to protest the toleration of a "Communist colony" in the Western hemisphere.[103] In late July 1963 a House Republican task force on Cuba urged the president to take " 'speedy action' to halt free world trade with Fidel Castro's Communist regime. . . . If a request is not enough, we would favor closing the ports of this country to all vessels of any nation which permit any of its ships to carry to or from Cuba, directly or indirectly."[104]

Congressional dicta on the peril from Cuba remained lively through the spring of 1963. In May the Senate Armed Services Committee issued an "Interim report on the Cuban Military Buildup" so somber that Khrushchev's retreat months earlier seemed not to have registered. Apart from posing an open question "whether missiles and other strategic weapons" remained in Cuba, the report found "the source of the real threat" to be that "international communism now has a firm foothold in this hemisphere." Unless the United States removed this threat, "the nations of this hemisphere may be subverted one by one . . . until the entire hemisphere is lost. . . ." The report recommended giving the "entire Cuban problem . . . the highest possible priority by our governmental officials to the end that the evil threat which the Soviet occupation of Cuba represents will be eliminated at an early date."[105]

At dinner with Benjamin Bradlee, the editor of the *Washington Post*, Kennedy observed that Americans could not reasonably complain about the Soviet troops in Cuba when there were 27,000 American troops in Turkey on the Soviet border. The demands for renewed confrontation in Cuba appalled him as being insensitive to the sacrifices Khrushchev had already made. "Can you imagine the Russians backing up like this and not seeing it as a victory?" he exclaimed. "We would never be allowed to back down like this. If we did, you can imagine what Congress and the press would say." But Kennedy made sure to keep such balanced judgments off the record, because "It isn't wise politically to understand Khrushchev's problems in quite this way."[106]

5. "No 'Deal' of any Kind"

SECRECY over the pledge to remove missiles from Turkey proved more enveloping and enduring than the sieve of Washington politics would have given grounds for hope. Although some in the military suspected a trade, others, like Lauris Norstad, commander of NATO forces, merely urged against making one. On November 1, 1962, he wrote the president, "To permit the question of missiles in Turkey to be raised again would seem to deny the soundness of your position on the Soviet missiles in Cuba."[107] Averell Harriman, an early supporter of a trade of bases, never learned he had been a prophet with honor. Instead Harriman continued to advise removal of the missiles, unaware that his counsel had already prevailed.[108] Raymond Hare, the ambassador to Turkey who had first suggested a secret deal, was himself kept ignorant; Rusk cabled him (and the ambassador to NATO, Thomas Finletter) on October 29 that "no 'deal' of any kind was made involving Turkey."[109]

Even Soviet and American diplomats assigned to coordinate implementation of the settlement argued over the Jupiters in Turkey without suspecting that a deal had already been struck. At one meeting Soviet Deputy Foreign Minister Vasily Kuznetsov pressed for their removal while John J. McCloy insisted for the U.S. government that this lay outside the scope of their talks. According to Philip Nash, "It was a lunch of the mutually uninformed."[110]

Kennedy's aides stonewalled possible critics in closed congressional hearings. When Senator Stennis asked McNamara point-blank whether withdrawal of the Jupiter missiles "has nothing to do with the Cuban situation or anything like that," McNamara assured him, "Absolutely not . . . the Soviet Government did raise the issue . . . [but the] President absolutely refused even to discuss it. He wouldn't even reply other than that he would not discuss the issue at all." Senator Hickenlooper cross-examined Rusk with equal futility, asking, "The removal of the missiles from Turkey . . . was in no way, shape or form, directly or indirectly, connected with the settlement, the discussions or the manipulations of the Cuban situation?" Rusk replied, "That is correct, sir."[111]

There were signs that the lustrous veneer of a Soviet surrender hid murkier arrangements, but in an era of wide public faith in government, the desire to see America as invincible—and unwavering—overcame most suspicions. Typical of such doublethink, the *Hartford Courant* opined, "The news that the rough and tough Mr. Khrushchev had caved in, seems too good to be true"—but then assumed it to be fully credible and pronounced it "a turning point in history."[112]

NATO governments, insulated from the secret pact to remove the Jupiters, paid homage to the president's firmness on their behalf. British Prime Minister Macmillan led the way, writing to Kennedy on October 28, "It was indeed a trial of wills and yours has prevailed. Whatever dangers and difficulties we may have to face in the future I am proud to feel that I have so resourceful and so firm a comrade."[113]

The most exultant and apparently trusting were the target of Kennedy's cover-up, the Turks themselves. "I feel as though we [have] won," a Turkish newspaper editor wrote after the announced settlement of the crisis. "This is the payoff for our policy of strength and reliance on the United States."[114]

The administration's staunch denials of a deal accompanied the most urgent efforts to remove the Turkish missiles by April 1, 1963, as Robert Kennedy had promised Dobrynin. Taking his cue from the president just a day after the crisis formally concluded, McNamara told John McNaughton, the Department of Defense general counsel, "John, get those missiles out of Turkey. . . . Cut them up. Saw them up. Take photographs of them. Deliver the photographs to me . . . Do it!" McNamara's further instructions reflected Kennedy's secretive approach: "I don't want you to ask any questions about it. I don't want you to say to anybody else why it's being done, 'cause I'm not going to tell you." McNaughton resolved, "Those [Jupiters] are going to be out of there by April 1 if we have to shoot them out."[115]

Robert Komer, an influential staff member of the National

Security Council, cautioned his superior, McGeorge Bundy, that "early removal" of the Jupiters "could create one hell of a mess" with NATO allies because it "would revive all their latent fears" about the U.S. commitment to distant allies. Despite myths to the contrary, Komer wrote, Turkey "is not the strong-man of the Middle East; it's in the throes of a continuing domestic political crisis" and could be demoralized by a sudden removal of the missiles. The repercussions, moreover, would range well beyond Turkey:

> I am convinced that a withdrawal of JUPITERS (regardless of how we play it) would be widely regarded, and played up by the Soviets, as a retraction of US power. However wrong it may be, the history of European sensitivity on this point is painfully clear. Doubt as to US intentions is at the core of our NATO problems, and we have *not* swept it away by our recent actions.[116]

Even with the deliberate pace of NATO's multilateral decision-making, the administration nearly met its hidden deadline. Allied governments, including Turkey, ratified a plan to replace the Jupiters with Polaris submarines armed with nuclear missiles. The administration's rationale was simply that the submarines would be more secure than the Jupiters, which of course was so, but neither the whole truth nor even the main truth. No matter: the first of sixteen Polaris submarines began its Mediterranean patrol on March 30, 1963. The dismantling of the Jupiters began on April 1 and concluded within a month.

Kennedy sustained this diplomatic legerdemain as the price for finessing two irresistible but seeming irreconcilable demands: to negotiate a peaceful settlement with the Russians while avoiding concessions that would brand him an "appeaser" either in NATO or at home. His secret pledge to withdraw the Turkish missiles deftly cut the Gordian knot of this contradictory mandate by compromising to keep the peace while concealing a key feature of that compromise. His profile in camouflage suggests the extent to which Kennedy made prudence his chief virtue as he sought with a single policy to placate the Soviets, NATO, and the American public.

The Missile Crisis
in Historical Perspective

IN HIS HISTORY of nuclear policy, *Danger and Survival*, McGeorge Bundy acknowledged, "Forests have been felled to print the reflections and conclusions of participants, observers, and scholars" on the Cuban missile crisis.[1] The first great wave of coverage occurred in the mid-1960s, as the nation savored a cold war triumph and saluted a martyred leader of untold promise. A second wave peaked in the 1970s, as critics dissected the episode not to extol President Kennedy's supreme feat but to expose his feet of clay. Beginning in the mid-1980s the deforestation again accelerated, as declassified sources and meetings by former officials from America, Russia, and Cuba provided a wealth of factual corrections to early, long unchallenged recollections. Yet this crisis, perhaps the most intensely scrutinized fortnight in American history, is just beginning to come into historical focus.

1. Early Histories: Kennedy's Matchless "Crisis Management"

KENNEDY'S ADMIRERS were first to the ramparts in the battle over the president's historical reputation. The president's speech writer and special counsel Theodore Sorensen, historian Arthur Schlesinger, Jr., columnists and presidential intimates Joseph Alsop and Charles Bartlett, NBC correspondent Elie Abel, and the president's brother and attorney general, Robert Kennedy (in his posthumously published memoir *Thirteen Days*), all depicted the Soviet placement of missiles in Cuba as a brazen, nuclear-tipped challenge that the president could not decline without compromising credibility and tempting still bolder provocations. Brimming with insiders' revelations of tense national security meetings, their narratives formed a paradigm of successful crisis management that, they suggested, future policymakers should study and emulate.[2]

The early histories lauded President Kennedy for cool judgment "in steering a safe course between war and surrender."[3] Although he had discounted diplomacy alone as inadequate to dislodge the missiles and, in any case, a poor answer to nuclear blackmail, Kennedy had rejected urgings to bomb the missile sites (possibly followed by an invasion of Cuba), which would likely have killed many Russians. According to Robert Kennedy, at least six of twelve top aides, both civilian and military, had pressed this doubtful "surgical" solution, prompting him to muse that had any of them been president, "the world would have been very likely plunged in a catastrophic war."[4]

Kennedy drew further praise for conjuring a diplomatic miracle from an unpromising and increasingly volatile standoff. Elie Abel reported that Khrushchev's public demand that America remove its Jupiter missiles from Turkey was "a doubled sense of shock" to Kennedy, who "distinctly remembered having given instructions, long before" to remove the obsolete Jupiters. Now the president "reflected sadly on the built-in futilities of big government," for "not only were the missiles still in Turkey but they had just become pawns in a deadly chess game."[5] Still, Sorensen observed, "The President had no intention of destroying the Alliance by backing down."[6]

As the story was told: After much wrangling and confusion among Ex Comm members, Robert Kennedy offered "a thought of breathtaking simplicity and ingenuity: why not ignore the second Khrushchev message and reply to the first?"[7] With his brother's approval, he informed the Soviet ambassador that while "there could be no quid pro quo or any arrangement made under this kind of threat or pressure. . . . President Kennedy had been anxious to remove those missiles" and still hoped to do so "within a short time after this crisis was over."[8] The attorney general served this carrot on a stick, adding that either the Soviets must remove the missiles promptly or the Americans would do so. The next morning Khrushchev publicly acceded to these terms.

In the heady aftermath of the crisis, President Kennedy saluted the Soviet premier for his "statesmanlike" decision and privately cautioned aides that there should be "no boasting, no gloating, not even a claim of victory. We had won by enabling Khrushchev to avoid complete humiliation—we should not humiliate him now."[9] Robert Kennedy recalled, "What guided all [the president's] deliberations was an effort not to disgrace Khrushchev," to leave the Soviets a path of graceful retreat.[10]

For a nation emerging from a week of terror of the missile crisis, Henry Pachter wrote in the book *Collision Course*, the "style" and "art" of Kennedy's leadership had "restored America's confidence in her own power."[11] Sorensen, haggard from two weeks of stress and fatigue, recalled pondering the president's achievement as he leafed through a copy of *Profiles in Courage* and read the introductory quotation from Burke's eulogy of Charles James Fox: "He may live long, he may do much. But here is the summit. He never can exceed what he does this day."[12]

2. Revisionist Histories: Reckless Kennedy Machismo

WHETHER OR NOT history moves in cycles, historians typically do, and by the 1970s the once-standard odes to President Kennedy had given way to hard-edged, often hostile studies.[13] As portrayed by the new histories, the "brief shining moment" of Kennedy's Camelot was illumined by nothing more magical than the beacons of modern public relations. From his youth Kennedy had flaunted a reckless self-indulgence encouraged by the family's founding tyrant, Joseph P. Kennedy, who imparted to his male children his own ambition, opportunism, and a shameless *machismo* toward women. A succession of affairs unencumbered by emotional involvement; publication of an intelligent but amateurish senior thesis courtesy of family friends; embellishment of a war record marked by heroism but also by some unexplained lapses in leadership; and reception of a Pulitzer Prize for *Profiles in Courage*, written in significant part by his aide, Sorensen, all reflected a pursuit of expedience more than excellence.

Critics found that Kennedy's performance as president confirmed and extended rather than overcame this pattern of flamboyant mediocrity. They discerned in his conduct of foreign policy a dismal amalgam of anti-Communist hysteria, reckless posturing, and a disturbingly gleeful crisis orientation. The results were accordingly grim, ranging from the early disaster at the Bay of Pigs to the placement—or misplacement—of more than fifteen thousand U.S. military personnel in Vietnam by the time of Kennedy's death. Scarcely learning from his early mistakes, Kennedy ignored legitimate Cuban concerns for defense against American intervention and needlessly flirted with the apocalypse in order to force the removal of missiles that scarcely affected the world military balance. To judge from their skeptical recounting, this harrowing superpower confrontation might better be termed the "misled crisis," for it stemmed from Kennedy's perception of a threat to his personal and political prestige rather than (as Americans were misinformed) to the nation's security.

No crisis existed, then, until Kennedy himself created one by forgoing private diplomacy for a public ultimatum and blockade. Considering that the United States had already planned to remove its obsolete missiles from Turkey, Kennedy should have heeded Adlai Stevenson's advice to propose immediately a trade of bases, rather than rush into a confrontation whose outcome he could neither foresee nor fully control. Instead, "From the first, he sought unconditional surrender and he never deviated from that objective."[14] "He took an unpardonable mortal risk without just cause," Richard J. Walton wrote. "He threatened the lives of millions for appearances' sake."[15]

The prime historical mystery to the revisionists was why any American president would needlessly play Russian roulette in the nuclear age. Critics conceded that the president may have felt "substantial political pressures" over Cuba but blamed him for having largely created those pressures with shrill, alarmist speeches. "He had been too specific about what the United States would and would not tolerate in Cuba, and his statements reduced his options," Louise FitzSimons wrote.[16] Garry Wills also saw Kennedy as a prisoner of his own superheated rhetoric about Khrushchev, Communists, and missiles, which aroused a false sense of crisis: "If he was chained to a necessity for acting, he forged the chains himself. . . . Having fooled the people in order to lead them, Kennedy was forced to serve the folly he had induced."[17]

Revisionist writers detected a sad consistency in Kennedy's anti-Communist hyperbole, so that the missile crisis appeared to be a logical by-product of his style rather than simply a grisly aberration. During his bid for the presidency in 1960 Kennedy had stirred voters by charging his Republican opponent, Vice President Richard Nixon, with failing to "stand up to Castro" and to Khrushchev, or to prevent a potentially lethal "missile gap" with the Soviets (in fact Americans had a vast lead). Such ideological zeal remained evident in the Ex Comm, where, David Detzer claimed, Kennedy was "more Cold Warrior" than many, "worrying about America's reputation (and maybe his own) for toughness. . . ."[18]

Scholars in the rising genre of psychohistory traced the nation's "perilous path" in the missile crisis to "the neuroticism of Kennedy's machismo."[19] According to Nancy Gager Clinch, the president viewed the Cuban missiles "as a personal challenge to

[his] courage and status," and "In the Kennedy lexicon of man-liness, not being 'chicken' was a primary value."[20] This interpre-tation radiated to other fields: Sidney Lens, in his study of the military-industrial complex, found in Kennedy's "willingness to gamble with the idea of nuclear war . . . a loss of touch with re-ality, almost a suicidal impulse."[21]

The more judicious of the new historians, like Richard J. Walton, tempered their personal indictments by depicting the president as "an entirely conventional Cold Warrior."[22] Still, in addition to "his fervent anti-communism, and his acceptance of the basic assumptions of American postwar foreign policy," "the *machismo* quality in Kennedy's character"[23] pushed him to em-bark on "an anti-communist crusade much more dangerous than any policy Eisenhower ever permitted."[24] Burdened by both personal flaws and political pressures, Kennedy failed dur-ing the missile crisis to keep American policy from exhibiting, in his own words, "a collective death-wish for the world."[25]

Like traditional historians of the missile crisis, the revision-ists identified a hero, but it was the Soviet premier, Nikita Khrushchev, who withdrew the missiles at risk to his prestige. "Had Khrushchev not done so, there might well have been no later historians to exalt Kennedy,"[26] for then Kennedy and his aides, so set on victory at any cost, "would burn the world to a cinder."[27] In effect the new histories inverted the earlier images of Kennedy as a sentry for international order standing firm against a ruthless Soviet Union. To the revisionists, Kennedy's belligerence itself posed the chief threat of global annihilation, and only the belated prudence of his counterpart in the Krem-lin salvaged the peace.[28]

3. New Evidence, Old Myths

FOR MORE THAN two decades after the missile crisis, scholarship churned along these two interpretive poles, grinding ever finer a limited cache of primary sources. Denied access to most records of the Ex Comm meetings, historians continued to rely on memoirs by several of President Kennedy's aides. As for the Soviets, a commentator for *Izvestia* later lamented that their press "treated the episode with socialist surrealism," refusing even to concede Khrushchev's placement of nuclear weapons in Cuba. "The word 'missiles' never appeared in the newspapers, though later, in the Kennedy-Khrushchev letters, the phrase 'weapons the United States considers offensive' was used."[29]

As late as 1982 a writer surveying the historical literature could reasonably assert, "There are no new facts about the Kennedys, only new attitudes."[30] Seldom has an insight aged more rapidly or spectacularly. Beginning in the mid-to-late eighties the volcanic flow of information and inquiry in the era of *glasnost* enabled several conferences on the missile crisis in which Soviet and American scholars and former officials shared facts and feelings long guarded like vital national secrets.[31] These exchanges, coinciding with the declassification of various Ex Comm conversations, overturned much of what both traditional and revisionist scholars had long believed, extending even to shared assumptions about the basic facts of the crisis.[32]

The entire twenty-five-year debate over whether Kennedy was warranted in not pledging to withdraw the Turkish missiles was abruptly exposed as based on a faulty record of events. In 1987 former Secretary of State Dean Rusk revealed that Kennedy had secretly prepared a fallback plan to have UN Secretary General U Thant propose a mutual dismantling of missiles in

Cuba and Turkey. This would have let the president appear to comply only with a UN request rather than a Soviet demand. Whether Kennedy would have resorted to this gambit is uncertain, but clearly he had been seeking ways to defuse the risk of war.[33]

Kennedy's back-channel efforts to end the crisis went further still. At a conference in Moscow in 1989, the former Soviet ambassador to the United States, Anatoly Dobrynin, recalled an explicit American agreement to withdraw the missiles from Turkey, not simply a vague expression of hope that this might eventually occur. Robert Kennedy had asked him not to draw up any formal exchange of letters, saying it was important not to publicize the accord, for it could show the administration to be purveying a falsehood to the American public.[34] Sorensen deepened the panelists' astonishment by confirming that Robert Kennedy's diaries, which formed the basis of the posthumously published book *Thirteen Days*, were indeed explicit on this part of the deal. But at the time it was still a secret even on the American side, except for the president and a few officials within the Ex Comm. Sorensen explained that in preparing *Thirteen Days* for publication, "I took it upon myself to edit that out of his diaries."[35]

As a result of Sorensen's editing discretion, Kennedy's conciliatory policy on the Turkish missiles was distorted by histories of the crisis into a symbol of either his valiant resolve or his confrontational bent. Similarly historians had long emphasized the imminent danger of a U.S. attack on the Cuban missile sites, whether to highlight the president's grave choices or to further indict him for war-mongering. Yet McNamara insisted in 1987, "There was no way we were going to war on Monday or Tuesday [October 29 or 30]. No way!"[36] McNamara had suggested in the Ex Comm an intermediate step of tightening the quarantine to include petroleum, oil, and lubricants, and felt "very certain" that the president would have preferred this step to authorizing an attack.[37]

Some of the new evidence is considerably less flattering to President Kennedy's image as a peacemaker. Records of the first day of Ex Comm meetings, October 16, show both John and Robert Kennedy inclined, with most other participants, to a quick air strike. The president's vaunted containment of the risks of war also appears less reassuring than in the idealized portrayals of early histories and memoirs. The perennial boast that he only modestly opened a Pandora's box of nuclear dangers lost much of its luster as scholars inventoried what had nearly escaped. The president never learned that U.S. destroyers might have crippled a Soviet submarine with depth charges near the quarantine line,[38] an episode that could have triggered a wider naval clash. Kennedy also did not know of a series of false nuclear alerts that, in combination with the Strategic Air Command's heightened combat readiness, DEFCON (Defense Condition) 2, posed risks of inadvertent escalation.

Still more alarming, on October 27 a U.S. reconnaissance pilot strayed into Soviet territory, a violation that Khrushchev indignantly likened to a preparation for a preemptive nuclear strike. "There's always some son of a bitch who doesn't get the word," the president said on learning of this provocation. Kennedy would have been still more displeased had he known that because of the heightened military alert, U.S. fighter planes scrambling to protect the lost pilot from Russian MiGs were armed not with conventional weapons but with nuclear missiles. Scott D. Sagan, whose resourceful study *The Limits of Safety* discloses various military miscues and malfunctions during the crisis that might have led to a wider conflict, concludes that while "President Kennedy may well have been prudent," he lacked "unchallenged final control over U.S. nuclear weapons."[39]

Nor did the danger of unwanted escalation stem entirely

from U.S. nuclear forces. According to Anatoli Gribkov, who headed operational planning for the Soviet armed forces in 1962, the Russians had placed in Cuba not only medium-range missiles but also twelve *Luna* tactical missiles with nuclear warheads designed for ground combat support. Had Kennedy ordered an invasion, the Soviet commander in Cuba, General Issa Pliyev, in the event he lost contact with Moscow, had authority to fire the *Lunas* at the American landing force.[40] On hearing this in 1992, a stunned McNamara exclaimed, "No one should believe that a U.S. force could have been attacked by tactical nuclear warheads without the U.S. responding with nuclear warheads. And where would it have ended? In utter disaster."[41]

Even Ex Comm veterans who had long exalted the Kennedy administration's "rational crisis management" have renounced the very notion as romantic—and dangerous. President Kennedy's National Security Adviser, McGeorge Bundy, acknowledged, "The most important part of crisis management is not to have a crisis, because there's no telling what will happen once you're in one."[42] McNamara agreed, " 'Managing' crises is the wrong term; you don't 'manage' them because you *can't* . . ."[43] On the twenty-fifth anniversary of the missile crisis, Sorensen, Kennedy's loyal aide and biographer, termed the confrontation "unwise, unwarranted and unnecessary."[44]

The new scholarship has further chipped at the Kennedys' larger-than-life image by crediting the much maligned foreign policy establishment with contributions hitherto unknown or attributed wholly to the president and his brother. Secretary of State Dean Rusk, belying later charges that he was ineffectual in the Ex Comm and nearing a breakdown, originated the contingency plan to have UN Secretary General U Thant request the withdrawal of missiles in both Turkey and Cuba. With the president's approval, Rusk prepared Andrew Cordier, the president of Columbia University and a former UN parliamentarian, to approach U Thant. Had Khrushchev not accepted an earlier American offer, Rusk's idea might have served as the basis for a settlement under UN auspices.[45]

The administration's celebrated "acceptance" of Khrushchev's tacit proposals on October 26 rather than his sterner public demands the next day—a ploy once credited to Robert Kennedy alone—in fact had a complex patrimony. Llewellyn Thompson, the former ambassador to the Soviet Union, whom Robert Kennedy's memoir credits generously but generally for "uncannily accurate" advice that was "surpassed by none,"[46] may have first suggested the outlines of this strategy. Bundy, Assistant Secretary of State for Latin American Affairs Edwin Martin, and others also offered variations on this gambit in informal discussions.[47] Robert Kennedy formally proposed the idea in an Ex Comm meeting and drafted a response with Sorensen. But the view that this was his exclusive brainchild—a view nurtured by his own seemingly definitive account—underscores that memoirs seldom reveal an author's limitations other than a selective memory.

The very machinery of government, long viewed as a cumbersome, bumbling foil to a dynamic chief executive, now appears to have been a responsive (if not fully respected) partner. Contrary to early accounts, the failure to remove American missiles from Turkey before the crisis did not stem from unwitting bureaucratic sabotage of a presidential directive. Rather, Kennedy himself had acquiesced in the delay to avoid embarrassing a Turkish government that had only recently hinged its prestige on accepting the missiles.[48] The president may well have been dismayed by their continued presence, but he was in no way surprised by it in the Ex Comm meetings. Rusk dismissed reports of the president's alleged betrayal by a lazy State Department, saying, "He never expressed any irritation to me because he had been fully briefed by me on that situation."[49]

These and other discoveries all augur a far richer, more precise understanding of Kennedy's role in the missile crisis. But they have yet to produce an interpretive framework to encompass them. Should historians conclude that the president was less militant than once thought because he sanctioned a trade of missile bases? Or more militant because he initially leaned toward bombing Cuba? Does he now appear more adept at crisis management, given his elaborate fallback plans for a possible settlement through the UN? Or simply lucky to survive his own ignorance of swaggering American officers, false nuclear alerts, and nuclear-equipped Soviet forces in Cuba? Was the president more dependent on the Ex Comm in light of contributions by unsung heroes such as Llewellyn Thompson? Or did he treat the Ex Comm as having limited relevance, as in his concealment from most members of the private deal on the Turkish missiles? On these and other issues, the additions to our knowledge have been individually striking but cumulatively chaotic.

A way to make sense of these seemingly disparate and even conflicting pieces of evidence is to view President Kennedy as a moderate leader in a militant age. His vision at all times extended beyond the Ex Comm's deliberations, encompassing the formidable national consensus that the Soviet base in Cuba should be challenged militarily. Honing his policies on the grindstone of political necessity, Kennedy ordered a blockade of the island and considered still bolder action because he knew that Soviet leaders and the American public alike would otherwise view him as fatally irresolute. Yet within his circumscribed political setting, he proved more willing than most Americans, both in and outside his circle of advisers, to limit bellicose displays and to offer the Russians timely, if covert, concessions.

Despite a growing awareness of Kennedy's political constraints,[50] the revisionist image of a man driven by both insecurity and arrogance to rash policies has proven extraordinarily resilient. Thomas G. Paterson, who incisively recounts the covert war against Castro waged by two administrations, judges Kennedy's brand of cold war leadership more dangerous than Eisenhower's. "Driven by a desire for power," Paterson writes, "Kennedy personalized issues, converting them into tests of will."[51] Far from simply continuing "his predecessor's anti-Castro policies," Kennedy "significantly increased the pressures against the upstart island" out of an obsession with Castro. "He thus helped generate major crises, including the October 1962 missile crisis. Kennedy inherited the Cuban problem—and he made it worse."[52]

In *The Dark Side of Camelot* (1997) the award-winning journalist Seymour Hersh cranks up to full strength the assault on Kennedy's character that had stamped revisionist writings of the 1970s. Contrasting Khrushchev's "common sense and dread of nuclear war" with Kennedy's "fanaticism" during the missile crisis,[53] Hersh concludes: "For the first time in his presidency, Kennedy publicly brought his personal recklessness, and his belief that the normal rules of conduct did not apply to him, to his foreign policy. . . . The Kennedy brothers brought the world to the edge of war in their attempts to turn the dispute into a political asset."[54]

Textbooks too have incorporated into their "objective" look at American history the notion that Kennedy's belligerence is the key to understanding his foreign policy. In a leading work, *Promises to Keep: The United States Since World War II* (1999), Paul Boyer finds that "Kennedy's approach to Cold War leadership differed markedly from Eisenhower's. Shaped by an intensely competitive family and a hard-driving father whom he both admired and feared, he eagerly sought to prove his toughness to the Soviet adversary."[55]

The focus on Kennedy's supposed confrontational bent to explain his policies reaches its fullest—and most problematic—

development in the aptly titled study by Thomas C. Reeves, *A Question of Character*. Reeves's Kennedy was "deficient in integrity, compassion, and temperance,"[56] defects that "clearly influenced his Cuban policy, from the decision [in 1961] to ignore the moral and legal objections to an invasion, through the creation of Operation Mongoose."[57] During the missile crisis too, "Kennedy at times seemed unduly militant, and his aggressive and competitive instincts led him to grant the [diplomatic] initiative to the Soviets at critical points where more skilled diplomacy might have avoided it."[58] Reeves dismisses claims that the president sought never to "challenge the other side needlessly," with the comment, "Neither, of course, were the Kennedys prepared to accept anything short of victory."[59] Faced with the mounting evidence of Kennedy's prudence, Reeves allows that the president's "personal agony over the conflict, his several efforts to avoid bloodshed, and his willingness to make a trade of Turkish for Cuban missiles, revealed a deeper concern for the nation and the world than many who knew him well might have suspected."[60] But little else leavens Reeves's generally dour portrait of a president whose personal failings compounded the risks of war.[61] Like other revisionist scholars, Reeves dutifully ingests the new scholarship on the missile crisis but cannot easily digest it.

The hazards of treating presidential character as the Rosetta stone to make sense of policies in the missile crisis should by now give pause to even the most confirmed of Kennedy's admirers or detractors. The emergence of contributions by Rusk, Thompson, Bundy, Martin, and other establishment figures has made it more difficult to portray the Kennedys as lonely titans striding across the political stage with ideas and policies uniquely their own. And, granted that Kennedy was "the key decisionmaker,"[62] he nonetheless acted within tightly defined parameters that had little to do with the character of the chief executive.

The amplified record of decision-making has also recast or removed issues that long galvanized and framed debates over Kennedy's character. Interpretations of the president's supposedly tough policy on the Jupiter missiles now appear to have rested on accounts that, by embellishment and concealment alike, exaggerated his brinkmanship. The puncturing of those distortions should deflate as well the images of Kennedy as either a surpassingly valiant leader or a Neanderthal cold warrior.

Traditional historians, it is now clear, both sanitized and romanticized the historical record in portraying President Kennedy as an ideal fusion of hawkish resolve and dovish reserve, who forced out the Cuban missiles without making needless concessions or taking heedless risks. In fact Kennedy resolved the crisis not simply through toughness and diplomatic bluff but also by pledging to remove the missiles from Turkey, a deal he publicly spurned and his partisans long proudly but wrongly denied. And while Kennedy's defenders lauded his rejection of calls for air strikes and invasion, they overlooked the provocation of his actual policies, including the plots against Castro, the push for ever greater American nuclear superiority, and, of course, the blockade of Cuba.

The historical record is even more resistant to revisionist portraits of a president whose psychological deformities impelled him to risk peace for the sake of personal glory or catharsis. These accounts were from the first suspect, whether in drawing tortured connections between Kennedy's womanizing and his foreign policy or deriding him for sharing the beliefs of his own generation rather than a later one. They simply collapse under the weight of evidence that, during the gravest crisis of the cold war, Kennedy repeatedly proved more prudent than many aides, both civilian and military. As he told his brother

Robert on October 26, "If anybody is around to write after this, they are going to understand that we made every effort to find peace and every effort to give our adversary room to move. I am not going to push the Russians an inch beyond what is necessary."[63]

Ernest May and Philip Zelikow, editors of an invaluable annotated record of the Ex Comm sessions, marvel that "[Kennedy] seems more alive to the possibilities and consequences of each new development than anyone else." On October 27, with pressure mounting for decisive action, the president "is the only one in the room who is determined not to go to war over obsolete missiles in Turkey."[64] May and Zelikow acknowledge Kennedy's partial responsibility for this superpower clash but deem it "fortunate" that "[he] was the president charged with managing the crisis."[65]

The most telling dismissal of revisionist rhetoric comes from Kennedy's adversaries themselves. Shortly after the crisis ended, Khrushchev admitted to an American journalist, "Kennedy did just what I would have done if I had been in the White House instead of the Kremlin."[66] In his memoirs the former Soviet leader lamented Kennedy's death as "a great loss," for "he was gifted with the ability to resolve international conflicts by negotiation, as the whole world learned during the so-called Cuban crisis. Regardless of his youth he was a real statesman."[67] As for those "clever people" who "will tell you that Kennedy was to blame for the tensions which might have resulted in war," Khrushchev said, "You have to keep in mind the era in which we live."[68] Castro, for his part, believed Kennedy "acted as he did partly to save Khrushchev, out of fear that any successor would be tougher."[69]

The misrepresentations of Kennedy's leadership go deeper than the debates over whether he was heroic or merely reckless, idealistic or expedient, poised or impulsive. Scholars have so focused on Kennedy's style, aura, temperament, and character as to slight, if not obscure, the crucial framework of national values that he necessarily accommodated and largely shared. The missile crisis, as much as anything, is the story of how Kennedy faithfully reflected a remarkable consensus in political institutions and public opinion regarding America's role as Free World champion in the nuclear age.

Contrary to the impression left by Kennedy's partisans, the Executive Committee he formed to advise him during the missile crisis was never a sealed laboratory for reinventing American policy. Nor was it, as the revisionists later had it, a forum for venting personal demons at public expense. Rather, like any leader in a democracy, Kennedy self-consciously labored under constraints imposed by public opinion, the Congress, the military, the CIA, and a host of civilian constituencies. To argue that he could or should have disdained these pressures is to imply a preference for philosopher kings over accountable presidents. Whatever the appeal of such arguments, they leave little room for either the ideal or the reality of American democracy.

Americans in the early sixties overwhelmingly regarded the prospect of missiles in Cuba as intolerably threatening and judged leaders by their firmness against Soviet encroachments. Whoever occupied the Oval Office would therefore have faced intense pressures to demand removal of the missiles, direct low-level military action against Cuba, and avoid apparent concessions to the Russians. Buffeted by partisan sniping, public opinion, and the force of inherited policies, President Kennedy pursued all of these options. Throughout he sought to minimize confrontation with the Soviet Union to a degree consistent with his political survival.

Accounting for the full political weight of entrenched national attitudes can help resolve the central paradox of Kennedy's policies during the missile crisis, which reflected elements of both recklessness and restraint. Considered against the background of his times, Kennedy appears a rational leader, conciliatory and even empathetic towards his counterpart in the Kremlin. Yet he also represented a political culture marked by fear and bluster, qualities stoked by an uncontrolled arms race and Manichean visions of the East-West divide. To ask which was the "real" Kennedy is to speak of a chimera: a leader somehow extricable from his era.

Kennedy embodied the anti-Soviet, anti-Communist values—and obsessions—of his day, though with more skepticism and caution than most contemporaries. His relative detachment from cold war dogmas was not enough to avoid a crisis caused by mutual misjudgments. Still, it allowed for a crucial modicum of flexibility and restraint that helped keep this crisis from spiraling toward war.

It may be tempting to conclude that Kennedy's avoidance of a wider conflict warrants cynicism rather than celebration, as the bare minimum one should expect of any sane leader in the nuclear age. Yet the obstacles to military restraint between states are no less daunting simply because the dangers are so great. Whatever Kennedy's missteps, he proved—together with Soviet Premier Khrushchev—that leaders can resist the lures of unchecked escalation even while mired in a climate of mutual suspicion, fear, and hostility. This achievement may yet gain new luster as nuclear weapons spread to other nations steeped in their own bitter rivalries, a development auguring two, three, many missile crises to come.

Selected Chronology

1960

July 9. Soviet Premier Khrushchev declares that "Speaking figuratively, in case of necessity, Soviet artillerymen can support the Cuban people with rocket fire. . . ."

July 12. Premier Khrushchev declares the Monroe Doctrine "dead."

October 19. The U.S. ends all exports to Cuba except nonsubsidized foodstuffs, medicines, and medical supplies.

1961

April 17–19. The CIA-sponsored invasion by Cuban exiles at the Bay of Pigs fails.

June 3–4. President Kennedy and Premier Khrushchev meet in Vienna.

1962

February 3. President Kennedy embargoes all trade with Cuba except for medical necessities.

Selected Chronology

May 24. The Soviet Defense Ministry formally decides to send nuclear missiles to Cuba.

August 31. Republican Senator Kenneth B. Keating warns of possible Soviet "rocket installations in Cuba" and urges President Kennedy to act, a refrain that echoes in Congress through the first three weeks of October.

September 4. President Kennedy issues a press statement that denies evidence of offensive military weapons in Cuba but warns, "Were it otherwise, the gravest issues would arise."

September 13. At a press conference, President Kennedy declares that if Cuba were to "become an offensive military base of significant capacity for the Soviet Union, then this country would do whatever must be done to protect its own security and that of its allies."

September 20. The Senate resolves by a vote of 86 to 1 to sanction the use of force, if necessary, "to prevent the creation or use of an externally supported offensive military capability endangering the security of the U.S." Six days later the House of Representatives passes this resolution by a vote of 384 to 7.

Monday, October 15. CIA analysis of aerial photography over Cuba reveals the presence of Soviet nuclear missile sites.

Tuesday, October 16. President Kennedy secretly convenes a group of advisers, later known as the Executive Committee of the National Security Council, or "Ex Comm."

Monday, October 22. At 7 p.m., E.D.T., President Kennedy informs the nation of nuclear missiles in Cuba and announces a naval "quarantine" as a first step to secure their removal.

Wednesday, October 24. The quarantine goes into effect at 10 a.m., E.D.T.

Friday, October 26. At 7:50 a.m., E.D.T., the freighter *Marucla* is boarded by quarantine forces.

At 6 p.m., E.D.T., the State Department begins receiving a cable from Premier Khrushchev that hints at removal of the missiles from Cuba were the U.S. to pledge not to attack the island.

Saturday, October 27

At 9 a.m., E.D.T., Premier Khrushchev publicly proposes a settlement that would include removal of U.S. Jupiter missiles from Turkey.

Around noon, E.D.T., U-2 pilot Major Rudolph Anderson is fatally downed over Cuba.

At 7:45 p.m., E.D.T., Robert Kennedy meets with Soviet Ambassador Anatoly Dobrynin. He emphasizes the urgency of a settlement and reaches an understanding regarding the Jupiter missiles in Turkey.

Sunday, October 28. In a message to President Kennedy broadcast over Radio Moscow at 9 a.m., E.D.T., Premier Khrushchev agrees to remove "the weapons which you describe as offensive" in return for assurances that the U.S. will not invade Cuba.

November 20. After further negotiations, Premier Khrushchev agrees to remove IL-28 warplanes stationed in Cuba. President Kennedy lifts the blockade and cancels the heightened alert status of the Strategic Air Command.

Notes

1. Rethinking the Cuban Missile Crisis

1. George W. Ball, *The Past Has Another Pattern: Memoirs* (New York: W. W. Norton, 1982), pp. 297–298.
2. Theodore C. Sorensen, *Kennedy* (New York: Harper & Row, 1965), p. 705.
3. James G. Blight and David Welch, *On the Brink: Americans and Soviets Reexamine the Cuban Missile Crisis*, 2d ed. (New York: Farrar, Straus and Giroux, 1989), p. 378.
4. Nikita S. Khrushchev, *Khrushchev Remembers*, translated and edited by Strobe Talbott (Boston: Little, Brown, 1970), p. 497.
5. Michael R. Beschloss, *The Crisis Years: Kennedy and Khrushchev, 1960–1963* (New York: Edward Burlingame, 1991), p. 571.
6. David Detzer, *The Brink: Cuban Missile Crisis, 1962* (New York: Thomas Y. Crowell, 1979), p. 257.
7. Arthur M. Schlesinger, *A Thousand Days: John F. Kennedy in the White House* (Boston: Houghton Mifflin, 1965), pp. 840, 841.
8. Theodore C. Sorensen, *The Kennedy Legacy* (New York: Macmillan, 1969), p. 192.
9. Henry Fairlie, *The Kennedy Promise: The Politics of Expectation* (Garden City, N.Y.: Doubleday, 1973), p. 301.
10. Ibid., p. 289.
11. Nancy Gager Clinch, *The Kennedy Neurosis* (New York: Grosset & Dunlap, 1973), p. 205.
12. Beschloss, *The Crisis Years*, p. 350.

13. Ibid., p. 702.
14. Ibid., p. 438.
15. Samuel I. Rosenman, *Working with Roosevelt* (New York: Harper & Brothers, 1952), p. 167.
16. Schlesinger, *A Thousand Days*, p. 674.
17. Louis J. Paper, *The Promise and the Performance: The Leadership of John F. Kennedy* (New York: Crown, 1975), p. 377.

2. Cold War Alarms and the 1960 Campaign

1. Robert A. Divine, *Foreign Policy and U.S. Presidential Elections, 1952–1960* (New York: New Viewpoints, 1974), p. 246.
2. "50-State Survey: What the Voters Are Thinking . . . And What Will Swing Their Votes in November," *Newsweek*, Aug. 1, 1960, p. 26.
3. Robert G. Spivack, "It's Up to Kennedy," *Nation*, CXCI (Oct. 8, 1960), pp. 220–221.
4. "Cold War Goes On," *Time*, July 25, 1960, p. 8.
5. James Reston, "Democratic Plans Backfire in Senate," *New York Times* [hereafter *NYT*], Aug. 17, 1960, p. 30.
6. William G. Carleton, "Nixon or Kennedy: The People Have Decided," *Nation*, CXCI (Sept. 10, 1960), p. 124.
7. Theodore H. White, *The Making of the President 1960* (New York: Atheneum, 1961), p. 153.
8. Richard A. Aliano, *American Defense Policy from Eisenhower to Kennedy: The Politics of Changing Military Requirements, 1957–1961* (Athens, Ohio: Ohio University Press, 1975), p. 236.
9. Divine, *Foreign Policy and U.S. Presidential Elections*, p. 228.
10. Ibid., p. 229.
11. "Ike v. Dick," *Time*, Oct. 27, 1958, p. 13.
12. "Rocky & the Issues," *Time*, Dec. 28, 1959, p. 12.
13. David Lawrence, "JFK Alone Doesn't Hold Key," *Birmingham News*, Jan. 17, 1961, p. 10.
14. *NYT*, Aug. 25, 1960, p. 20.
15. Divine, *Foreign Policy and U.S. Presidential Elections*, p. 227.
16. Ibid., p. 261.
17. Ibid., p. 263.
18. Ernest K. Lindley, "Will They Regret It?" *Newsweek*, Oct. 24, 1960, p. 53.
19. Henry Hazlitt, "What Are We Deciding?" *Newsweek*, Oct. 24, 1960, p. 116.

20. Divine, *Foreign Policy and U.S. Presidential Elections*, p. 266.
21. Theodore C. Sorensen, *Kennedy* (New York: Harper & Row, 1965), p. 205.
22. See, for example, Averell Harriman, "My Alarming Interview with Khrushchev," *Life*, July 13, 1959, p. 36; "Peaceful Coexistence," *Time*, July 13, 1959, p. 10.
23. John Newhouse, *War and Peace in the Nuclear Age* (New York: Alfred A. Knopf, 1989), p. 125.
24. The reference to Khrushchev's inebriated state is in ibid.
25. Instances of Americans taking Khrushchev's boast as a threat of war are legion. See, for example, Howard V. Andrews, Titonka, Iowa, in *Des Moines Register*, Oct. 27, 1962, p. 6.
26. Nixon proudly detailed his encounter with Khrushchev in his memoir *Six Crises* (Garden City, N.Y.: Doubleday, 1962), pp. 235–292. Divine, *Foreign Policy and U.S. Presidential Elections*, pp. 222–223, notes the political benefits that Nixon reaped from the "kitchen debate."
27. "The Key to the White House?" *Newsweek*, Jan. 4, 1960, p. 12.
28. Beschloss, *The Crisis Years*, p. 23; also see "Nixon—To the Attack," *Newsweek*, Nov. 7, 1960, p. 33.
29. Divine, *Foreign Policy and U.S. Presidential Elections*, p. 207.
30. "The New Campaign," *Time*, June 13, 1960, p. 23.
31. Vladislav Zubok and Constantine Pleshakov, *Inside the Kremlin's Cold War: From Stalin to Khrushchev* (Cambridge, Mass.: Harvard University Press, 1996), p. 207.
32. Ben Pearse, "Defense Chief in the Sputnik Age," *NYT*, Nov. 10, 1957, sec. 6 (magazine), p. 20.
33. Fred Kaplan, *The Wizards of Armageddon* (Stanford: Stanford University Press, 1983), p. 141.
34. Ibid., p. 142.
35. Chalmers Roberts, *Washington Post*, Dec. 20, 1957, p. 1.
36. "United States Objectives and Programs for National Security" (NSC 68), in United States Department of State, *Foreign Relations of the United States 1950*, vol. I (Washington, D.C.: U.S. Government Printing Office, 1977), pp. 234–292.
37. Ibid., p. 245.
38. Ibid., p. 238.
39. Ibid., p. 251.
40. Ibid., p. 287.
41. Among many earlier documents of similar pitch, see "U.S. Objectives with Respect to the USSR to Counter Soviet Threats to U.S. Security" (NSC 20/4), Nov. 23, 1948, in United States Department of

State, *Foreign Relations of the United States 1948*, vol. I, part 2 (Washington, D.C.: U.S. Government Printing Office, 1976), pp. 662ff. The memorandum asserted, "The gravest threat to the security of the United States within the foreseeable future stems from the hostile designs and formidable power of the USSR, and from the nature of the Soviet system" (p. 666), a conclusion that NSC 68 declared "remains valid" (ibid., p. 288).

42. In his memoir *Present at the Creation: My Years in the State Department* (New York: W. W. Norton, 1969), p. 373, former Secretary of State Dean Acheson brushed aside charges that NSC 68 had exaggerated the Soviet threat: "The task of a public officer seeking to explain and gain support for a major policy is not that of the writer of a doctoral thesis. Qualification must give way to simplicity of statement, nicety and nuance to bluntness, almost brutality, in carrying home a point. . . . If we made our points clearer than truth, we did not differ from most other educators and could hardly do otherwise."

43. Kaplan, *The Wizards of Armageddon*, p. 131.

44. "The Build-Up, the Letdown," *Newsweek*, Dec. 16, 1957, p. 65.

45. "General Overhaul," *Time*, Dec. 16, 1957, p. 9. The resulting worldwide ridicule of American space efforts is sampled in "Vanguard's Aftermath: Jeers and Tears," *Time*, Dec. 16, 1957, p. 12.

46. "Signals from Moscow," *Time*, Oct. 21, 1957, p. 29.

47. "The Power for Now," *Time*, Nov. 25, 1957, p. 27.

48. "The Muddle—Now a Method?" *Newsweek*, Dec. 2, 1957, p. 23.

49. *Time*, Jan. 6, 1958.

50. "Satellites and Our Safety: Stepping Up the Pace—A Special Section," *Newsweek*, Oct. 21, 1957, p. 30.

51. "The U.S., Ike, and Sputnik," *Newsweek*, Oct. 28, 1957, p. 31.

52. "Ready for the Brawl," *Time*, Jan. 6, 1958, p. 9.

53. "One Man Show," *Time*, Jan. 20, 1958, p. 13.

54. "The U.S.S.R.'s Challenge," *Time*, Jan. 13, 1958, p. 10.

55. "What About the Missile Gap?" *Time*, Feb. 9, 1959, p. 12.

56. Albert Wohlstetter, "The Delicate Balance of Terror," *Foreign Affairs*, vol. 37, no. 2 (January 1959), p. 217.

57. Ibid., p. 234.

58. Bernard Brodie, *Strategy in the Missile Age* (Princeton: Princeton University Press, 1965, reprint of 1959 edition issued by the RAND Corporation), pp. 393-394.

59. See Herman Kahn, *On Thermonuclear War* (Princeton: Princeton University Press, 1960).

60. "If the Enemy Should Attack," *Newsweek*, Feb. 15, 1960, pp. 29-35.

61. On February 28, 1961, CIA director Allen W. Dulles submitted for President Kennedy a compendium of statements on Soviet rocket power by Khrushchev and other Kremlin leaders since mid-1957. See National Security Archive, *Cuban Missile Crisis, 1962*, microfiche collection (Alexandria, Va.: Chadwyck-Healey, 1990), document 37.
62. "The Russian Threat" in "Power Struggle—A Special Section," *Newsweek*, Jan. 25, 1960, p. 20.
63. "The Bold Stroke," *Time*, Aug. 1, 1960, p. 11.
64. Aliano, *American Defense Policy*, pp. 232, 234.
65. Kaplan, *The Wizards of Armageddon*, pp. 249–250, explores the ties between RAND personnel and the Kennedy campaign.
66. John F. Kennedy, *The Strategy of Peace*, ed. Allan Nevins (New York: Harper & Brothers, 1960), p. 139.
67. Ibid., pp. 132–133.
68. *NYT*, July 10, 1960, p. 2.
69. *NYT*, July 13, 1960, p. 6; "Khrushchev's Protectorate," *Time*, July 18, 1960, p. 26.
70. *NYT*, Sep. 21, 1960, p. 1.
71. *NYT*, July 16, 1960, p. 18.
72. *Atlanta Constitution*, June 25, 1960, p. 1.
73. "Further Shocks Loom in Crisis With Castro," editorial, *Atlanta Constitution*, July 19, 1960, p. 4.
74. *Atlanta Constitution*, Aug. 9, 1960, p. 1.
75. William S. White, "Will Castro Issue Help Democrats?" *Atlanta Constitution*, Sept. 16, 1960, p. 4.
76. Ibid., and "Cheering Throngs Hail Sen. Johnson in Toccoa, Gainesville and Atlanta/Rips Loss of Cuba to Red Bloc," *Atlanta Constitution*, Oct. 12, 1960, p. 1.
77. White, *The Making of the President 1960*, p. 208.
78. Beschloss, *The Crisis Years*, p. 28.
79. "The Menace of the Red Foothold in Cuba ... We Sharpen Our Weapons to Meet It," *Newsweek*, July 11, 1960, p. 36.
80. "Khrushchev's Protectorate," *Time*, July 18, 1960, p. 26.
81. Schlesinger, *A Thousand Days*, p. 224.
82. *NYT*, Oct. 20, 1960, p. 1; Divine, *Foreign Policy and U.S. Presidential Elections*, p. 268.
83. Beschloss, *The Crisis Years*, pp. 29ff, examines the ambiguous evidence on whether and to what extent Kennedy had been briefed by CIA director Allen Dulles.
84. Divine, *Foreign Policy and U.S. Presidential Elections*, pp. 268–269.

85. Schlesinger, *A Thousand Days*, p. 73.
86. Divine, *Foreign Policy and U.S. Presidential Elections*, p. 269.
87. Ibid., p. 287.
88. *New Orleans Times-Picayune*, Jan. 19, 1961, sec. 1, p. 12.
89. David Lawrence, "Will Administration Face Up to Threat, Call Red Bluff?" *Houston Chronicle*, Jan. 8, 1961, sec. 6, p. 2.
90. "Global Crises Stacked Up for Mr. Kennedy: A Special Section," *Newsweek*, Jan. 23, 1961, p. 25.
91. Rowland Evans, Jr., "Kennedy Task Not to Be Easy," *Birmingham News*, Jan. 5, 1961, p. 5.
92. Clarence Manion, "We're at War; Will We Fight or Are We to Surrender?" *Houston Chronicle*, Jan. 17, 1961, sec. 1, p. 10.
93. See, for example, *Monthly Survey of American Opinion on International Affairs*, no. 236 (Jan. 3, 1961), p. 11, Folder: "Monthly Survey—1961," Box 13, U.S. State Department, Office of Public Opinion Studies 1943–1965 (Schuyler Foster papers), RG 59, General Records of the Department of State, National Archives.
94. Daniel James, "14 of 20 Latin American Republics Sitting on Dynamite," *Birmingham News*, Jan. 3, 1961, p. 7.
95. "Could-Be Hero Lost His Chance," *Birmingham News*, Jan. 8, 1961, p. 14.
96. "Master of Latin-American Intrigue Appears to Control Our Diplomacy," *Houston Chronicle*, Jan. 1, 1961, sec. 2, p. 2.
97. "To What Lengths Will Castro Go?" editorial, *New Orleans Times-Picayune*, Jan. 5, 1961, sec. 1, p. 14.
98. "Fairly Good Year Behind Us, as Good or Better in Prospect," editorial, *Houston Chronicle*, Jan. 1, 1961, sec. 2, p. 2.
99. "Your Election Blue Extra: Castro—We Draw the Line," *Newsweek*, Nov. 14, 1960, pp. 27–28.

3. The New Frontier Under Siege

1. "Excellent on Foreign Policy," editorial, *New Orleans Times-Picayune*, Jan. 21, 1961, sec. 1, p. 8; "The Two Leaders, Two 'Peaces,'" editorial, *New Orleans Times-Picayune*, Jan. 22, 1961, sec. 2, p. 4.
2. Samuel Lubell, "The People Speak: Public Anxiously Awaits New President's Actions," *New Orleans Times-Picayune*, Jan. 9, 1961, sec. 2, p. 2.
3. "The Speeches," *Time*, Oct. 6, 1961, p. 26.
4. Charles E. Bohlen, *Witness to History, 1929–1969*, with the editorial as-

sistance of Robert H. Phelps (New York: W. W. Norton, 1973), p. 476.

5. Beschloss, *The Crisis Years*, p. 20.

6. Zubok and Pleshakov, *Inside the Kremlin's Cold War*, p. 239.

7. Beschloss, *The Crisis Years*, p. 70.

8. *NYT*, Jan. 4, 1961, p. 1.

9. Thomas G. Paterson, "Fixation with Cuba: The Bay of Pigs, Missile Crisis, and Covert War Against Fidel Castro," in Paterson, ed., *Kennedy's Quest for Victory: American Foreign Policy, 1961–1963* (New York: Oxford University Press, 1989), pp. 129–130.

10. James Reston, "On the Art and Wisdom of Slamming Doors," *New York Times*, Jan. 6, 1961, p. 26.

11. "Final Break with Cuba Is Lesson for Future," editorial, *Atlanta Constitution*, Jan. 5, 1961, p. 4. See also "Reaching Limit of Endurance, U.S. Breaks Relations with Cuba," editorial, *Houston Chronicle*, Jan. 4, 1961, sec. 4, p. 2, on the "crowning insult" by Castro's "insufferable," "outlaw regime" to "long-suffering Uncle Sam."

12. See, for example, Paterson, "Fixation with Cuba," p. 123; McNamara's comment is in 94th Congress, 1st session of U.S. Senate, Select Committee on Intelligence Activities, Report no. 94–465, Nov. 20, 1975, *Alleged Assassination Plots Involving Foreign Leaders: An Interim Report of the Select Committee to Study Governmental Operations with Respect to Intelligence Activities* (Washington, D.C.: U.S. Government Printing Office, 1975), pp. 157–158.

13. "How *Not* to Overthrow Castro," in Theodore Draper, *Castro's Revolution: Myths and Realities* (New York: Praeger, 1962), p. 59.

14. *Birmingham News*, Jan. 5, 1961, p. 1.

15. "Yankee Si, Castro No!" ibid., Jan. 4, 1961, p. 14. The "temptation" fed on confidence that "a couple of battalions of Marines" would so overpower Castro's "jerry-built forces" that "Fidel's men would be neatly picked off through stealth and in such a manner that the city would suffer no more than a few bullet nicks here and there, and the rumpots would hardly have been disturbed." See "Castro's Weird Defense," ibid., Jan. 6, 1961, p. 4.

16. Ace Lambert, "Resume Relations and Annex Cuba," letter, *Houston Chronicle*, Jan. 12, 1961, sec. 2, p. 4.

17. "Castro's Tactics," editorial, *Dallas Morning News*, Jan. 21, 1961, sec. 4, p. 2.

18. William B. Ruggles, "Reds' Toehold in the Caribbean," a review of *Red Star Over Cuba* by Nathaniel Weyl, in *Dallas Morning News*, Jan. 19, 1961, sec. 4, p. 2.

19. Paterson, "Fixation with Cuba," p. 126.

20. David Binder, "Intervention? We've Done It 90 Times in 164 Years," *Detroit Free Press*, Oct. 23, 1962, p. 8-D. The same author tallied 160 instances of U.S. military intervention throughout the world during this period.
21. Beschloss, *The Crisis Years*, p. 102.
22. Stephen G. Rabe, *Eisenhower and Latin America: The Foreign Policy of Anticommunism* (Chapel Hill: University of North Carolina, 1988), p. 129.
23. Beschloss, *The Crisis Years*, pp. 135–137, makes a strong circumstantial case that Richard Nixon gave the approval.
24. Rabe, *Eisenhower and Latin America*, p. 168.
25. John Lewis Gaddis, *Strategies of Containment: A Critical Appraisal of Postwar American National Security Policy* (New York: Oxford University Press, 1982), p. 159, citing a letter from President Eisenhower to Lewis Douglas, Mar. 29, 1955, Eisenhower Papers, Whitman File: Dwight D. Eisenhower Diary, Box 6, "Mar. 55 (1)."
26. See, for example, Rabe, *Eisenhower and Latin America*, pp. 172–173.
27. Dwight D. Eisenhower, *The White House Years: Waging Peace, 1956–1961* (Garden City, N.Y.: Doubleday, 1965), p. 612.
28. Clark M. Clifford, "Memorandum on Conference Between President Eisenhower and President-elect Kennedy and Their Chief Advisers on January 19, 1961," Jan. 24, 1961, p. 5, Box 29A, President's Office Files, John F. Kennedy Library, Boston [hereafter JFKL].
29. Beschloss, *The Crisis Years*, p. 121, citing Nestor T. Carbonell, *And The Russians Stayed: The Sovietization of Cuba* (New York: William Morrow, 1989), p. 190.
30. Beschloss, *The Crisis Years*, pp. 144–145.
31. "Notes by General Eisenhower of April 22 Meeting with President Kennedy. Failure of Bay of Pigs Operation," Augusta-Walter Reed Series, Cuba (2), Box 1, Post-Presidential Papers, 1961–1969, p. 3, reprinted in *Foreign Relations of the United States 1961–1963*, vols. 10–12, microfiche supplement, document 258.
32. Beschloss, *The Crisis Years*, pp. 145–146, citing Nixon in *Reader's Digest*, November 1961; Richard Nixon, *RN: The Memoirs of Richard Nixon* (New York: Grosset & Dunlap, 1978), pp. 232–236; and *NYT*, Apr. 21, 1961.
33. *NYT*, Feb. 12, 1962, p. 20.
34. Beschloss, *The Crisis Years*, p. 129.
35. Paul B. Fay, Jr., *The Pleasure of His Company* (New York: Harper, 1966), p. 188.
36. Arthur M. Schlesinger, Jr., *Robert Kennedy and His Times* (Boston:

Houghton Mifflin, 1978), pp. 453–454, citing an interview by the author with Tom Wicker, July 8, 1975.

37. "Special Section: Cuba: The Consequences," *Newsweek*, May 1, 1961, p. 23.

38. George H. Gallup, *The Gallup Poll: Public Opinion 1935–1971*, vol. 3, 1959–1971 (New York: Random House, 1972), p. 1721, citing Gallup poll, survey #643-A Q#6C.

39. Ibid., p. 1717, citing Gallup poll, survey #643-A Q#7.

40. Ibid., pp. 1786–1787, citing Gallup poll, survey #663-K Q#20, results on p. 1787.

41. "The Right to Intervene," *Time*, May 19, 1961, p. 20.

42. Marc Scott Zicree, *The Twilight Zone Companion*, 2d ed. (Los Angeles: Silman-James, 1982), p. 258; italics added.

43. Ibid., p. 258.

44. Memorandum of Conversation, Vienna Meeting Between the President and Chairman Khrushchev, June 3, 1961, 3 p.m., p. 6, Box 126, President's Office Files, JFKL.

45. Ibid., 12:45 p.m., p. 5.

46. Ibid., p. 6.

47. Ibid., p. 7.

48. Ibid., 3 p.m., p. 2.

49. Ibid., 12:45 p.m., p. 3.

50. Ibid., 3 p.m., p. 3.

51. Ibid.

52. Ibid., p. 4.

53. Ibid., June 4, 1961, 10:15 a.m., p. 3.

54. Ibid., June 3, 1961, 3 p.m., p. 7.

55. Ibid., p. 8.

56. Ibid., p. 7.

57. Ibid., p. 10.

58. Ibid.

59. Ibid., p. 12.

60. Ibid., p. 3.

61. Ibid., 12:45 p.m., p. 5.

62. Ibid., June 3, 1961, 3 p.m., p. 10.

63. Ibid., p. 11.

64. Vladislav Zubok, "Working Paper #6: Khrushchev and the Berlin Crisis (1958–62)," Cold War International History Project (http://cwihp.si.edu), citing his interview with Khrushchev's interpreter, Oleg Troyanovsky, March 23, 1993.

65. Memorandum of Conversation, Vienna Meeting Between the Presi-

dent and Chairman Khrushchev, June 4, 1961, 10:15 a.m., p. 13, Box 126, President's Office Files, JFKL.

66. Ibid., p. 14.

67. Zubok and Pleshakov, *Inside the Kremlin's Cold War*, p. 247.

68. Memorandum of Conversation, Vienna Meeting Between the President and Chairman Khrushchev, June 4, 1961, 3:15 p.m., p. 3, Box 126, President's Office Files, JFKL.

69. Beschloss, *The Crisis Years*, p. 234.

70. Edwin O. Guthman and Jeffrey Shulman, eds., *Robert Kennedy: In His Own Words: The Unpublished Recollections of the Kennedy Years* (Toronto: Bantham, 1988), p. 28.

71. Beschloss, *The Crisis Years*, p. 224, citing author's interview with Rusk. See also Dean Rusk, as told to Richard Rusk, *As I Saw It*, ed. Daniel S. Papp (New York: W. W. Norton, 1990), p. 221.

72. Nikita S. Khrushchev, *Khrushchev Remembers: The Last Testament* (Boston: Little, Brown, 1974), p. 499.

73. Beschloss, *The Crisis Years*, p. 224. See also James Reston's accounts in *NYT*, June 5, 1961, p. 1, and Nov. 15, 1964, sec. 6, p. 126.

74. Newhouse, *War and Peace in the Nuclear Age*, p. 150, citing a conversation with Arkady Schevchenko, Nov. 11, 1986.

75. Kenneth Crawford, "The Test of Nerves," *Newsweek*, July 10, 1961, p. 19, and "The Berlin Switch," *Newsweek*, Sept. 25, 1961, p. 38.

76. "Taking the Initiative," *Time*, Aug. 4, 1961, pp. 9–10.

77. Mrs. Niles Chapman, Seattle, Washington, letter to *Time*, July 21, 1961, p. 4.

78. McGeorge Bundy, *Danger and Survival: Choices About The Bomb in the First Fifty Years* (New York: Random House, 1988), p. 368.

79. Beschloss, *The Crisis Years*, pp. 279–280.

80. Ibid., p. 280.

81. Ibid.

82. Kenneth P. O'Donnell and David F. Powers, with Joe McCarthy, *"Johnny, We Hardly Knew Ye": Memories of John Fitzgerald Kennedy* (Boston: Little, Brown, 1970), p. 303.

83. Khrushchev's remarks at the Conference of first secretaries of Central Committees of Communist and workers parties of socialist countries for the exchange of views on the questions related to preparation and conclusion of German peace treaty, August 3–5, 1961, second session, August 4, in "Soviet Foreign Policy During the Cold War: A Documentary Sampler," *Cold War International History Project Bulletin*, no. 3 (Fall 1993), pp. 60, 61.

84. Newhouse, *War and Peace in the Nuclear Age*, p. 160, citing WGBH interview with Valentin Falin, Tape #89, Side A, pp. 1–2.
85. Beschloss, *The Crisis Years*, p. 334.
86. Ibid., citing an interview with Valentin Falin by WGBH Television.
87. William Kaufmann, ed., *Military Policy and National Security* (Princeton: Princeton University Press, 1956), p. 252.
88. Ibid., p. 119.
89. Ibid., p. 118.
90. At a conference on the missile crisis in Havana in 1992, Sergei Khrushchev recalled, "At one point [in 1961] Khrushchev said that we built missiles like sausages. I said then, 'How can you say that, since we only have two or three?' He said, 'The important thing is to make the Americans believe that. And that way we prevent an attack.' And on these grounds our entire policy was based. We threatened with missiles we didn't have. . . . But it happened that in 1962 the United States discovered the real balance of forces in terms of missiles." See James G. Blight, Bruce J. Allyn, and David A. Welch, with the assistance of David Lewis, *Cuba on the Brink: Castro, the Missile Crisis, and the Soviet Collapse* (New York: Pantheon, 1993), p. 130.
91. Roger Hilsman, *To Move a Nation: The Politics of Foreign Policy in the Administration of John F. Kennedy* (New York: Doubleday, 1967), p. 163.
92. Hugh Sidey, *John F. Kennedy, President* (New York: Atheneum, 1963), p. 266.
93. Peter Wyden, *Wall: The Inside Story of Divided Berlin* (New York: Simon and Schuster, 1989), p. 258.
94. Viktor Adamsky and Yuri Smirnov, "Moscow's Biggest Bomb: The 50-Megaton Test of October 1961," *Cold War International History Project Bulletin*, no. 4 (Fall 1994), pp. 3, 19, 20.
95. Stewart Alsop, "Kennedy's Grand Strategy," *Saturday Evening Post*, Mar. 31, 1962, p. 14.
96. Bundy, *Danger and Survival*, p. 418, citing *Pravda*, May 20, 1962, reported in *Current Digest of the Soviet Press*, June 13, 1962, p. 7.
97. Ibid., pp. 418–419.
98. U.S. Senate, *Alleged Assassination Plots Involving Foreign Leaders*, p. 141.
99. Former Defense Secretary McNamara stated in 1989, "I can state unequivocally that we had *absolutely no intention* of invading Cuba," only routine contingency plans, in Bruce J. Allyn, James G. Blight, and David A. Welch, eds., *Back to the Brink: Proceedings of the Moscow Conference on the Cuban Missile Crisis, January 27–28, 1989* (Cambridge, Mass.: Center for Science and International Affairs, Harvard Univer-

sity, Occasional Paper No. 9, 1992), p. 9 (emphasis in original). Blight, Allyn, and Welch, *Cuba on the Brink*, p. 423, n. 83, concur. Scholars who find a more serious U.S. threat to Cuba include Thomas G. Paterson, "Fixation with Cuba," pp. 23–55, and James G. Hershberg, "Before 'The Missiles of October': Did Kennedy Plan a Military Strike Against Cuba?" *Diplomatic History* 14, no. 12 (Spring 1990), pp. 163–199.

100. Khrushchev, *Khrushchev Remembers*, p. 493.

101. Zubok and Pleshakov, *Inside the Kremlin's Cold War*, p. 261.

102. Aleksandr Fursenko and Timothy Naftali, *"One Hell of a Gamble": Khrushchev, Castro, and Kennedy, 1958–1964* (New York: W. W. Norton, 1997), p. 180.

103. Beschloss, *The Crisis Years*, p. 387.

104. Zubok and Pleshakov, *Inside the Kremlin's Cold War*, p. 261.

105. Fursenko and Naftali, *"One Hell of a Gamble,"* p. 191.

106. Ibid., p. 181.

107. Khrushchev, *Khrushchev Remembers*, p. 494.

108. Blight, Allyn, and Welch, *Cuba on the Brink*, pp. 59–60.

109. Ibid., p. 60.

110. Fursenko and Naftali, *"One Hell of a Gamble,"* p. 198.

111. James G. Blight and David A. Welch, *On the Brink: Americans and Soviets Reexamine the Cuban Missile Crisis* (New York: Hill and Wang, 1989), p. 241. General Gribkov rebuked a Soviet general in Cuba who had mocked the troops' winter outfits, saying, "Try to think like an adult. Remember the secrecy of this operation. It's called ANADYR for a reason. We could have given away the game if we had put any tropical clothing in your kits." See General Anatoli I. Gribkov and General William Y. Smith, *Operation ANADYR: U.S. and Soviet Generals Recount the Cuban Missile Crisis*, ed. Alfred Friendly, Jr. (Chicago: edition q, 1994), p. 15.

112. James Reston, "United States and Cuba: The Moral Question—I," *NYT*, Apr. 12, 1961, p. 40.

113. James Reston, "Will Khrushchev Overplay His Hand?" *NYT*, Apr. 19, 1961, p. 38.

4. "We Just Had to Get Them Out of There"

1. *Current Public Attitudes Toward President Kennedy's Handling of Foreign Affairs*, Nov. 2, 1961, p. 2, Folder: "Current Public Concerns About U.S. Foreign Policy 1961," Special Reports on Public Attitudes To-

ward Foreign Policy, 1943–1965, Box 1, Office of Public Opinion Studies 1943–1965 (Schuyler Foster papers), RG 59, General Records of the Department of State, National Archives.

2. David Lawrence, "Retreat," *U.S. News*, Sept. 24, 1962, p. 136; "The Durable Doctrine," *Time*, Sept. 21, 1962, pp. 21, 27; Claire Booth Luce, "Cuba—and the Unfaced truth: Our Global Double Bind," *Life*, Oct. 5, 1962, pp. 53–56; the quotation is on pp. 55–56; Arthur Krock, "A New Name for the Monroe Doctrine," *NYT*, Sept. 18, 1962, p. 38.

3. "The Reluctant Power," *Wall Street Journal*, Sept. 12, 1962, p. 18.

4. "No Time for Double Talk—Is the Monroe Doctrine Dead?" *San Diego Union*, Sept. 7, 1962, p. b-2; *Monthly Survey of American Opinion on International Affairs* No. 256, September 6, 1962, pp. 10–11, folder: "Monthly Survey—1962," Box 13, Office of Public Opinion Studies, 1943–1965 (Schuyler Foster papers), RG 59, General Records of the Department of State, National Archives.

5. "What Must Cuba and Russia Do to Wake Kennedy Up?" *Alliance (Nebr.) Daily Times-Herald*, Sept. 8, 1962, p. 7.

6. William S. White, "Castro's Red Boast Leaves No Alibis," *Atlanta Constitution*, Dec. 8, 1961, p. 4; Raymond Moley, "A Living Doctrine," *Newsweek*, June 26, 1961, p. 100; *NYT*, Sept. 17, 1962, p. 1; "The Praise of Weakness," *Wall Street Journal*, Sept. 19, 1962, p. 8.

7. "Capehart: U.S. Should Act, Stop 'Examining' Cuba," *U.S. News & World Report*, Sept. 10, 1962, p. 45; Louise Fitzsimons, *The Kennedy Doctrine* (New York: Random House, 1972), p. 129, cites Capehart's speech of Aug. 28, 1962, at a Republican meeting. See also *Congressional Record*, Sen. Capehart of Indiana, speaking on "Soviet Exports to Cuba," 87th Cong., 2d sess., vol. 108, pt. 13, Aug. 29, 1962, p. 18063.

8. Elie Abel, *The Missile Crisis* (Philadelphia: J.B. Lippincott, 1966), p. 17. David Detzer, *The Brink: Cuban Missile Crisis, 1962* (New York: Thomas Y. Crowell, 1979), p. 65, tallies twenty-five warnings by Keating in seven weeks.

9. Dino A. Brugioni, *Eyeball to Eyeball: The Inside Story of the Cuban Missile Crisis* (New York: Random House, 1990), p. 113.

10. Ibid.; *Congressional Record*, Rep. Fountain of North Carolina, speaking on "The Military Threat of Cuba to the United States," 87th Cong., 2d sess., vol. 108, pt. 15, Sept. 26, 1962, p. 20898.

11. Ibid., Sen. Miller of Iowa, speaking on "A War Materiel Blockade of Cuba?" pt. 14, Sept. 6, 1962, p. 18754, and Sen. Winston L. Prouty of Vermont, speaking on "U.S. Policy with Respect to Cuba," pt. 15, Sept. 20, 1962, p. 20030.

12. Ibid., Sen. Dirksen of Illinois, speaking on "Protection of Hemisphere

from European and Asiatic Aggression," pt. 14, Sept. 11, 1962, p. 19004.

13. *NYT*, Sept. 15, 1962, pp. 1, 7; *Congressional Record*, Sen. Thurmond of South Carolina, speaking on "Foreign Policy Toward Communist Cuba," 87th Cong., 2d sess., vol. 108, pt. 14, Sept. 6, 1962, pp. 18774–18775; and Sen. Javits of New York, speaking on "The President's Authority to Call Up Reserves—Cuba and Berlin," Sept. 7, 1962, p. 18864. See also *Congressional Record*, Sen. Javits of New York, speaking on "The Cuban Situation," Sept. 6, 1962, p. 18713.

14. Ibid., Sen. Pearson of Kansas, speaking on "Buildup in Cuba," speech entitled, "Will Cuba Be Another 'Wall of Shame'?" Sept. 6, 1962, p. 18731, and Sen. Lausche of Ohio, speaking on "Presidential Authority to Mobilize Reservists," Sept. 11, 1962, p. 18987.

15. *Hartford Courant*, Sept. 12, 1962, p. 17.

16. "A Hostile Presence Close to Home," *Newsweek*, Sept. 17, 1962, p. 19; *Congressional Record*, Sen. Thurmond of South Carolina, speaking on "Foreign Policy Toward Communist Cuba," 87th Cong., 2 sess., vol. 108, pt. 14, Sept. 6, 1962, pp. 18775–18776.

17. Ibid., Sen. Tower of Texas, speaking on "Protection of Hemisphere from European and Asiatic Aggression," Sept. 11, 1962, p. 19003, and Sen. Keating of New York, speaking on "U.S. Policy with Respect to Cuba," pt. 15, Sept. 20, 1962, p. 20055.

18. *Boston Herald Traveler*, Oct. 16, 1962, p. 8.

19. *Congressional Record*, Rep. Selden of Alabama, speaking on "Cuba," 87th Cong., 2d sess., vol. 108, pt. 14, Sept. 6, 1962, pp. 18674–18675, Sen. Young speaking on "Castro," pt. 17, Oct. 8, 1962, pp. 22778–22780; Sen. Joseph S. Clark of Pennsylvania, speaking on "U.S. Policy with Respect to Cuba," pt. 15, Sept. 20, 1962, p. 20000; Rep. Pelly of Washington, speaking on "The President and Cuba," pt. 14, Sept. 4, 1962, p. 18431; Rep. Celler of New York, speaking on "Expressing the Determination of the United States with Respect to the Situation in Cuba," pt. 15, Sept. 26, 1962, p. 20863; Sen. Engle of California, speaking on "Soviet Aid to Cuba," pt. 14, Sept. 5, 1962, p. 18652; and Sen. Humphrey of Minnesota, speaking on "A Forceful U.S. Response to Soviet Provocation in Cuba," pt. 15, Sept. 20, 1962, p. 19552.

20. Ibid., Rep. Selden of Alabama, speaking on "Cuba," pt. 14, Sept. 6, 1962, p. 18675.

21. Ibid., Sen. Mansfield of Montana, speaking on "The Situation in Cuba," Sept. 7, 1962, p. 18868; and Sen. Morse of Oregon, speaking on "Cuba," pt. 17, Oct. 9, 1962, p. 22872.

22. Mrs. C. V. Lynn, Minneapolis and M. H. Bell, New York City, letters to *Time*, Sept. 21, 1962, p. 12.

23. Angus L. MacLean, Jr., San Francisco, letter to *Time*, Oct. 5, 1962, pp. 9–10.

24. Ellsworth Culver, Palo Alto, California, letter to *Time*, Sept. 28, 1962, p. 7.

25. *Congressional Record*, Sen. Dodd of Connecticut, speaking on "The Future of Latin America and the Problem of the Soviet Quisling Regime in Cuba," 87th Cong., 2d sess., vol. 108, pt. 14, Sept. 10, 1962, p. 18957.

26. Ibid., Sen. Keating of New York, speaking on "Cuba," pt. 17, Oct. 9, 1962, p. 22889. Keating cited columnist Joseph Alsop for comments by the California resident.

27. Ibid., Sen. Wiley of Wisconsin, speaking on "Peace with Justice," pt. 14, Sept. 7, 1962, pp. 18824–18825.

28. Ibid.; Sen. Dodd of Connecticut, speaking on "The Future of Latin America and the Problem of the Soviet Quisling Regime in Cuba," Sept. 10, 1962, p. 18960; and Sen. Keating of New York, speaking on "Buildup in Cuba," Sept. 6, 1962, p. 18727.

29. Blight, Allyn, and Welch, *Cuba on the Brink*, p. 446, n. 182.

30. Brugioni, *Eyeball to Eyeball*, p. 113.

31. "'Cuba' Issue Most Cited by Congressmen, Editors," *Congressional Quarterly Weekly Report*, vol. XX, no. 42, Week Ending Oct. 19, 1962, p. 1933; *NYT*, Oct. 17, 1962, pp. 1, 24; quotation is on p. 24.

32. Memorandum of Conversation Between President Kennedy and Alexei Adzhubei, Jan. 30, 1962, p. 2, Box 190, Countries Series, National Security Files, JFKL.

33. *Chicago Tribune*, Oct. 22, 1962, part 1, p. 20.

34. Montague Kern, Patricia W. Levering, and Ralph B. Levering, *The Kennedy Crises: The Press, the Presidency, and Foreign Policy* (Chapel Hill: University of North Carolina Press, 1988), p. 100.

35. "A Hostile Presence Close to Home," *Newsweek*, Sept. 17, 1962, p. 20.

36. "The Praise of Weakness," *Wall Street Journal*, Sept. 19, 1962, p. 18.

37. *Congressional Record*, Sen. Dodd of Connecticut, speaking on "The Future of Latin America and the Problem of the Soviet Quisling Regime in Cuba," 87th Cong., 2d sess., vol. 108, pt. 14, Sept. 10, 1962, p. 18962; and Sen. Miller of Iowa, speaking on "Presidential Authority to Mobilize Reservists," Sept. 11, 1962, p. 18988.

38. *NYT*, Oct. 2, 1961, p. 19; *NYT*, Mar. 17, 1962, pp. 1, 2; *NYT*, July 17, 1962, p. 1.

39. *Atlanta Constitution*, Sept. 5, 1961, p. 1.

40. *NYT*, Aug. 6, 1962, p. 1; *NYT*, Oct. 27, 1962, p. 4; *Washington Post*, Oct. 25, 1962, A2. On the likely impact of the Soviet buildup in Cuba, see *NYT*, Oct. 27, 1962, p. A1.

41. *Congressional Record*, Sen. Keating of New York, speaking on "Soviet Activities in Cuba," 87th Cong., 2d sess., vol. 108, pt. 14, Aug. 31, 1962, p. 18360; and Sen. Cannon of Nevada, speaking on "The Military Space Program," pt. 17, Oct. 5, 1962, vol. 108, p. 22519.

42. Ibid., "S.J. Res. 230," pt. 15, Sept. 20, 1962, p. 20058, and Sept. 26, 1962, p. 20910.

43. Ibid., Sen. Prouty of Vermont, speaking on "U.S. Policy with Respect to Cuba," speech entitled "No Principle to Light Our Way," Sept. 20, 1962, p. 20030.

44. Ibid., Sen. Bennett of Utah, speaking on "Needed: A Policy of Firmness and Action Toward Cuba," Sept. 20, 1962, p. 20002.

45. Schlesinger, *Robert Kennedy and His Times*, p. 505.

46. David L. Larson, ed., *The "Cuban Crisis" of 1962: Selected Documents and Chronology* (Boston: Houghton Mifflin, 1963), p. 3.

47. *Public Papers of the Presidents of the United States*, John F. Kennedy, 1962 (Washington, D.C.: U.S. Government Printing Office, 1963), pp. 674–675.

48. Beschloss, *The Crisis Years*, p. 420. Sorensen later claimed that President Kennedy's warnings to the Soviets over Cuba in September 1962 actually sought to avoid provocation: "One reason the line was drawn at zero [offensive missiles] was because we simply thought the Soviets weren't going to deploy any there anyway." See James G. Blight and David Welch, *On the Brink: Americans and Soviets Reexamine the Cuban Missile Crisis*, 2d ed. (New York: Noonday, 1990), p. 43.

49. Ernest R. May and Philip D. Zelikow, eds., *The Kennedy Tapes: Inside the White House During the Cuban Missile Crisis* (Cambridge, Mass.: Belknap Press of Harvard University Press, 1997), p. 92.

50. The Executive Committee of the National Security Council was formally constituted only on October 22, nearly a week after it had begun meeting. The term "Ex Comm," like "hawks" and "doves," became commonplace only after the crisis, never during the actual deliberations of Kennedy's advisers. See Sorensen, *Kennedy*, p. 679. Robert F. Kennedy, *Thirteen Days: A Memoir of the Cuban Missile Crisis* (New York: W. W. Norton, 1969), p. 30, lists beside the president and himself the following regular participants: "Secretary of State Dean Rusk; Secretary of Defense Robert McNamara; Director of the Central Intelligence Agency John McCone; Secretary of the Treasury Douglas Dillon; President Kennedy's adviser on national-security affairs,

McGeorge Bundy; Presidential Counsel Ted Sorensen; Under Secretary of State George Ball; Deputy Under Secretary of State U. Alexis Johnson; General Maxwell Taylor, Chairman of the Joint Chiefs of Staff; Edward Martin, Assistant Secretary of State for Latin America; originally, Chip Bohlen, who, after the first day, left to become ambassador to France and was succeeded by Llewellyn Thompson as the adviser on Russian affairs; Roswell Gilpatric, Deputy Secretary of Defense; Paul Nitze, Assistant Secretary of Defense; and, intermittently at various meetings, vice-President Lyndon B. Johnson; Adlai Stevenson, Ambassador to the United Nations; Ken O'Donnell, Special Assistant to the President; and Don Wilson, who was Deputy Director of the United States Information Agency."

51. Sorensen, *Kennedy*, p. 679.
52. Kennedy, *Thirteen Days*, p. 46.
53. Ball, *The Past Has Another Pattern*, p. 290.
54. Paul H. Nitze with Ann M. Smith and Steven L. Rearden, *From Hiroshima to Glasnost: At the Center of Decision, a Memoir* (New York: Grove Weidenfeld, 1989), p. 226.
55. McGeorge Bundy, *Danger and Survival: Choices About the Bomb in the First Fifty Years* (New York: Random House, 1988), p. 400.
56. Kennedy, *Thirteen Days*, p. 116.
57. Rusk, *As I Saw It*, p. 231.
58. Kennedy, *Thirteen Days*, pp. 116-117.
59. U. Alexis Johnson, *The Right Hand of Power* (Englewood Cliffs, N.J.: Prentice-Hall, 1984), pp. 384-386. Johnson coordinated his meticulous diplomatic scenarios with plans by Assistant Secretary of Defense Paul Nitze to mobilize the armed forces.
60. Maxwell D. Taylor, *Swords and Plowshares* (New York: W. W. Norton, 1972), p. 268.
61. Kennedy, *Thirteen Days*, p. 38.
62. Abel, *The Missile Crisis*, p. 50, citing particularly the recollections of Dean Rusk and of Assistant Secretary of Defense Roswell Gilpatric.
63. "Radio and Television Report to the American People on the Soviet Arms Buildup in Cuba," October 22, 1962, *Public Papers of the Presidents of the United States*, John F. Kennedy, 1962, p. 807.
64. Kennedy, *Thirteen Days*, p. 45; May and Zelikow, *The Kennedy Tapes*, p. 342.
65. Bundy, *Danger and Survival*, pp. 410-411, incisively distills the case for action as meeting both domestic and international exigencies.
66. May and Zelikow, eds., *The Kennedy Tapes*, pp. 90, 180, 182.

67. Raymond Garthoff, Special Assistant for Soviet Bloc, of Politico-Military Affairs, "The Military Significance of the Soviet Missile Bases in Cuba," Oct. 27, 1962, pp. 1, 2, reprinted in *Foreign Relations of the United States 1961–1963*, vols. 10–12, microfiche supplement, document no. 434.

68. Blight and Welch, *On the Brink*, p. 261.

69. May and Zelikow, *The Kennedy Tapes*, pp. 89, 90.

70. Ibid., pp. 92, 182.

71. Ibid., p. 236.

72. Ibid., pp. 88, 105, 106.

73. Ibid., p. 107.

74. Newhouse, *War and Peace in the Nuclear Age*, p. 170, citing conversation with Arkady Shevchenko, Nov. 11, 1986.

75. Douglas Dillon, "Memorandum for the President," Oct. 17, 1962, p. 1, reprinted in Laurence Chang and Peter Kornbluh, eds., *The Cuban Missile Crisis, 1962: A National Security Archive Documents Reader* (New York: New Press, 1992), p. 126.

76. Beschloss, *The Crisis Years*, p. 459; Dean Acheson, "Dean Acheson's Version of Robert Kennedy's Version of the Cuban Missile Affair," *Esquire* (February 1969), pp. 76–77; Douglas Brinkley, *Dean Acheson: The Cold War Years, 1953–71* (New Haven: Yale University Press, 1992), pp. 154–164, 172–174.

77. Bernstein, "Reconsidering the Missile Crisis," p. 58; see also p. 109, n. 16.

78. Beschloss, *The Crisis Years*, p. 104.

79. Bruggioni, *Eyeball to Eyeball*, p. 346; Richard Reeves, *President Kennedy: Profile of Power* (New York: Simon and Schuster, 1993), pp. 391–392, citing Eisenhower's memo of Oct. 22, 1962, in Post-presidential Papers, Box 10, Dwight D. Eisenhower Library.

80. CIA Special National Intelligence Estimate, "Major Consequences of Certain U.S. Courses of Action on Cuba," Oct. 20, 1962, p. 5, reprinted in Chang and Kornbluh, eds., *The Cuban Missile Crisis, 1962*, p. 144.

81. "Major Consequences of Certain U.S. Courses of Action on Cuba," p. 6, in ibid., p. 145.

82. Theodore Sorensen, "Summary of Objections to Airstrike Option and Advantages of Blockade Option," Oct. 20, 1962, ibid., p. 143.

83. Theodore C. Sorensen, "Conversation with Ambassador Dobrynin—#2," Sept. 6, 1962, p. 1, Box 185A, Countries Series, National Security Files, JFKL.

84. Ibid., pp. 1, 2.

85. Adlai Stevenson to Dean Rusk, Sept. 7, 1962, Box 185A, Countries Series, National Security Files, JFKL.
86. Bruce J. Allyn, James G. Blight, and David A. Welch, eds., *Back to the Brink: Proceedings of the Moscow Conference on the Cuban Missile Crisis, January 27–28, 1989* (Lanham, Md.: University Press of America, 1992), p. 146. During the Ex Comm meetings, the subject of Dobrynin's good faith briefly arose. Bundy expressed doubts, but Robert Kennedy, despite his anger toward the Russians, cleared Dobrynin, saying, "He didn't know." See May and Zelikow, *The Kennedy Tapes*, p. 105.
87. "Memorandum of Conversation Between President Kennedy and Foreign Minister Gromyko," Oct. 18, 1962, Part II, Subject—Cuba, pp. 2, 4–5, Box 187, Countries Series, National Security Files, JFKL.
88. Ibid., p. 5.
89. Robert Lovett, interviewed by Dorothy Fosdick, Nov. 19, 1964, part 2, pp. 50–51, Oral History Collection, JFKL.
90. "Memorandum of Conversation Between Secretary Rusk and Foreign Minister Gromyko on 'Germany and Berlin,'" Oct. 18, 1962, p. 7, Box 186A, Countries Series, National Security Files, JFKL.
91. Department of State telegram to the U.S. Ambassador to Moscow (Foy Kohler), Oct. 17, 1962, Box 187, Countries Series, National Security Files, JFKL.
92. Ball, *The Past Has Another Pattern*, p. 292; Paul H. Nitze with Ann M. Smith and Steven L. Rearden, *From Hiroshima to Glasnost: At the Center of Decision, A Memoir* (New York: Grove Weidenfeld, 1989), p. 224.
93. May and Zelikow, *The Kennedy Tapes*, p. 65.
94. Ibid., p. 114.
95. Ibid., pp. 202–203. The quotations are from Theodore C. Sorensen, interview by Carl Kaysen, Apr. 6, 1964, pp. 60, 64, Oral History Collection, JFKL.
96. Douglas Dillon to Theodore C. Sorensen, Oct. 18, 1962, Box 48, Theodore Sorensen Papers, JFKL.
97. May and Zelikow, *The Kennedy Tapes*, p. 127.
98. Ibid., p. 157.
99. Ibid., p. 172.
100. Adlai Stevenson to President Kennedy, Oct. 17, 1962, in Walter Johnson, ed., *The Papers of Adlai E. Stevenson*, 8 vols. (Boston: Little, Brown, 1972–1979), VIII, pp. 299–301; quotations are on p. 300.
101. Abel, p. 60.

5. The Decision to Blockade

1. *NYT*, Oct. 19, 1960, p. 1.
2. *NYT*, Jan. 29, 1962, p. 1; *NYT*, Feb. 1, 1962, p. 2; "Cuba Embargo Statement and Text," *NYT*, Feb. 4, 1962, p. 22.
3. *NYT*, Oct. 5, 1962, p. 1.
4. "The Embargo on Castro," editorial, *NYT*, Oct. 5, 1962, p. 32.
5. Schlesinger, *Robert Kennedy and His Times*, p. 471, citing Robert Kennedy to Kenneth O'Donnell for the President, Apr. 19, 1961.
6. Ibid.
7. Beschloss, *The Crisis Years*, p. 147.
8. Stephen G. Rabe, *The Most Dangerous Area in the World: John F. Kennedy Confronts Communist Revolution in Latin America* (Chapel Hill: University of North Carolina Press, 1999), p. 73.
9. Abel, *The Missile Crisis*, p. 102.
10. Elizabeth Cohn, "President Kennedy's Decision to Impose a Blockade in the Cuban Missile Crisis: Building Consensus in the ExComm After the Decision," in Nathan, ed., *The Cuban Missile Crisis Revisited*, pp. 221–235; quotations are on pp. 221, 226–227.
11. "Castro Apparently to Get No Aid From Increased Canadian Trade," editorial, *Houston Chronicle*, Jan. 9, 1961, sec. 3, p. 4.
12. Arthur Krock, "But a Naval Patrol Is Not 'Invasion,'" *NYT*, Aug. 30, 1962, p. 28; "What Should the Monroe Doctrine Mean? Blockade," *Life*, Sept. 21, 1962, p. 4; "The Soviets' Immunity," *Wall Street Journal*, Sept. 18, 1962, p. 12; also see "Policy, Politics and People," *Wall Street Journal*, Sept. 28, 1962, p. 16.
13. See, for example, Rep. Arends of Illinois, speaking on "Expressing the Determination of the United States with Respect to the Situation in Cuba," *Congressional Record*, 87th Cong., 2d sess., vol. 108, pt. 15, Sept. 26, 1962, pp. 20868–20870. Leslie Arends, the House Republican whip, celebrated House passage of a resolution backing presidential action against Cuba by advocating enforcement of the Monroe Doctrine and demanding that the Russians leave Cuba, though like most of his colleagues he declined to specify how to accomplish this.
14. Rep. Derounian of New York, speaking on "Blockade of Military Shipments to and from Cuba," *Congressional Record*, pt. 14, Sept. 11, 1962, p. 19128.
15. See, for example, Sen. Pearson of Kansas, speaking on "Buildup in Cuba," *Congressional Record*, pt. 14, Sept. 6, 1962, pp. 18731–18732,

Notes for pages 117-120

and Sen. Miller of Iowa, speaking on "Proposed Presidential Authority to Employ Armed Forces," pt. 14, Sept. 7, 1962, p. 18879.

16. *NYT*, Sept. 9, 1962, p. 41; James Reston, "How About a Blockade on Nonsense?" *NYT*, Sept. 16, 1962, sec. 4, p. 10E. Thurmond sometimes favored an outright invasion of Cuba, as in a newsletter in late August, cited in *Congressional Quarterly Almanac*, vol. 18, 1962 (Washington, D.C.: Congressional Quarterly, 1963), p. 333.

17. Rep. Dole of Kansas, speaking on "Red Arms Buildup in Cuba Threatens U.S. Security," *Congressional Record*, 87th Cong., 2d sess., vol. 108, pt. 17, Oct. 6, 1962, pp. 22738–22739; Sen. Bush of Connecticut, speaking on "A Way to Stop the Buildup of a Communist Military Base in Cuba," pt. 17, Oct. 9, 1962, p. 22902.

18. Sen. Dodd of Connecticut, speaking on "The Future of Latin America and the Problem of the Soviet Quisling Regime in Cuba," ibid., pt. 14, Sept. 10, 1962, pp. 18960–18961; "The Cuba Debate," *Time*, Oct. 12, 1962, p. 23.

19. *NYT*, Sept. 17, 1962, p. 3; *NYT*, Sept. 19, 1962, pp. 1, 3.

20. Sen. Wiley of Wisconsin, speaking on "OAS Investigation of Red Arms Shipments to Cuba," *Congressional Record*, 87th Cong., 2d sess., vol. 108, pt. 14, Sept. 4, 1962, p. 18440; Rep. Hosmer of California, speaking on "Seven-Point Program and Joint Resolution to Prevent Communist Penetration in the Americas, Reapply Monroe Doctrine, and Contraband Red Arms and Munitions," pt. 14, Sept. 6, 1962, p. 18669.

21. Ibid., Sen. Stennis of Mississippi, speaking on "The Situation in Cuba," vol. 108, pt. 17, Oct. 9, 1962, p. 22967.

22. George H. Gallup, *The Gallup Poll: Public Opinion 1935–1971*, 3 vols. (Wilmington, Del.: Scholarly Resources, 1972), vol. III, p. 1787, Survey #663-K, conducted September 20 to 25, 1962.

23. Sen. Keating of New York, speaking on "Buildup in Cuba," *Congressional Record*, 87th Cong., 2d sess., vol. 108, pt. 14, Sept. 6, 1962, p. 18727, in which Keating responded to a friendly query by the like-minded Senator Smathers; Sen. Keating of New York, speaking on "A Policy for Cuba," pt. 16, Oct. 2, 1962, p. 21626; Rep. Van Zandt of Pennsylvania, speaking on "The Military Threat of Cuba to the United States," pt. 15, Sept. 26, 1962, p. 20899; Sen. Stennis, speaking on "The Growing Menace in Cuba," pt.14, Sept. 7, 1962, p. 18865.

24. Lou [sic] Harris to the President, memorandum on "The New Shape of This Campaign," Oct. 4, 1962, p. 2, Box 105, President's Office

239

Files, JFKL; "How U.S. Voters Feel About Cuba," *Newsweek*, Oct. 22, 1962, p. 21; "Two Big Issues," *Time*, Oct. 26, 1962, p. 23.

25. May and Zelikow, *The Kennedy Tapes*, p. 72.

26. Theodore C. Sorensen, *Decision-Making in the White House* (New York: Columbia University Press, 1963), p. 30. Sorensen here compressed a statement in "After Two Years—A Conversation with the President." December 17, 1962, *Public Papers of the Presidents* (Washington, D.C.: U.S. Government Printing Office, 1963), p. 889.

27. May and Zelikow, *The Kennedy Tapes*, pp. 100–101. Robert Kennedy unknowingly echoed a proposal by President Eisenhower's secretary of state, Christian Herter, to justify an invasion of Cuba. At a meeting of top advisers on January 3, 1961, Herter had proposed that "we should stage an 'attack' on Guantanamo," copying the technique Hitler had used in 1939 on the German-Polish border before he invaded Poland. See Stephen E. Ambrose, *Eisenhower: Soldier and President* (New York: Simon and Schuster, 1991), p. 533.

28. Kennedy, *Thirteen Days*, p. 9.

29. Others had earlier mentioned a blockade in passing. General Maxwell Taylor appears to have been the first to refer to a naval blockade, though as a follow-up to an air strike; McNamara later proposed "a declaration of open surveillance: a statement that we would immediately impose a blockade against offensive weapons entering Cuba in the future." See May and Zelikow, *The Kennedy Tapes*, pp. 58, 86.

30. Ibid., p. 115.

31. Ibid., pp. 143; Ball, *The Past Has Another Pattern*, p. 291.

32. Kennedy, *Thirteen Days*, p. 39; May and Zelikow, *The Kennedy Tapes*, p. 149.

33. *Foreign Relations of the United States 1961–1963*, vol. XI, *Cuban Missile Crisis and Aftermath* (Washington, D.C.: U.S. Government Printing Office, 1996), p. 119; Abel, *The Missile Crisis*, p. 81; see also Dillon's remarks in George Plimpton, ed., *American Journey: The Times of Robert Kennedy*, interviews by Jean Stein (New York: Harcourt Brace Jovanovich, 1970), p. 136. Alexis Johnson of the State Department offered a comparable verdict—"Bobby Kennedy's good sense and his moral character were perhaps decisive," in Johnson, *The Right Hand of Power*, p. 382.

34. Schlesinger, *Robert Kennedy and His Times*, p. 508.

35. Acheson, "Dean Acheson's Version of Robert Kennedy's Version of the Cuban Missile Affair," p. 16.

36. Theodore C. Sorensen, interviewed by Carl Kaysen, Apr. 6, 1964, pp. 51–52, Oral History Collection, JFKL.

37. May and Zelikow, *The Kennedy Tapes*, p. 138.

38. Bundy, *Danger and Survival*, p. 399.
39. Robert Lovett, interviewed by Dorothy Fosdick, Nov. 19, 1964, p. 51, Oral History Collection, JFKL.
40. May and Zelikow, *The Kennedy Tapes*, pp. 133–134.
41. Ibid., p. 97.
42. Ibid.
43. Ibid., p. 145, emended by Sheldon M. Stern.
44. May and Zelikow, *The Kennedy Tapes*, p. 175.
45. Ibid., p. 176.
46. Ibid., p. 178.
47. Ibid., pp. 222–223.
48. Ibid., p. 223.
49. Ibid., p. 213.
50. Letter from President Kennedy to Chairman Khrushchev, in U.S. Department of State, *Foreign Relations of the United States 1961–1963* (Washington, D.C.: U.S. Government Printing Office, 1996), vol. VI, *Kennedy–Khrushchev Exchanges*, p. 166.
51. *Buffalo Courier-Express*, Oct. 16, 1962, p. 1.
52. May and Zelikow, *The Kennedy Tapes*, p. 231.
53. I. F. Stone, "The Brink," *New York Review of Books* 6 (Apr. 14, 1966), p. 13.
54. John McCone, Memorandum for the file, "Conversation Between McCone and Former President Eisenhower on Cuban Developments," Oct. 17, 1962, in *Foreign Relations of the United States 1961–1963*, vols. 10–12, microfiche supplement, document no. 329; John McCone, "Memorandum of Discussion Between the President and McCone, October 21. Conclusions of McCone's discussion with Former President Eisenhower on Military Procedures to Follow in Cuba," Oct. 21, 1962, in *Foreign Relations of the United States 1961–1963*, vols. 10–12, microfiche supplement, document no. 350.
55. *San Francisco News-Call Bulletin*, Oct. 22, 1962, p. 1.
56. May and Zelikow, *The Kennedy Tapes*, pp. 258–262.
57. Sen. J. William Fulbright, speaking on "Some Reflections Upon Recent Events and Continuing Problems," *Congressional Record*, 87th Cong., 1 sess., vol. 107, pt. 9, June 29, 1961, p. 11704.
58. May and Zelikow, *The Kennedy Tapes*, p. 271; John McCone, Memorandum for the File, "Leadership Meeting on October 22nd at 5:00 p.m.," Oct. 24, 1962, in Mary S. McAuliffe, ed., *CIA Documents on the Cuban Missile Crisis 1962* (Washington, D.C.: Central Intelligence Agency, 1992), p. 278.
59. May and Zelikow, *The Kennedy Tapes*, pp. 271–272.

60. Brugioni, *Eyeball to Eyeball*, pp. 361–362. Brugioni's detailed notes of conversations with Lundahl during the crisis seem authoritative here, though May and Zelikow, eds., *The Kennedy Tapes*, p. 246, do not list Wiley among the senators at this meeting, nor is Wiley's participation featured on the taped portion of the conversation. But the exchange with Wiley, coming at the very end of the meeting, may well have gone unrecorded.

61. Special Gallup poll of 553 adults in 30 areas across the nation, Oct. 22, 1962, copy courtesy of the Gallup organization; Detzer, *The Brink*, p. 192, citing poll by Samuel Lubell.

62. *St. Louis Post-Dispatch*, Oct. 23, 1962, p. 1A; Ralph McGill, "N.Y. Hears the President," *Atlanta Constitution*, Oct. 23, 1962, p. 1.

63. *Denver Post*, Oct. 23, 1962, p. 12.

64. Charles D. Strong of Denver, letter to editor, "Courage on Cuba," in *Denver Post*, Oct. 27, 1962, p. 12.

65. *NYT*, Oct. 28, 1962, p. 4E; "Tar Heels Back Cuba Quarantine," *Raleigh News and Observer*, Oct. 23, 1962, p. 1; North Carolina's governor, Terry Sanford, and Ervin's junior colleague, Everett Jordan, added their own emphatic endorsements of Kennedy's actions, quoted in *Raleigh News and Observer*, Oct. 24, 1962, p. 1.

66. *NYT*, Oct. 28, 1962, p. 4E; "The Backdown," *Time*, Nov. 2, 1962, p. 16.

67. "New Belligerence Shows in Midwest," by Joseph Alsop, *Denver Post*, Oct. 23, 1962, p. 18, "based on two days of intensive door-to-door polling by Oliver Quayle of Louis Harris Associates."

68. *NYT*, Oct. 28, 1962, p. 4E; "Our Nuclear Credibility on Test," editorial, *Boston Herald Traveler*, Oct. 23, 1962, p. 22.

69. Marshall L. Gates, Succasunna, New Jersey, letter to the editor, *Newark Evening News*, Oct. 28, 1962, sec. 2, p. C3; *Denver Post*, Oct. 23, 1962, p. 12.

70. *Denver Post*, Oct. 24, 1962, p. 8; *NYT*, Oct. 24, 1962, p. 25; *NYT*, Oct. 28, 1962, p. 4E; *San Francisco News-Call Bulletin*, Oct. 24, 1962, p. 1; Detzer, *The Brink*, p. 192.

71. "Opposition to Blockade Voiced by Student Union," *Pittsburgh Post-Gazette*, Oct. 25, 1962, p. 7.

72. John Gerhard, Jersey City, New Jersey, letter to the editor, *Newark Evening News*, Oct. 28, 1962, sec. 2, p. C3.

73. See, for example, the editorial "A Soviet Pledge to Withdraw," *Philadelphia Inquirer*, Oct. 29, 1962, p. 16: "As The Inquirer has said repeatedly in the past, the situation in Cuba can be viewed in proper perspective only by studying it in relationship to the worldwide Communist struggle for power."

74. Mrs. H.W., Springfield, Pennsylvania, letter to the editor, ibid., Oct. 27, 1962, p. 8.
75. Mrs. Zelma Hoy, Adel, Iowa, letter to the editor, *Des Moines Register,* Oct. 25, 1962, p. 6; Howard V. Andrews, Titonka, Iowa, letter to the editor, *Des Moines Register,* Oct. 27, 1962, p. 6.
76. Sorensen, for example, comments in Blight and Welch, eds., *On the Brink,* 2d ed., p. 285, "But let us not forget that what we did in the first place was to bring the world closer to the brink of nuclear destruction than it has ever been. That is nothing to be proud of. And, for that reason, Bob McNamara is absolutely right that the first lesson of the Cuban missile crisis is the importance of avoiding crises in the first place."
77. Beschloss, *The Crisis Years,* p. 487, citing *Boston Herald,* Oct. 25, 1962.
78. *Hartford Courant,* Oct. 27, 1962, p. 11.
79. Franklin Clark Fry, D.D., chairman, Central Committee, World Council of Churches, letter to *Time,* Nov. 9, 1962, pp. 9–10.
80. "Hurray for Kennedy," editorial, *New York Daily News,* Oct. 23, 1962, p. 31; "The President's Solemn Call," editorial, *Philadelphia Inquirer,* Oct. 23, 1962, p. 12; "Kennedy Chose Between Dangers, Took the Course of Self-Defense," editorial, *Denver Post,* Oct. 23, 1962, p. 18; "A Course of Courage," editorial, *Raleigh News and Observer,* Oct. 23, 1962, p. 4; "A Tough Cuban Policy Too Long in Coming," editorial, *Detroit Free Press,* Oct. 23, 1962, p. 6-A; "At This Critical Hour," editorial, *Chattanooga Daily Times,* Oct. 23, 1962, p. 8; "'Quarantine' on Cuba," editorial, *NYT,* Oct. 23, 1962, p. 36; "Behind the Blockade," editorial, *Newark Evening News,* Oct. 23, 1962, p. 26; "Meeting the Cuban Crisis," editorial, *Washington Post,* Oct. 23, 1962, p. A16.
81. "The Cuban Quarantine," *Pittsburgh Post-Gazette,* Oct. 24, 1962, p. 8.
82. "The United States Draws the Line," editorial, *Denver Post,* Oct. 24, 1962, p. 26; "To Defend the Americas," editorial, *New York Herald Tribune,* Oct. 23, 1962, p. 24; "The Role of Power," editorial, *Wall Street Journal,* Oct. 25, 1962, p. 12.
83. "The End of Forbearance," editorial, *Atlanta Constitution,* Oct. 25, 1962, p. 1.
84. James Reston, "To Deal or Not to Deal: That's the Question," *NYT,* Oct. 28, 1962, p. 10E.
85. *Denver Post,* Oct. 23, 1962, p. 12; "To the Abyss," editorial, *Hartford Courant,* Oct. 23, 1962, p. 18; Chalmers M. Roberts, "The 1930s Revisited: U.S. Won't Repeat Delay of Hitler's Day," *Philadelphia Inquirer,* Oct. 23, 1962, p. 13.
86. George Gallup, "The Gallup Poll: 84 Pct. of Americans Back JFK Blockade Edict," *Denver Post,* Oct. 24, 1962, p. 10.

87. *Cleveland Plain Dealer,* reported in "How Other Papers See Cuban Crisis," *Detroit Free Press,* Oct. 23, 1962, p. 6-A; "A Tough Cuban Policy Too Long in Coming," editorial, *Detroit Free Press,* Oct. 23, 1962, p. 6-A; *St. Louis Globe-Democrat,* reported in "How Other Papers See Cuban Crisis," *Detroit Free Press,* Oct. 23, 1962, 6-A. "The President's Next Task," *Wall Street Journal,* Oct. 24, 1962, p. 16; "For Khrushchev, A Way Out," editorial, *Chattanooga Daily Times,* Oct. 24, 1962, p. 10.

88. *Denver Post,* Oct. 23, 1962, p. 12.

89. *Buffalo Courier-Express,* Oct. 23, 1962, p. 1; Jack Bell (Associated Press), "Party Leaders Grimly Accept A-War Risk," *Denver Post,* Oct. 24, 1962, p. 17; *NYT,* Oct. 24, 1962, p. 15. Robert Kennedy's memory was not so short. Briefed on the range of Soviet nuclear missiles in Cuba, he mused with a wry smile, "Will [they] reach Oxford, Mississippi?" See Brugioni, *Eyeball to Eyeball,* p. 224.

90. *Buffalo Courier-Express,* Oct. 23, 1962, p. 1; Jerry Greene, "Capitol Stuff," *New York Daily News,* Oct. 23, 1962, p. 5.

91. *Philadelphia Inquirer,* Oct. 25, 1962, p. 8; *Denver Post,* Oct. 23, 1962, p. 12.

92. *San Francisco News-Call Bulletin,* Oct. 23, 1962, p. 3.

93. Sorensen, *Kennedy,* p. 717.

94. Kennedy, *Thirteen Days,* p. 61.

95. Abel, *The Missile Crisis,* pp. 135–137; Blight and Welch, *On the Brink,* p. 64.

96. Kennedy, *Thirteen Days,* p. 83.

6. Kennedy's Hidden Concession—to Public Opinion

1. Philip Nash, *The Other Missiles of October: Eisenhower, Kennedy, and the Jupiters, 1957–1963* (Chapel Hill: University of North Carolina Press, 1997), is indispensable to a study of this subject. See also Barton J. Bernstein, "Reconsidering the Missile Crisis: Dealing with the Problems of American Jupiters in Turkey," in Nathan, *The Cuban Missile Crisis Revisited,* pp. 55–129, and Barton J. Bernstein, "The Cuban Missile Crisis: Trading the Jupiters in Turkey?" *Political Science Quarterly* 95, no. 1 (Spring 1980), pp. 97–125.

2. "Cuban Blockade," *Des Moines Register,* Oct. 24, 1962, p. 6; "President Had No Choice," *Milwaukee Journal,* Oct. 23, 1962, p. 12.

3. "Good Sense So Far," editorial, *Chattanooga Daily Times,* Oct. 25, 1962, p. 6; "A Course of Courage," *Raleigh News and Observer,* Oct. 23,

1962, p. 4; "This Time of Testing," *Raleigh News and Observer*, Oct. 27, 1962, p. 4.

4. *Denver Post*, Oct. 26, 1962, p. 10; "A Time for Diplomacy," *NYT*, Oct. 28, 1962, sec. 4, p. 10E.

5. Nash, *The Other Missiles of October*, pp. 11, 18.

6. "The Specific Threat," *Time*, Oct. 21, 1957, p. 21.

7. Nash, *The Other Missiles of October*, pp. 82–84.

8. Albert Wohlstetter, "The Delicate Balance of Terror," *Foreign Affairs*, vol. 37, no. 2 (January 1959), pp. 222–230; Bernard Brodie, *Strategy in the Missile Age* (Princeton: Princeton University Press, 1959), pp. 343–345; Kahn, *On Thermonuclear War*, p. 283.

9. Nash, *The Other Missiles of October*, p. 81.

10. James M. Gavin, *War and Peace in the Space Age* (New York: Harper & Brothers, 1958), p. 9; Maxwell D. Taylor, *The Uncertain Trumpet* (New York: Harper, 1959), p. 142.

11. Nash, *The Other Missiles of October*, p. 33; John Newhouse, *De Gaulle and the Anglo-Saxons* (New York: Viking, 1970), p. 23.

12. Nash, *The Other Missiles of October*, pp. 53, 187–188, n. 44.

13. A. J. Goodpaster, June 19, 1959. "Memorandum of Conference with the President on June 16, 1959," p. 1 (original in Dwight D. Eisenhower Library), in National Security Archive, *The Cuban Missile Crisis*, microfiche collection (Alexandria, Va.: Chadwyck-Healey, 1990), document 12; A. J. Goodpaster, June 17, 1959, "Memorandum of Conversation with the President, June 17, 1959," p. 2 (original in Dwight D. Eisenhower Library), ibid., document 11.

14. John S. D. Eisenhower, January 17, 1961, "Memorandum of Conference with the President, January 13, 1961" (original in Dwight D. Eisenhower Library), in National Security Archive, *The Cuban Missile Crisis*, ibid., document 31.

15. Nash, *The Other Missiles of October*, pp. 64, 71.

16. Ibid., p. 3, citing McNamara in *The Cuban Missile Crisis: At the Brink*, episode 5 of *War and Peace in the Nuclear Age* (documentary) (Boston: WGBH, 1988); Bundy, *Danger and Survival*, p. 435; Blight and Welch, eds., *On the Brink*, p. 172.

17. Nash, *The Other Missiles of October*, p. 88.

18. "A Review of North Atlantic Problems for the Future," March 1961, pp. 8, 61, Box 220, Regional Security Series, National Security Files, JFKL.

19. Nash, *The Other Missiles of October*, p. 96.

20. U.S. Senate, Committee on Foreign Relations, executive session, Feb.

28, 1961, Dean Rusk testifying, p. 220, in National Security Archive, *The Cuban Missile Crisis, 1962*, document 38.

21. Nash, *The Other Missiles of October,* p. 95.

22. Thomas K. Finletter to President Kennedy, May 29, 1961, p. 3, Box 220A, Regional Security Series, National Security Files, JFKL.

23. Record of Meeting between President Kennedy and Dirk Stikker, June 16, 1961, pp. 1, 12, Box 220A, Regional Security Series, National Security Files, JFKL.

24. Nash, *The Other Missiles of October*, p. 97.

25. Nitze, *From Hiroshima to Glasnost*, p. 233; George McGhee to McGeorge Bundy, June 22, 1961, Box 226A, Regional Security Series, National Security Files, JFKL.

26. Nash, *The Other Missiles of October,* p. 112.

27. Ibid., p. 91.

28. Ibid., p. 1.

29. Ibid., p. 106, citing Alexei Adzhubei, interview, in British Broadcasting Corporation, *Cuban Missile Crisis*, part 1, "Defying Uncle Sam"; Allyn, Blight, and Welch, *Back to the Brink*, p. 46.

30. Memorandum of Meeting with the President, Aug. 23, 1962, in McAuliffe, ed., *CIA Documents on the Cuban Missile Crisis*, p. 28; National Security Action Memorandum No. 181, Cuba (A), Aug. 23, 1962, p. 1, Meetings and Memoranda, Box 338, National Security Files, JFKL.

31. Chester Bowles to McGeorge Bundy, Oct. 15, 1962, and Bowles to President Kennedy, "Report of Conversation with Ambassador Dobrynin on Saturday, Oct. 13th, Regarding Cuba and Other Subjects," Oct. 14, 1962, pp. 2–3, Box 185A, Countries Series, National Security Files, JFKL.

32. Stewart Alsop and Charles Bartlett, "In Time of Crisis," *Saturday Evening Post*, vol. 235, no. 44 (Dec. 8, 1962), p. 20.

33. Adlai Stevenson to President Kennedy, Oct. 17, 1962, in Johnson, ed., *The Papers of Adlai E. Stevenson*, vol. 8, p. 300.

34. May and Zelikow, eds., *The Kennedy Tapes*, p. 199.

35. Ball, *The Past Has Another Pattern*, pp. 295–296.

36. O'Donnell, *"Johnny, We Hardly Knew Ye,"* p. 323.

37. Jeff Broadwater, *Adlai Stevenson and American Politics: The Odyssey of a Cold War Liberal* (New York: Twayne, 1994), p. 210, citing Memorandum by Adlai Stevenson, Oct. 21, 1962, in Johnson, ed., *The Papers of Adlai E. Stevenson*, vol. 8, pp. 304–306.

38. Sorensen, *Kennedy*, p. 696.

39. Schlesinger, *A Thousand Days*, p. 811.

40. May and Zelikow, *The Kennedy Tapes*, pp. 60, 156.

41. Ibid., p. 100.

42. Ibid., pp. 142, 165.
43. U.S. Department of State, *Foreign Relations of the United States 1961–1963*, vol. 11, *Cuban Missile Crisis and Aftermath* (Washington, D.C.: U.S. Government Printing Office, 1996), pp. 121; May and Zelikow, *The Kennedy Tapes*, p. 193.
44. May and Zelikow, *The Kennedy Tapes*, p. 199; Mark J. White, ed., *The Kennedys and Cuba: The Declassified Documentary History* (Chicago: Ivan R. Dee, 1999), p. 201.
45. Nitze, *From Hiroshima to Glasnost*, p. 227.
46. Abram Chayes, *The Cuban Missile Crisis: International Crises and the Role of Law* (New York: Oxford University Press, 1974), pp. 81–82, 95.
47. Theodore C. Sorensen, "Notes to Speech Draft," Oct. 20, 1962, pp. 1–2, Box 48, Theodore C. Sorensen Personal Papers, Classified Subjects, 1961–1964, JFKL.
48. Averell Harriman, "Memorandum on Kremlin Reactions," Oct. 22, 1962, Box 226A, Regional Security Series, National Security Files, JFKL.
49. Sorensen, "Synopsis of President's Speech," n.d. [ca. Oct. 22, 1962], p. 3, National Security Archive, *The Cuban Missile Crisis, 1962*, document 772.
50. Nash, *The Other Missiles of October*, p. 126.
51. May and Zelikow, *The Kennedy Tapes*, p. 235; Nash, *The Other Missiles of October*, p. 131.
52. Dean Rusk to U.S. Ambassador to Turkey Raymond Hare and U.S. Ambassador to NATO Thomas Finletter, Oct. 24, 1962, Box 226A, Regional Security Series, National Security Files, JFKL.
53. Walter Lippmann, "Crisis and This Election," *Washington Post*, Oct. 23, 1962, p. A17; Walter Lippmann, "Blockade Proclaimed," *Washington Post*, Oct. 25, 1962, p. A25.
54. William H. Stringer, "Choices for Khrushchev," *Christian Science Monitor*, Oct. 24, 1962, p. 1. See also the similar arguments in "On Leaving Khrushchev an Out," editorial, *Boston Herald*, Oct. 25, 1962, p. 38, and "With Devotion to Peace," editorial, *Chattanooga Daily Times*, Oct. 26, 1962, p. 16.
55. Ronald Steel, *Walter Lippmann and the American Century* (Boston: Little, Brown, 1980), p. 535.
56. *NYT*, Oct. 24, 1962, pp. 1, 20; Oct. 25, 1962, p. 20.
57. "Khrushchev Offers a Deal," editorial, *Philadelphia Inquirer*, Oct. 28, 1962, p. B6.
58. C. L. Sulzberger, "Mr. K's Own Huckster's Approach," *NYT*, Oct. 29, 1962, p. 28.
59. "'The First Imperative,'" editorial, *New York Herald Tribune*, Oct. 28,

1962, sec. 2, p. 5. See also "Their Bases & Ours," *Time*, Nov. 2, 1962, p. 16; "The Ethical Issue," editorial, *Christian Science Monitor*, Oct. 23, 1962, C(R).

60. "The Free World Responds," editorial, *Philadelphia Inquirer*, Oct. 24, 1962, p. 20.
61. "Why Cuba Isn't Like Turkey," editorial, *Chicago Tribune*, Oct. 24, 1962, part 1, p. 16F.
62. Richard Wilson, "Wilson: Can't Ease Up; Bases Must Go!" *Des Moines Register*, Oct. 28, 1962, sec. F, p. 4.
63. Bernstein, "Reconsidering the Missile Crisis," pp. 80, 81.
64. Thomas K. Finletter to Dean Rusk, Oct. 25, 1962, Box 226A, Regional Security Series, National Security Files, JFKL.
65. Nash, *The Other Missiles of October*, p. 137.
66. Secretary Rusk to Ambassadors Hare and Finletter, Oct. 24, 1962, Box 226A, Regional Security Series, National Security Files, JFKL.
67. Raymond Hare to Secretary of State, Oct. 26, 1962, sec. one of three, p. 1, Box 226A, Regional Security Series, National Security Files, JFKL. See also Thomas Finletter to Secretary of State, Oct. 25, 1962, and Raymond Hare to Dean Rusk, Oct. 28, 1962, in the same source.
68. Raymond Hare to Secretary of State, Oct. 26, 1962, sec. two of three, p. 2, ibid. Toward the end of a three-hour Ex Comm meeting on Saturday late afternoon, October 27, John McCone said without elaborating, "I would trade these Turkish things out right now. I wouldn't be talking to anybody about it." See May and Zelikow, *The Kennedy Tapes*, p. 585.
69. John F. Kennedy to Harold Macmillan, Oct. 27, 1962, Box 173, Countries Series, National Security Files, JFKL.
70. May and Zelikow, *The Kennedy Tapes*, pp. 497, 500.
71. Ibid., pp. 498–499.
72. Ibid., pp. 512, 517.
73. Brugioni, *Eyeball to Eyeball*, pp. 453–455.
74. May and Zelikow, *The Kennedy Tapes*, pp. 517–518; Bromley Smith, Summary Record of the Seventh Meeting of the Executive Committee of the National Security Council, Washington, October 27, 1962, 10 a.m., *Foreign Relations of the United States, 1961–1963*, vol. XI, *Cuban Missile Crisis and Aftermath* (Washington, D.C.: U.S. Government Printing Office, 1996), pp. 255–256.
75. May and Zelikow, *The Kennedy Tapes*, pp. 529, 530.
76. Ibid., pp. 542, 545.
77. Ibid., p. 548.
78. Ibid., p. 549–550.

79. Ibid., pp. 550, 553–555.
80. Ibid., p. 560.
81. Kennedy, *Thirteen Days*, p. 98.
82. May and Zelikow, *The Kennedy Tapes*, p. 563.
83. Ibid., pp. 582, 591. According to Brugioni, *Eyeball to Eyeball*, p. 470, Johnson had earlier summoned General Lemnitzer to the White House and admonished him not to fret over upsetting NATO: "[S]ince we damn well gave them [the missiles] to the Turks, we can damn well take them back," and added, as befitted a legendary deal-maker on Capitol Hill, "We can make it up to the Turks." Curiously, when the president returned to the discussion, Johnson shifted from dove to hawk, warning that a straight trade of bases would be disastrous because, "Why, then your whole foreign policy is gone. You take everything out of Turkey: 20,000 men, all your technicians, and all your planes, and all your missiles. And crumple." See May and Zelikow, *The Kennedy Tapes*, p. 602.
84. May and Zelikow, *The Kennedy Tapes*, p. 583.
85. McGeorge Bundy, transcriber, and James G. Blight, ed., "October 27, 1962: Transcripts of the Meetings of the ExComm," *International Security*, vol. 12, no. 3 (Winter 1987/1988), p. 45.
86. May and Zelikow, *The Kennedy Tapes*, pp. 554, 602.
87. In fact Soviet and American pilots clashed repeatedly over Korea, but Stalin took extraordinary steps to conceal these battles; and U.S. officials, fearing irresistible demands for escalation, kept the secret.
88. Roger Hilsman, *To Move a Nation: The Politics of Foreign Policy in the Administration of John F. Kennedy* (New York: Doubleday, 1967), p. 197.
89. Bundy, *Danger and Survival*, p. 433.
90. Ibid., pp. 432–433. Robert Kennedy described his meeting with Dobrynin in a memo to Secretary of State Dean Rusk, Oct. 30, 1962, p. 3, box 115, Countries Series, President's Office Files, JFKL. It stated, "He [Dobrynin] then asked me about Khrushchev's other proposal dealing with the removal of the missiles from Turkey. I replied that there could be no *quid pro quo*—no deal of this kind could be made." This document provides essentially the same account as that which Robert Kennedy later gave in his memoir *Thirteen Days*, p. 108.
91. According to Anatoly Dobrynin, Robert Kennedy stated that only "two other people besides the President know about the existing understanding: they are Rusk and Thompson." See "Telegram from Soviet Ambassador Dobrynin to the Soviet Foreign Ministry," Oct. 30, 1962, in White, ed., *The Kennedys and Cuba*, p. 252.
92. "Cable from Soviet Ambassador to the United States Anatoly F. Do-

brynin to the Soviet Foreign Ministry," Oct. 27, 1962, in ibid., p. 237. According to Dobrynin, the groundwork for this accord was laid as early as Friday evening, October 26, during one of many off-the-record meetings between him and Robert Kennedy. Allyn, Blight, and Welch, eds., *Back to the Brink*, p. 81. But Barton J. Bernstein casts doubt on this recollection in "Reconsidering the Missile Crisis: Dealing with the Problems of the American Jupiters in Turkey," in Nathan, ed., *The Cuban Missile Crisis Revisited*, pp. 125–126; Dobrynin himself makes no mention of an agreement on October 26 in his memoir, *In Confidence: Moscow's Ambassador to America's Six Cold War Presidents (1962–1986)* (New York: Times Books, 1995). For an analysis of Soviet documents of the accord on the Turkish missiles, see Jim Hershberg, "Anatomy of a Controversy: Anatoly F. Dobrynin's Meeting with Robert F. Kennedy, Saturday, October 27, 1962," *Cold War International History Project Bulletin*, no. 5 (Spring 1995), pp. 75, 77–80.

93. "Cable from Soviet Ambassador to the United States Anatoly F. Dobrynin to the Soviet Foreign Ministry," Oct. 27, 1962, in White, ed., *The Kennedys and Cuba*, p. 239.

94. Ibid., pp. 239–240.

95. "Telegram from Ambassador Dobrynin to the Soviet Foreign Ministry," Oct. 28, 1962, in ibid., p. 248.

96. "Telegram from Soviet Ambassador Dobrynin to the Soviet Foreign Ministry," Oct. 30, 1962, in ibid., p. 251.

97. See Anatoly Dobrynin, *In Confidence*, pp. 85–86; Fursenko and Naftali, *"One Hell of a Gamble,"* pp. 263, 270; Nash, *The Other Missiles of October*, pp. 132–133; Zubok and Pleshakov, *Inside the Kremlin's Cold War*, pp. 266–67.

98. " 'A Contribution to Peace,' " *New York Times Tribune*, Oct. 29, 1962, p. 24.

99. Richard Rovere, "Letter from Washington," *The New Yorker*, vol. 38, no. 39 (Nov. 17, 1962), p. 200.

100. Schlesinger, *Robert Kennedy and His Times*, p. 524, citing author's journal, Oct. 29, 1962. Anderson and LeMay had earlier objected to the president's agreement at a meeting of the Joint Chiefs: see Notes from Transcripts of JCS meetings, Oct. 28, 1962 [at 0900], p. 1, Department of Defense, Office of the Chairman of the Joint Chiefs of Staff, Office of Joint History, reprinted in U.S. State Department, *Foreign Relations of the United States 1961–1963*, vols. 10–12, microfiche supplement, document 441.

101. Beschloss, *The Crisis Years*, p. 581.

102. Television and Radio Interview: "After Two Years—A Conversation

with the President." December 17, 1962, in *Public Papers of the Presidents of the United States—John F. Kennedy (Containing the Public Messages, Speeches, and Statements of the President) 1962* (Washington, D.C.: U.S. Government Printing Office, 1963), pp. 898–899.

103. Thomas G. Paterson and William J. Brophy, "October Missiles and November Elections: The Cuban Missile Crisis and American Politics, 1962," in *Journal of American History*, vol. 73, no. 1 (June 1986), p. 108.

104. *Washington Post*, July 29, 1963, A2.

105. Preparedness Investigating Subcommittee, Senate Committee on Armed Services, "Interim Report on the Cuban Military Buildup," May 9, 1963, pp. 33–34, Departments and Agencies, Box 78, President's Office Files, JFKL.

106. Beschloss, *The Crisis Years*, p. 582; see also Benjamin C. Bradlee, *Conversations with Kennedy* (New York: W. W. Norton, 1975), p. 132.

107. Lauris Norstad to President Kennedy, Nov. 1, 1962, Box 103, Subjects, President's Office Files, JFKL. See also Charles Bohlen to Dean Rusk, Nov. 11, 1962, p. 1, Box 226A, Regional Security Series, National Security Files, JFKL.

108. Nash, *The Other Missiles of October*, p. 155, citing Schlesinger, *A Thousand Days*, p. 903.

109. Dean Rusk to Embassy, Ankara and Paris, Oct. 29, 1962, Box 226A, Regional Security Series, National Security Files, JFKL.

110. Nash, *The Other Missiles of October*, p. 156. See also Telegram from USSR Foreign Minister Gromyko to Deputy Foreign Minister Kuznetsov and Ambassador to the UN Zorin, Nov. 5, 1962, in "Russian Documents on the Cuban Missile Crisis," *Cold War International History Project Bulletin*, no. 8–9 (Winter 1996/1997), p. 324, in which Gromyko gives his negotiators in New York a sharply abridged version of the settlement: "The USA is giving assurances that no invasion will be inflicted on Cuba, not only on the part of the United States, but also on the part of their allies—the other countries of the Western hemisphere. The Soviet Union for its part will remove from the [sic] Cuba the missile weaponry that the President of the USA has called offensive, and will not install such types of weaponry in Cuba again. Such is the basis of the agreement, and we are adhering to it. . . ."

111. Nash, *The Other Missiles of October*, p. 157.

112. "Victory," editorial, *Hartford Courant*, Oct. 29, 1962, p. 16.

113. Harold Macmillan to John F. Kennedy, Oct. 28, 1962, Box 173, Countries Series, National Security Files, JFKL.

114. Nash, *The Other Missiles of October*, p. 150.

115. Ibid., pp. 150, 152.
116. Robert W. Komer to McGeorge Bundy, Nov. 12, 1962, p. 1, Box 226A, Regional Security Series, National Security Files, JFKL.

Epilogue: The Missile Crisis in Historical Perspective

1. Bundy, *Danger and Survival*, p. 391.
2. Early favorable accounts of Kennedy's leadership in the missile crisis include Stewart Alsop, "Our New Strategy: The Alternative to Total War," *Saturday Evening Post* 235 (Dec. 1, 1962), pp. 13–18, Stewart Alsop and Charles Bartlett, "In Time of Crisis," *Saturday Evening Post* 235 (Dec. 8, 1962), pp. 15–20; Henry M. Pachter, *Collision Course: The Cuban Missile Crisis and Coexistence* (New York: Frederick A. Praeger, 1963); Schlesinger, *A Thousand Days*, pp. 794–841; Sorensen, *Kennedy*, pp. 667–718; Abel, *The Missile Crisis*; Hilsman, *To Move a Nation*, pp. 159–229; Robert F. Kennedy's posthumously published *Thirteen Days*; Alexander L. George, "The Cuban Missile Crisis: Peaceful Resolution Through Coercive Diplomacy," in Alexander L. George and William E. Simons, eds., *The Limits of Coercive Diplomacy* (Boulder, Colo.: Westview, 1971), pp. 111–132; and (despite a focus on bureaucratic politics) Graham T. Allison, *Essence of Decision: Explaining the Cuban Missile Crisis* (Boston: Little, Brown, 1970).
3. Abel, *The Missile Crisis*, p. 217.
4. Schlesinger, *Robert Kennedy and His Times*, p. 525. A variant of Robert Kennedy's remarks, from the last interview he gave, are in David Frost, *The Presidential Debate, 1968* (New York: Stein and Day, 1968), pp. 115–116.
5. Abel, *The Missile Crisis*, p. 193. In *Thirteen Days*, p. 95, Robert Kennedy writes, "The President believed he was President and that, his wishes having been made clear, they would be followed and the missiles removed. . . . Now he learned that the failure to follow up on this matter had permitted the same obsolete Turkish missiles to become hostages of the Soviet Union. He was angry."
6. Sorensen, *Kennedy*, p. 714; see also Abel, *The Missile Crisis*, p. 189.
7. Schlesinger, *A Thousand Days*, p. 828.
8. Kennedy, *Thirteen Days*, pp. 108–109.
9. Sorensen, *Kennedy*, pp. 717–718.
10. Kennedy, *Thirteen Days*, p. 124.
11. Pachter, *Collision Course*, pp. 87–88.
12. Sorensen, *Kennedy*, p. 718.

13. Revisionist accounts of the missile crisis include such journalistic precursors as Roger Hagan, "Triumph or Tragedy?" *Dissent* 10 (Winter 1963), pp. 13–26; I. F. Stone, "The Brink," *New York Review of Books* 6 (Apr. 14, 1966), pp. 12–16; and Ronald Steel, "Endgame, Thirteen Days," *New York Review of Books* 12 (Mar. 13, 1969), pp. 15–22. Outstanding revisionist histories include Richard J. Walton, *Cold War and Counterrevolution: The Foreign Policy of John F. Kennedy* (Baltimore: Penguin, 1972), pp. 103–142; Barton J. Bernstein, "The Cuban Missile Crisis," in Lynn H. Miller and Ronald W. Pruessen, eds., *Reflections on the Cold War: A Quarter Century of American Foreign Policy* (Philadelphia: Temple University Press, 1974), pp. 108–142, and Barton J. Bernstein, "The Cuban Missile Crisis: Trading the Jupiters in Turkey?" *Political Science Quarterly* 95 (Spring 1980), pp. 97–125; Detzer, *The Brink*; and Herbert Parmet, *JFK: The Presidency of John F. Kennedy* (New York: Penguin, 1984), pp. 277–300. All evince a sharp sense of Kennedy's political constraints while also suggesting that Kennedy's limitations of character or temperament further stoked an already dangerous conflict. See also the provocative accounts by Henry Fairlie, *The Kennedy Promise: The Politics of Expectation* (Garden City, N.Y.: Doubleday, 1973), pp. 311–313; Nancy Gager Clinch, *The Kennedy Neurosis* (New York: Grosset & Dunlap, 1973), pp. 197–206; FitzSimons, *The Kennedy Doctrine*, pp. 126–172; Garry Wills, *The Kennedy Imprisonment: A Meditation on Power* (Boston: Little, Brown, 1994; originally 1981), pp. 258–274. An excellent introduction to the historiographical debate between traditional and revisionist writers is Robert A. Divine, ed., *The Cuban Missile Crisis*, 2d ed. (New York: Marcus Wiener, 1988). Arthur M. Schlesinger, Jr., a prime target of revisionist critiques, offers a penetrating retort in *Robert Kennedy and His Times*, pp. 530–531.
14. FitzSimons, *The Kennedy Doctrine*, p. 127.
15. Walton, *Cold War and Counterrevolution*, p. 123.
16. FitzSimons, *The Kennedy Doctrine*, p. 170.
17. Wills, *The Kennedy Imprisonment*, pp. 262–263.
18. Detzer, *The Brink*, p. 116.
19. Clinch, *The Kennedy Neurosis*, pp. 204–205. Earlier I. F. Stone, in "The Brink," p. 13, explained the missile crisis as "the best of therapies for Kennedy's nagging inferiority complex."
20. Clinch, *The Kennedy Neurosis*, p. 199.
21. Sidney Lens, *The Military Industrial Complex* (Philadelphia: Pilgrim Press and the National Catholic Reporter, 1970), p. 91.
22. Walton, *Cold War and Counterrevolution*, p. 224.

23. Ibid., p. 116.
24. Ibid., p. 10.
25. Ibid., p. 142, citing John F. Kennedy, *Public Papers*, 1963, p. 462.
26. Clinch, *The Kennedy Neurosis*, p. 204.
27. Fairlie, *The Kennedy Promise*, p. 311.
28. See Walton, *Cold War and Counterrevolution*, p. 134; Wills, *The Kennedy Imprisonment*, pp. 269, 271; Clinch, *The Kennedy Neurosis*, pp. 204, 206.
29. Stanislav Kondrashov, in *Back to the Brink*, p. 170.
30. John Gregory Dunne, "Elephant Man," *New York Review of Books*, Apr. 15, 1982, p. 10, cited in Thomas Brown, *JFK: History of an Image* (Bloomington: Indiana University Press, 1988), p. 94.
31. Records of these conferences have been preserved in three superbly annotated volumes: Blight and Welch, *On the Brink*, on the conference at Hawk's Cay, in the Florida Keys, March 5–8, 1987, and the conference in Cambridge, Massachusetts, October 11–12, 1987; Allyn, Blight, and Welch, eds., *Back to the Brink*, on the conference in Moscow, January 27–28, 1989; and Blight, Allyn, and Welch, *Cuba on the Brink*, on the conference in Havana, Cuba, January 9–12, 1992, hosted by Fidel Castro. See also Ray S. Cline, "The Cuban Missile Crisis," *Foreign Affairs* (Fall 1989), pp. 190–196, for a skeptic's view of Soviet oral histories of the missile crisis and the Soviets' political uses and misuses of *glasnost*.
32. In addition to published records of scholarly symposia on the crisis (see previous note), the burgeoning recent literature on Kennedy's leadership includes such indispensable volumes as May and Zelikow, *The Kennedy Tapes*; Chang and Kornbluh, *The Cuban Missile Crisis, 1962*, which contains an extensive bibliography, pp. 413–427; Beschloss, *The Crisis Years*, pp. 394–545; Nathan, *The Cuban Missile Crisis Revisited*; and Fursenko and Naftali, *One Hell of a Gamble*. Mark J. White insightfully distills and interprets the findings of recent scholarship in *Missiles in Cuba: Kennedy, Khrushchev, Castro, and the 1962 Crisis* (Chicago: Ivan R. Dee, 1997). McGeorge Bundy's brilliant insider's account in *Danger and Survival*, pp. 391–462, is an authoritative harbinger of the new scholarship.

Also notable among diverse other pioneering studies in recent years are Graham T. Allison and Philip D. Zelikow, *Essence of Decision: Explaining the Cuban Missile Crisis*, 2nd ed. (New York: Longman, 1999), a revised and updated version of Allison's pathbreaking political science study; Bruce J. Allyn, James G. Blight, and David A. Welch, "Essence of Revision: Moscow, Havana, and the Cuban Missile Crisis," *International Security* 14, no. 3 (Winter 1989/1990), pp. 136–172; Barton J. Bernstein, "Reconsidering the Missile Crisis: Dealing with the Problems of the American Jupiters in Turkey," in Nathan, *The Cuban Missile Crisis Revisited*, pp. 55–129; James G. Blight, Joseph S. Nye, Jr., and David A. Welch, "The Cuban Missile Crisis Revisited," *Foreign Affairs* (Fall 1987), pp. 170–188; Dino A. Brugioni, *The Inside Story of the Cuban Missile Crisis*, rev. ed. (New York: Random House, 1991); Raymond L. Garthoff, *Reflections on the Cuban Missile Crisis*, rev. ed. (Washington, D.C.: Brookings Institution, 1989); James N. Giglio, *The Presidency of John F. Kennedy* (Lawrence: University Press of Kansas, 1991), pp. 189–220; Fred Osler Hampson, "The Divided Decision-Maker: American Domestic Politics and the Cuban Crises," *International Security* 9 (Winter 1984–1985), pp. 130–165; James Hershberg, "Before 'The Missiles of October': Did Kennedy Plan a Military Strike Against Cuba?" *Diplomatic History* 14, no. 12 (Spring 1990), pp. 163–199; Nash, *The Other Missiles of October*; Richard Ned Lebow, "Domestic Politics and the Cuban Missile Crisis: The Traditional and Revisionist Interpretations Revisited," *Diplomatic History* 14 (Fall 1990), pp. 471–492; Richard Ned Lebow and Janice Gross Stein, *We All Lost the Cold War* (Princeton: Princeton University Press, 1994), pp. 19–145; Thomas G. Paterson, "Fixation with Cuba: The Bay of Pigs, Missile Crisis, and Covert War against Castro," in Paterson, ed., *Kennedy's Quest for Victory: American Foreign Policy, 1961–1963* (New York: Oxford University Press, 1989), pp. 123–155; Reeves, *President Kennedy*, pp. 349–425; Thomas G. Paterson and William J. Brophy, "October Missiles and November Elections: The Cuban Missile Crisis and American Politics, 1962," *Journal of American History* 73, no. 1 (June 1986), pp. 87–119; and David A. Welch and James G. Blight, "The Eleventh Hour of the Cuban Missile Crisis: An Introduction to the ExComm Transcripts," *International Security* 12, no. 3 (Winter 1987/1988), pp. 5–29; and Mark J. White, *The Cuban Missile Crisis* (Basingstoke, Hampshire: Macmillan, 1996), and White, *The Kennedys and Cuba*.

33. Blight and Welch, *On the Brink*, p. 84.
34. Allyn, Blight, and Welch, *Back to the Brink*, p. 93.
35. Ibid.
36. Blight and Welch, *On the Brink*, p. 189.
37. Ibid., p. 190.
38. Scott D. Sagan, "Nuclear Alerts and Crisis Management," *International Security*, vol. 9, no. 4 (Spring 1985), p. 117.
39. Scott D. Sagan, *The Limits of Safety: Organizations, Accidents, and Nu-*

clear Weapons (Princeton, N.J.: Princeton University Press, 1993), p. 116. Sagan unearths an instructive catalogue of potentially dangerous accidents during the missile crisis, pp. 53–155.

40. Blight, Allyn, and Welch, *Cuba on the Brink*, pp. 58–62, quoting General Anatoli Gribkov. According to May and Zelikow, *The Kennedy Tapes*, pp. 475–476, Kennedy was first briefed on October 26 on the possible deployment of Soviet short-range nuclear weapons. He maintained the option of invading Cuba then and later, though ruing that "by the time we get to these sites after a very bloody fight, [the missiles] will still be pointing at us." According to General William Y. Smith, special assistant to Maxwell Taylor, chairman of the Joint Chiefs of Staff in the Kennedy administration, "We knew that there were *Lunas* in Cuba; but to our knowledge, those *Lunas* had no nuclear warheads. At the time of the October crisis we had no evidence that there were any nuclear weapons in Cuba. So our forces were prepared to conduct any invasion that was ordered by the president with conventional forces." See Blight, Allyn, and Welch, *Cuba on the Brink*, p. 261. Smith offers similar testimony in Gribkov and Smith, *Operation ANADYR*, pp. 140–141.

Mark Kramer, "Tactical Nuclear Weapons, Soviet Command Authority, and the Cuban Missile Crisis," *Cold War International History Project Bulletin*, no. 3 (Fall 1993), pp. 40, 42–46, debunks claims that Pliyev ever had authority during the crisis to launch tactical nuclear weapons without approval from Moscow; in the same issue, James G. Blight, Bruce J. Allyn, and David A. Welch, "Kramer Vs. Kramer: Or, How Can You Have Revisionism in the Absence of Orthodoxy?" pp. 41, 47–50, find the evidence ambiguous, and add that neither Kennedy nor Khrushchev had enough confidence in the formal chain of command for the use of nuclear weapons to risk aggravating or prolonging the crisis. On February 21, 2001, at a forum at the Kennedy School of Government at Harvard, Robert McNamara, in response to a question from the author, dismissed as irrelevant whether authority to use nuclear weapons had been formally delegated to the local Soviet commander. Noting that Soviet forces in Cuba had already shot down a U-2 contrary to Khrushchev's wishes, McNamara concluded, "Would tactical nuclear weapons have been used in the face of a U.S. invasion? I guarantee you 100 percent they would have been."

41. Blight, Allyn, and Welch, *Cuba on the Brink*, p. 379.
42. Blight and Welch, *On the Brink*, p. 99.
43. Ibid., p. 100.

44. Ibid., p. 315, citing Sorensen's "Reflections on a Grim But Hopeful Anniversary," in *Miami Herald*, Nov. 1, 1987, p. C1.
45. See Blight and Welch, *On the Brink*, pp. 83–84, 173–174, and Rusk, *As I Saw It*, pp. 240–241; Mark J. White in *The Cuban Missile Crisis*, pp. 202–203, probes Rusk's recollection.
46. Kennedy, *Thirteen Days*, p. 116; see also Rusk *As I Saw It*, p. 240.
47. Rusk, *As I Saw It*, p. 240, credits Thompson. David A. Welch and James G. Blight, "The Eleventh Hour of the Cuban Missile Crisis: An Introduction to the ExComm Transcripts," *International Security*, vol. 12, no. 3 (Winter 1987/1988), p. 19; Blight and Welch, *On the Brink*, p. 369, n. 31, conclude that Bundy and Martin likely broached the plan first while Thompson "certainly persuaded the President that it might actually work." Bundy himself greatly credits Robert Kennedy, though subtly rethinking the conventional wisdom about his contribution, in *Danger and Survival*, p. 431.
48. See Rusk, *As I Saw It*, pp. 239–240; Blight and Welch, *On the Brink*, pp. 261–262; Bernstein, "Reconsidering the Missile Crisis," pp. 60–64. See also Ball, *The Past Has Another Pattern*, pp. 500–502, n. 2.
49. Dean Rusk to James G. Blight, Feb. 25, 1987, p. 2, cited in Welch and Blight, "The Eleventh Hour of the Cuban Missile Crisis," p. 18.
50. See, for example, the insightful analyses by Richard Ned Lebow, "Domestic Politics and the Cuban Missile Crisis: The Traditional and Revisionist Interpretations Revisited," *Diplomatic History* 14 (Fall 1990), pp. 471–492, and Fred Osler Hampson, "The Divided Decision-Maker: American Domestic Politics and the Cuban Crises," *International Security* 9 (Winter 1984–1985), pp. 130–165.
51. Paterson, *Kennedy's Quest for Victory*, p. 14.
52. Paterson, "Fixation with Cuba,", p. 129.
53. Seymour M. Hersh, *The Dark Side of Camelot* (Boston: Little, Brown, 1997), p. 345.
54. Ibid., pp. 345, 369.
55. Paul Boyer, *Promises to Keep: The United States Since World War II*, 2d ed. (Boston: Houghton-Mifflin, 1999), p. 170.
56. Thomas C. Reeves, *A Question of Character: A Life of John F. Kennedy* (Rocklin, Calif.: Prima, 1992), p. 419.
57. Ibid., p. 278.
58. Ibid., p. 391.
59. Ibid., p. 380.
60. Ibid., pp. 391–392.
61. Ibid., pp. 419–420, concludes that Kennedy "failed to be a true moral

leader of the American people because he lacked the conviction and commitment," though conceding that he "was showing signs of a new awareness in 1963"—that is, months *after* the missile crisis.

62. Bernstein, "Reconsidering the Missile Crisis," p. 104.

63. Kennedy, *Thirteen Days*, p. 98.

64. May and Zelikow, *The Kennedy Tapes*, pp. 691–692.

65. Ibid., p. 696.

66. "When One Man Sizes Up Another," *Newsweek*, Dec. 3, 1962, p. 3.

67. Khrushchev, *Khrushchev Remembers*, p. 505.

68. Khrushchev, *Khrushchev Remembers: The Last Testament*, p. 513.

69. Fidel Castro to Herbert Matthews in 1967, in Herbert L. Matthews, *Fidel Castro* (New York: Simon and Schuster, 1969), p. 225, cited in Schlesinger, *Robert Kennedy and His Times*, p. 531.

Index

Index

Index

Index

Index

McCormack, John W., 17, 145
McElroy, Neil H., 25
McGhee, George, 159, 160
McGill, Ralph, 143
McNamara, Robert, 44, 74,
    183; argument for air strikes,
    126; on crisis management,
    206; Cuban blockade and,
    115, 147–148, 204; as Ex
    Comm member, 94; Jupiter
    missiles in Turkey and, 156,
    157, 162, 166–167, 168, 176,
    192, 193; Robert Lovett and,
    126; on military significance
    of Cuban missiles, 98; on
    possible military response to
    Cuban missiles, 107,
    229(n99); proposal of open
    surveillance of Cuba,
    240(n29); reflections on
    Cuban missile crisis, 4; on
    tactical nuclear weapons in
    Cuba, 256(n40)
McNaughton, John, 193
Meany, George, 45
Media. *See* Press.
Medium-range ballistic missiles
    (MRBMs), 73, 98, 159, 166
Meeker, Leonard, 131, 167
*Meeting the Threat of Surprise
    Attack*, 24
Metiva, Raymond, 137
MiG aircraft, 73
Mikoyan, Anastas, 72
Military Assistance Program,
    157

"Military Significance of the
    Soviet Missiles in Cuba"
    (State Department), 98
Military spending, 25
Miller, Jack, 81, 90
Miller, William, 88, 146
Milwaukee Journal (newspaper),
    150
"Missile diplomacy," 24
"Missile gap" issue: American
    cold war fears and, 22–26,
    28; presidential campaign of
    1960 and, 29–30. *See also*
    Intercontinental ballistic
    missiles.
Missiles of October, The
    (television drama), 7
Moley, Raymond, 79
Mongoose. *See* Operation
    Mongoose.
Monroe Doctrine, 238(n13);
    American belief in, 33–34;
    critics of Kennedy's Cuban
    policy and, 78, 79, 81, 82, 90;
    Thomas Dodd and, 117;
    Hubert Humphrey and, 84;
    Kennedy's opinion of, 92;
    Khrushchev and, 13, 32,
    33–34; Soviet-Cuban
    relationship and, 8, 32–34
Morse, Wayne, 85
MRBMs. *See* Medium-range
    ballistic missiles.
Mundt, Karl, 117
Munich, 15–16, 83, 144
Murphy, Charles, 153

Index

Republican National
  Convention (1960), 17
Republicans: advocacy of armed
  action against Cuba, 189,
  190; criticism of Kennedy's
  Cuban policy, 79–80, 81–84;
  presidential campaign of
  1960, 15–16, 17; response to
  Bay of Pigs invasion, 48;
  support for Cuban blockade,
  116–117, 146
Reston, James, 14, 58, 75, 143
Roberts, Chalmers M., 144
Rockefeller, Nelson, 16–17, 29,
  48
Rockefeller Panel, 25, 153
Rocket programs: American, 24;
  Sputnik, 22, 24
Roosevelt, Franklin D., 10,
  131
Roper, Mrs. Steven, 137
Rosenstein, Joan, 139–140
Rovere, Richard, 188
Ruggles, William B., 44–45
Rusk, Dean, 104, 158, 183; air
  strike debate and, 124–125;
  argument for strong response
  to Cuban missiles, 108–109;
  Cuban blockade and,
  113–114; economic sanctions
  on Cuba and, 112; as Ex
  Comm member, 95; Andrei
  Gromyko and, 105; Jupiter
  missiles in Turkey and, 156,
  160, 166, 168, 169, 176, 192;
  on Khrushchev's threat of

war, 58; Robert Lovett and,
  126; on military significance
  of Cuban missiles, 99; UN
  fallback plan and, 203, 206
Russell, Richard, 134
Ryzhov, Nikita, 174

Sagan, Scott D., 205
Sakharov, Andrei, 70
Salinger, Pierre, 92, 186
San Diego Union (newspaper),
  78
San Francisco Chronicle
  (newspaper), 89
Sarper, Selim, 160
Saturday Evening Post
  (magazine), 70
Scali, John, 188
Schlesinger, Arthur M., Jr., 5,
  11, 15, 124, 141, 165, 189,
  197
Scott, Hugh, 21, 118
Seldon, Armistead, Jr., 84–85
Senate Armed Services
  Committee, 190–191
Senate Preparedness
  Subcommittee, 25
Serling, Rod, 50
Shelby Daily Star (newspaper),
  137
Shevchenko, Arkady, 59, 100
Short-range nuclear missiles: in
  Cuba, 73, 206, 256(n40)
Shoup, David, 128
Smathers, George A., 33, 34,
  88, 145

Index

Index

A NOTE ON THE AUTHOR

Robert Weisbrot was born in New York City and studied history at Brandeis University and at Harvard, where he received a Ph.D. He has written extensively on politics and society in the 1960s, including *Freedom Bound*, an award-winning history of the American civil rights movement. Mr. Weisbrot teaches American history at Colby College, where he is the Christian A. Johnson Distinguished Teaching Professor of History. He lives in Waterville, Maine.